'Elaine gifts us all with a beautifully intimate and powerful retelling of her ever unfolding journey. In sharing her joys, pitfalls, adventures, self doubt, and successes, she reminds us that through uncovering and discovering the many facets of ourselves, we are more than enough.'
Yara Shahidi

'Elaine's book is a call for young women to find their voice and spark their courage—it's a book I would have loved to have discovered as a young woman starting my own career.'
Reese Witherspoon

'*More Than Enough* is a guide for young people who want to find their voice, a crash course for those who want to challenge the status quo, and an adventure story for all of us. Young women can learn so much from Elaine's remarkable journey.'
Malala Yousafzai

'Elaine is a jolt of honesty, positivity, and inspiration. Anyone who has ever felt like she doesn't belong will feel less alone after reading *More Than Enough*. Elaine's voice couldn't be more important, and more important right now.'
Sophia Amoruso

'Elaine Welteroth has written the ultimate guide for how to come into your own, on your own terms. Packed with honesty and warmth, *More Than Enough* is a must read for women of all ages and walks of life.'
Karlie Kloss

'This isn't just a coming of age story, it's a book about coming into your own and embracing who you are. As we follow Elaine's journey, she sheds a bright light on what happens when a black girl not only decides to be the master of her own destiny but challenges what the world thinks a black girl's destiny should be.'
Lena Waithe

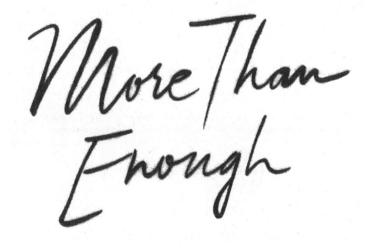

More Than Enough

CLAIMING SPACE FOR
WHO YOU ARE
(NO MATTER WHAT THEY SAY)

Elaine Welteroth

EBURY
PRESS

5 7 9 10 8 6 4

Ebury Press, an imprint of Ebury Publishing
20 Vauxhall Bridge Road
London SW1V 2SA

Ebury Press is part of the Penguin Random House group of companies
whose addresses can be found at global.penguinrandomhouse.com

Penguin
Random House
UK

First published in the United Kingdom by Ebury Press in 2019
First published in the United States by Viking in 2019

www.penguin.co.uk

A CIP catalogue record for this book is available from the British Library

ISBN 9781529105438

Printed and bound in Great Britain by Clays Ltd, Elcograf S.p.A.

Penguin Random House is committed to a sustainable future for
our business, our readers and our planet. This book is made
from Forest Stewardship Council® certified paper.

MIX
Paper from
responsible sources
FSC
www.fsc.org   FSC® C018179

For every girl who aspires to be great.

And to every woman who helped me realize
we already possess the greatness we seek.

If I didn't define myself for myself, I would be crunched into
other people's fantasies for me and eaten alive.

AUDRE LORDE

Contents

Foreword ix

Introduction: Intention xiii

CHAPTER 1
Born Enough 1

CHAPTER 2
White Paper Family 15

CHAPTER 3
Brown Girl Boss 23

CHAPTER 4
Pretty or Butt Ugly 37

CHAPTER 5
Ride or Die Syndrome 45

CHAPTER 6
Black Enough 63

CHAPTER 7
I Am Not My Hair 75

CHAPTER 8
A Different Kind of White 87

CHAPTER 9
The College Crisis 95

CHAPTER 10
Your Dreams Are Calling 111

CHAPTER 11
Started from the Bottom 123

CHAPTER 12
Are You My Husband? 143

CHAPTER 13
When It All Falls Down 165

CHAPTER 14
A Seat at the Table 181

CHAPTER 15
New World Order 193

CHAPTER 16
Disturbing the Peace 207

CHAPTER 17
New Highs, New Lows 225

CHAPTER 18
Lemonade 239

CHAPTER 19
Weight of the World 249

CHAPTER 20
The Ones We've Been Waiting For 259

CHAPTER 21
Burning Out 269

CHAPTER 22
End of an Era 281

CHAPTER 23
A Dream Realized 291

CHAPTER 24
Brave Enough 307

Conclusion: Just the Beginning 315
Acknowledgments 317

Foreword

BY AVA DUVERNAY

Nothing bad ever happens to me. It's all to learn and grow.

I was standing on the set during one of my film shoots in New York City when I heard these words. They hit my heart like a beam of light. One of my assistant directors said it to me very casually in the midst of a conversation on a different subject. "Nothing bad ever happens to me. It's all to learn and grow."

You know sometimes when you hear or read or see something that you need so deeply, but didn't even know it? This moment was like that for me. I was depleted. Emotionally. Physically. Spiritually. I was living far from home for six months filming a project about tough subject matter. It marked my third straight year of working on massive projects with no mental break in between. No full weekend off. No vacation. Just nonstop mentally and physically taxing work. I'd felt like I'd made choices that put me in a place of inner turmoil and lack, instead of nourishment and freedom. It was wearing on me. Every day. In every way.

Many of us have been there. We allow the expectations of others to shape our own expectations. We don't prioritize our time with ourselves. We rarely set aside moments to be still, to access our center. And the bottom line is, when we don't focus on our inner light, it dims. We feel put upon, distracted, out of balance. We feel that life is happening around us and we can't grasp it fully. It feels like bad things are happening to us. And it's all out of our control.

One of the things I love about the book you hold in your hands is its intention to share these kinds of challenges as a road map to the good within you. Elaine strips away the facade of success, the sheen and shimmer of social media, the shiny wrapping paper, to give us all a real gift. The true story of her climb. In all its clumsiness and elegance. Because if there is one thing we know for sure, each of our lives is filled with both. There are times when everything is in perfect balance. And times when we just aren't quite in sync.

But what if we chose to live with new vision? To not see the clumsiness as a bad thing, but to live in the space of "nothing bad ever happens to me." To embrace an idea that my friend Oprah Winfrey told me some years ago: "This bad thing isn't happening to you. It is happening for you." That, my friends, is a game-changing notion. It is a powerful truth. And when I abide by it, I am whole.

When my father passed on suddenly a few years ago and my heart was shattered into a million pieces, I held onto this. I knew that his Life had happened for his family, that he lived it exquisitely like a work of art, and that his passing was a triumphant one because he powerfully fulfilled his purpose on this earth. I choose gratitude in that moment, instead of despair. And it saved me. Whenever I remember that Life is for me, not against me, I hear and see and feel it all. And I can find good in every shadow, in every cloud. It makes every day brighter.

How do we get there? It's a spiritual practice. It takes time. And repetition. And as you can see, we all need to be reminded to stay on course just as I was reminded that day in New York on set. But if you're open, you'll receive those reminders. In fact, you're holding one in your hand right now. Elaine's book is a gorgeous reminder that each day we have the chance to gain lessons from Life. We can observe how human nature unfolds before us. We can begin to read the world around us, the people we meet and the places we go, as if they are letters written by a divine pen. A person whose soul has awakened to this fact is so abundantly aware that every interaction, situation, even blade of grass reveals something worth knowing. And in that knowing, the truth is that nothing bad can ever happen to you. We can see it and process it as bad. Or we can see it and process it as something happening for us, not to us.

In these pages, you'll find a story of a woman who learned that lesson along the way. Every fall was actually a step. Every confusion was actually insight. Every risk was actually a reward waiting to happen.

I hope you enjoy Elaine's story as much as I did. Her journey is a testament to shaping what we experience for our own good. For crafting positivity as our path. For knowing that the bad is our choice and the good is our choice. And to work to choose the good. Every day. In every way.

Intention

What comes from the heart touches the heart.

DEBRA WELTEROTH, MY MOM

Growing up, Oprah was my favorite imaginary auntie. She lived inside the TV and I looked forward to visiting her every day at 4:00 P.M. sharp. For one hour every Monday through Friday, I got to watch a Black woman command dominion over the world. As a little brown girl in a big White world, that's a powerful thing to witness. Especially in a culture where you do not see yourself positively reflected in the media.

Research tells us that, on average, a girl's confidence peaks at just nine years old.

Nine.

That *pains* me.

Though sadly, it's not surprising to me.

My baby cousin, Joy, was just five when I noticed her standing in front of a mirror with a tan towel wrapped around her tiny head. She was looking at her reflection, examining her smooth, mahogany brown skin with eyes that lit up like little half moons. As I watched, she got caught up in a reverie, whipping that towel back and forth like it was Rapunzel's long golden locks blowing in the wind.

"What are you doing?" I asked.

She looked at me, and with one final swing just as the towel fell to the floor, she said, "I wish my hair wasn't so ugly."

I was only a kid then, too, but her words gave me a sinking feeling in the pit of my stomach. It wasn't just sympathy, but also a quiet recognition of my own internalized struggle to accept what was looking back at me in the mirror.

The kind of beauty we saw celebrated around us at school, in magazines, and on television had a way of making us feel like the bodies we were born in were somehow inferior. Apart from Auntie Oprah, the media's portrayal of Black women was grossly limited in scope and variety. Luckily, I had strong examples of women of color in my real life who watered the seeds that helped me believe I could dream beyond what I saw around me.

Fast-forward to when I was appointed by Anna Wintour to lead *Teen Vogue*. I thought I was just a girl getting a dream job. But then the headlines hit: suddenly, I was a Black girl making history. At twenty-nine, I had become the second Black person and the youngest ever to helm a Condé Nast magazine. I was now the one holding the pen in one of the most divisive political climates in recent history.

Shonda Rhimes coined the term: "First. Only. Different." Being an "FOD" in your field comes with a unique responsibility and a powerful opportunity: to rewrite rules, to redefine norms, to represent for the communities that haven't had a seat at the table before. But what good is a trailblazer who isn't willing to leave signposts along the way that make it a little less confusing, less lonely, less disorienting for the next woman or person of color to follow?

With my promotions, I had an opportunity to help ensure the Joys of the world never doubted their value. I was able to help undo some of the damaging narratives I grew up with by recasting pages to make them more reflective of my world, and to create space for the most pressing issues of our time. While it all played out like a career fairy tale online, none of it was easy.

Unlike the days when the integrity and authenticity of women's stories reigned supreme on *The Oprah Winfrey Show*, we now scroll headlines and highlight reels, collecting clues from each other's filtered lives for how to navigate our own. Yet what you see is rarely what it is. As a journalist and a truth seeker, I believe there are universal gems buried in the stories women never tell.

While I still have much more life to live and so much more work to do in the world, I am ready to offer some of my own signposts from my path thus far. Because no one can share my truth but me.

I have often found myself situated in the in-between, stretched like a bridge between worlds: Black and White, beauty and activism, the past and the future. But in this sliver of space, this intersection I now own, I have learned to create magic.

Which brings me back to Oprah, who is a master of many things, but reminding us of the power of intention setting might be her greatest gift to us all.

As I embark on telling this slice of my own story—a story that is still being written—it is important that I lay out my intentions clearly: This is my offering to the next generation as much as it is a tribute to the women who have come before me and offered their shoulders to stand on.

This book is not a career manual, because I believe only you can write your own blueprint for success, though I do share some of my hard-earned lessons that I am still learning to live by.

This is not intended as self-help, though I do open up about how I have overcome fear—again and again—through faith.

This also isn't the story of how *Teen Vogue* got woke, though I do reflect on how I woke up to the power of my own voice, and how I learned to use it to advocate for what I believe in.

Instead, consider this book a love letter—to anyone who's felt othered, overlooked, overwhelmed, underestimated, undervalued, and still chooses to overcome.

This is for all my fellow POCs and FODs out there, standing proudly as First, Only, and Different, who know what it is to be the only one of you in the room. My story is your story.

This is for the first-generation college student plotting your way to the top, and every parent who wants to see you get there. Know that your dreams are valid and that you belong.

This is for every mixed-race kid who knows what it means to exist in the in-between. There is power in any intersection. You will find your rhythm and carve out space to thrive in your own lane.

This is for anyone in your dream job facing perils no one talks about. You are not alone. When you exist in spaces that weren't built for you, remember sometimes that just being you is the revolution.

This is especially for the ones who are Next Up. Those of you who are responsible for taking the same systems my generation is disrupting and building better ones.

As you continue crafting the life you want, I hope you are reminded that it is the very things you underestimate about yourself that will help you create your own magic.

Find it. Use it. Trust it.

We spend too much time hearing and telling ourselves we are not enough. Not smart enough. Not beautiful enough. Not successful enough. Not young enough. Not old enough. Not woke enough. I want this book to be the voice reminding you to say ENOUGH with all that. You are enough. You were BORN enough.

The world is waiting on you.

Let's go.

xo, E

CHAPTER 1

Born Enough

I am my ancestors' wildest dreams.

BRANDAN ODUMS, AKA BMIKE

T HANK YOU, JESUS!"

My mother's multi-octave praise assailed everyone within earshot of her hospital bed. She is a gospel singer— a rare female contralto in a traveling church quintet called the Angelic Voices. Those lungs could project.

Her booming voice moved like a praise dance down the long hallways of the Good Samaritan maternity ward, sweeping my aunts, who were anxiously awaiting my arrival, into a kind of contagious joy only she can conjure—we had our very own chorus cheering from the waiting room. I was conceived in love, born into celebration, and it seems almost prophetic now that the first words I'd ever hear were filled with the unmistakable delight of a woman getting exactly what she wanted.

But let's rewind for a second, to the moments before my mother's cry of joy. Shortly after I was born, I was rushed off to the baby ICU with an oxygen-deprived face the color of a Smurf. The umbilical cord strangled me during delivery, so even during those first celebratory moments on planet Earth I appropriately had more pressing matters to tend to than listening to my mother. To this day she jokes that I was busy putting people to work right out of the womb.

Meanwhile, the frenzy around the circumstances of my delivery was so great that it distracted even the doctors from fact-checking one very critical piece of the birth story before reporting it:

"It's a boy!" they proclaimed as I was whisked away.

"Joseph Tyler!" My dad rejoiced, halfway hoping his excitement would distract my mother from the panic of not being able to see or hold her newborn.

My mom will tell you her prayers were simply to give birth for the second time to a healthy baby, but her heart's desire was for a baby girl; a daughter with a gang of hair to braid; a little sister for her firstborn son to protect; a woman to guide throughout her walk in the world. Luckily for her, just as the pigment was returning to my skin and as soon as the doctors could stabilize me, all that baby boy business went out the window—right along with my mom's coy charade. The delivery nurse took a closer look at me and immediately filed a correction.

"Um, excuse me, ma'am. I've been doing this a long time and I know the difference between a girl and a boy when I see it," the nurse said, placing me into my mom's arms. *"This* is a baby *girl."*

My mother's life was now complete. She finally had the boy and girl she had always dreamed of.

As a newborn I looked like an exact replica of my older brother, Eric Charles, who was born two and a half years earlier, but Mom was quick to spot one distinguishing characteristic: "You see this jawline?" Her finger traced the only visible bone structure on an otherwise puffy mound of flesh. "She gets *that* from her mama. This ain't no Joseph Tyler. *This* is Elaine Marie."

And *that's* when she let it rip: *"THANK YOU, JESUS!"*

BORN ENOUGH

⸻

As any family legend goes, the earliest stories of our lives are passed on like hand-me-downs, stretched in some places and covered in the owner's loving fingerprints. Are they always true? Mostly. Are there some exaggerations? Knowing my mother, no doubt. But regardless of what drama actually went down in that hospital room that day, what I've known for sure every day since is the profound impact of a mother's love. And for as long as I can remember, it has always been there to remind me that *I was born enough*.

When a girl is born, a universe of possibilities is born within her. When a little Black girl is born, she is born with the promise of a better future; her life represents new hope for breaking generational chains—of systemic oppression, of discrimination, of abuse—that have plagued our lineage. And it is because of the struggles of the strong women who came before that she is born with the potential to dream beyond what any of them ever could.

We are all born with a sense of possibility and limitlessness. This is before the labels are placed upon us, those social stratifications of race, gender, sexuality, and status that start to shape our idea of who we are and that often erode the dreams of what we can become. We are also born with a certain indestructibility that can withstand every one of those tests—if only we recognize it. And it is the power of our own possibilities that keeps us fighting to get back to who we were born to be.

Throughout my childhood, my mom often reminded me that I was born to go further than any woman in our family: in school, in work, in love, in the world. She was certain that I would get to go deeper into my purpose than she was able to in her own life. And she was insistent that I should never settle for anything less. "Because *you* won't have to," she'd say. "We went through what we went through so that you could live, baby girl. So you gotta *live*. Run after it. And know that we are all with you. All of us—are all right there with *you*."

I WAS BORN ON DECEMBER 10, 1986, and according to the card I found in my Easter basket one year and taped up onto my bedroom wall, Elaine means "ray of light." Combine that with "world of fire," the translation of my German surname, and you get what my mom describes as a girl with a "sho 'nuff fire in her belly."

I was two years old when my parents bought our family home in Newark, California, just thirty-five minutes south of San Francisco. It is a small, middle-class town: one freeway exit on I-880, one mall, one junior high, one high school. Green lawns, four-bedroom ranch-style homes, and a flagpole that kids pledge allegiance to every day in public school. Suburbia, USA. It was the quiet city where my parents were able to afford a home and lay down roots. To me, it was the city where nothing ever happened.

My dad saw Newark as a diverse place to raise us. My mother disagreed on the diversity front, but she always found his optimism to be one of his most redeeming traits. Even with its smattering of first-generation Mexican, Indian, and Asian families, Newark was then and is still a predominantly White town. As an interracial family, we were in the slim minority, though we never felt like an oddity in the Bay Area. Even in our diversity, there was a sameness to all of our lives then. Economically, we were all a part of a similar blue-collar existence in middle-class America. No matter what color kid you were, we all had parents who were just trying to hold on to jobs that promised pensions and the security of a full-term retirement. That was the American dream I came from.

Yet I yearned for the bigness of a life elsewhere. Someplace where people dreamed bigger and walked a little faster. Where houses came with winding, custom staircases and fancier cars. Where men carried briefcases to boardrooms and women wore power suits to work. I didn't know anyone who was even remotely a part of that world back then—but I knew from an early age that was the world I was desperate to live in.

My mom never thought she would wind up on the West Coast. She was born the eldest of three in Macrae, Georgia, a tiny backwoods town where she spent her summers pacing dirt roads with her cousins and mastering the art of soul food in her grandmothers' kitchens. She is a self-professed "down-home, southern girl" at heart—and she has the cooking chops to prove it—but during the school year, she was raised fifteen hundred miles north in Rochester, New York's bustling, blue-collar city life with her two brothers, Tyrone and Tyson.

To pay for their private Catholic school education, my grandfather worked backbreaking shifts driving trucks for Kodak and my grandmother served in the cafeteria at the University of Rochester. My great-grandmother Maggie, who has skin as smooth as butter and is still vibrant today at ninety-eight, was a domestic worker all her life—her parents were the first generation removed from slavery on my mother's side of the family.

While our people were still being pillaged and suppressed at polls down South, up North my mother was elected class president at Nazareth Academy, a private, nearly all-White, all-girls high school. She grew up in the postsegregation duality of the 1960s and '70s, in a country that promised more for Black people than ever before. She had the privilege of being raised in a two-parent dual-income household, where James Brown's transcendent message of being Black and proud reverberated. Meanwhile, her strict parents instinctively shielded their children from the racism they still faced daily—even in integrated working-class neighborhoods in New York.

Young Debra Elaine Southerland (never call her Debby—trust me) was a sheltered, overachieving student with a smiley, preternaturally joyful disposition. Genetically blessed with high cheekbones, a megawatt smile, and a naturally slim, tall frame, she was the kind of woman you might hate if she wasn't so damn sweet. Her plan was to attend the University of Rochester; marry her high school sweetheart, John; have a couple of Black babies; maybe become a teacher; and live happily ever after, close to family on the East Coast.

But you know what they say about God and plans—we make 'em, God laughs.

Life managed to get in the way of my mom's girlhood dreams coming true. At the age of eighteen, after a family dispute, she was shipped off to San Jose, California, alone, where she struggled to start over. The painful details of that journey are hers to share, but my mother's story isn't one of victimhood; she managed to do more than just survive the blows life dealt her—she was always determined to thrive.

She got a job bagging groceries, then became a temp receptionist at San Jose State University, and by twenty she landed a gig as a temp typist at a Fortune 500 aerospace corporation. On her first day of work an older White man escorted her to her desk, leading her through workstations where lewd pictures of nude women hung in plain sight. The year was 1979, and she was a single, young Black woman with no family and no friends in a new city, entering into a male-dominated industry of engineers who swore like sailors and ogled titty magazines at their desk. Even so, my mother felt entitled to her dignity. With more to lose than anyone, she turned to look into the eyes of a man who seemed utterly oblivious to the assault on her morning routine, and said plainly:

"If I have to come into this room every day to do my job, can you please take down those images?"

The man laughed nervously, taken aback by the audacity of her request, but the images were gone the next day.

Word got around that my mom was the "snitch" who made the men clean up their act around the office, but the OG office matriarch warmed up to her right away. Mary Patricia Welteroth was a little old Irish lady with big blue eyes, and in a pod of lily-white typists, she was the queen of the roost. Over daily lunch dates, she taught my mom everything she knew about life, love, family, and putting men in their place. One day at Frankie, Johnnie and Luigi's pizzeria in Mountain View, she said:

"Well, you know, Deb, you really should consider dating my son Jackie."

My mom told Pat she loved her to pieces but that she wasn't having any of it: "Patty, my life is hard enough," she retorted. "Ain't no way I am gonna make it harder by going out with a White man. No, ma'am."

"Oh, now, Debra, what does any of that matter?" Pat responded, as if race were just a bump in the road you could simply sidestep in a relationship.

Clearly, my grandma Pat was way ahead of her time. Or perhaps just as naive as her son.

PATRICIA WELTEROTH WAS AN avid reader who studied social justice and literature at University of California, Berkeley. She was head of the debate team and the pep club. Which is just to say you couldn't win an argument with this charismatic, pint-sized woman if you tried. She married her college sweetheart, a stoic, second-generation German American boy named Chuck, who wrote her romantic letters after serving as an Air Force lieutenant in World War II. He worked as an executive at the same aerospace company where she was a typist. Together, they raised a family of four kids in a liberal, Irish Catholic household.

Their youngest son, Jack, was then a thirtysomething-year-old blue-eyed boy; a carpenter at the same company where his parents held office jobs. According to my mother, he spent his workdays "looking like a dust-bowl." He lived in a bachelor pad in the foothills of Cupertino with two cats, Lumpy and Blondie, and an acoustic Gibson Gospel guitar named Maple. To let him tell it, he's always had "soul," for a White guy from Sara-toga. Growing up in the 1950s in a scenic town in Northern California with beautiful, rolling hills and sprawling orchards that go on for miles, Black people were merely figments of his musical imagination. He claims as a kid he was the only one in his whole milk-white neighborhood racing home after his paper route to listen to B. B. King and Dionne Warwick records.

Over long lunches with chatty Patty, my mom came to know every inti-mate detail of Jack's and his siblings' lives. When tragedy struck the Wel-teroth family with the sudden passing of the eldest son, Bobby, my mom sang at his funeral. Afterward she showed up on Jack's doorstep with a home-cooked meal—a gesture she still offers anyone in crisis. She knew from Pat that Bobby was not only Jack's brother, he was his bandmate and his very best friend.

That day my mom and dad formed a friendship, rooted in vulnerability and honesty, and eventually he even found his way into her heart. It was a relationship they both say was beyond skin deep right from the start—and it had to be in order to sustain the inevitable blows of any lifelong, interra-cial love affair.

Decades later, at my mom's fiftieth birthday party, there wasn't a dry eye in the room when my dad described seeing my mom sing at his brother's funeral: "The way the light from the church's stained-glass window shined on her—it was just like an angel came down to remind me that there was a God in a godless moment in my life." He ended the tribute holding up a glass of water, barely getting out the words: "She's the best thing that ever happened to me."

When my dad proposed, it took my mom some time to wrap her head around the notion of marrying a White man. She lives in the "real world," as she puts it; he was the hopeless romantic. She knew it was going to be harder than he realized, but ultimately their love transcended their cultural differences and any discrimination that their union would invite.

They got married in 1982 at Antioch Baptist Church. It was the same Black church where my brother and I would be baptized and forced to follow our mom's footsteps into the choir stand. She'd put a white bow in my hair and "grease up" my knees before church on Sundays, always adding a dollop of Vaseline to a healthy serving of lotion for extra sheen. "See, your daddy's people, they just use lotion," she'd say under her breath. "But we need something a little heavier on our skin. I can't have my babies looking ashy. No, sir."

I AM NOT ACTUALLY SURE when I became consciously aware of the fact that my mom is Black and my dad is White. But there was never any doubt in my mind that they viewed the world and moved through it rather differently. They grew up in diametrically opposing backgrounds, on two different coasts. She loved singing gospel music. He was always playing classic rock songs on his acoustic guitar. She was a prayer-slanging, pie-baking purist. He was a chain-smoking wild child who cussed like a sailor and drank a little too much. But above all, he was a family man with a huge heart. My mom and dad were a radically unlikely but fiercely loving pair—two people with absolutely nothing in common except a love for music and an unwavering commitment to their family.

Despite their differences, in our household there was always an understanding between my parents that they were raising Black children. Yes, we were technically biracial, but they knew that the world wouldn't see it that way. So, in order to prepare us for a society that would require us to check a box—"Black" or "White"—they decided before we were born that we would check "Black." It was all presumably some interracial parenting scheme to preempt their mixed-race children from having an identity crisis down the line (as if preventing that were possible).

Meanwhile, my brother and I never felt like we fit neatly into boxes of any kind. Throughout our childhood, every time we were handed one of those anxiety-inducing personal information cards in school that were required by law for the US Census Bureau, Eric and I decided that we would buck the system, challenge racial norms, and defy our parents by checking both Black *and* White. The way we saw it then, checking just one was a dismissal of half of our family tree. Plus, we were kids and breaking rules was fun. Checking both felt like a little victory—our very own tiny act of resistance, a small but powerful way to tell the world who we are.

My DAD HAS ALWAYS celebrated the ways in which my mom instilled a full embrace of Black culture in our household, from her catfish and cornbread dinners to the Black history books strategically placed throughout our home. And yet, we didn't grow up with any rigid definitions of what it meant to be Black or White. Apart from making sure we knew who James Brown was and that we couldn't leave the house without glazing our knees and elbows with Vaseline, there were no subtle suggestions about how we "should" dress or speak, what music we "should" listen to, who we "should" date. All that would come from the world beyond our walls—but inside our home, our parents gave me and my brother all the room we needed to become exactly who we were born to be.

And it was a good thing they did, because right from the start, my brother rejected any suggestion of conformity. The way my parents tell it, this kid basically popped out of the womb with a little Mohawk and an electric guitar. He was Afropunk long before the festival—the brown kid fronting a punk band and starting mosh pits when no one who looked like him even entered those spaces. At school, he was bullied and teachers treated him like some kind of problem child who needed to be fixed with doses of Ritalin and detention sentences. They'd single him out in the classroom, label him as a troublemaker, and send him to the principal's office for things any hyperactive ten-year-old boy would do. Eric was not only a Black boy in a White school system, he was the lone alt-Black kid who was so often misunderstood.

Making heavy metal music seemed to be his way of metabolizing it all. He gets that from our dad, along with his general proclivity toward guitars and loud rock music, which seems appropriate considering he was named after my dad's rock-and-roll hero, Eric Clapton.

My dad has always been my brother's biggest advocate. And Lord knows he needed one. While I was more of a social chameleon, Eric was routinely rejected by kids at school. Black kids said he acted "too White." White kids would slam him with racial slurs and get away with it. Any time Eric's behavior issues came up, the school administrators would call our mom. But whenever the N-word flew in his face, they would conveniently call our dad. Go figure. Maybe they were expecting a more sympathetic response? Once, in grade school, when my brother was the one sent home for clocking some jerk kid who called him the N-word, my dad marched straight into that principal's office to demand that the administration acknowledge the racist incident for what it was. He stood nose to nose with the principal—White man to White man—and refused to allow his son to be singled out and punished for defending himself in an environment that was not invested in protecting him equally. For parents of Black kids in a White school system, protecting your children can feel like a tireless fight from a powerless position. But my dad raised my brother and me with the guts to stand up for ourselves.

While my brother and I are dissimilar in as many ways as our parents, we share the same rebellious spirit—it just looks a little different on the outside: his interpretation is more curly green Mohawk in a mosh pit. Mine is more cornrows at a corporate office. But we were both born independent thinkers with a deep sense of justice and a willingness to fight for anything— or anyone—we believed in. While my parents encouraged this, at times it worked against them. Before I could even speak, I'd stare down my mom after she spanked my brother. And when Eric got into his first fight in elementary school, they couldn't peel me off the other guy's backpack.

"Nobody puts baby in a corner."

My mom loves a classic one-liner. If you give her five minutes she will bend your ear retelling the "Pink Reeboks" story, her favorite story of all.

Apparently, when I was an infant, my parents would place me in one of those baby-walker contraptions that give newly discovered legs the chance to glide around the room on wheels. I would scoot all around the house with reckless abandon, but if I ever found myself in a corner, I would break out in hives. "Homegirl was maaaaaa-ad"—my mother cracks herself up telling this one. "Your face would get beet red just like your dad's when his temper flares." She conveniently blames the other side of the family tree for my insufferable impatience: "There goes that Welteroth fire again," she'll snicker.

When I was ten months old, she bought me a pair of pink Reebok sparkly sneakers. ("This was before you had a tooth in your little head," she likes to add for color.) As the family legend goes, as soon as I had them on, I was off and running. Just like that. No baby steps. No tumbles. Just off! Apparently, I cut a look at my mom as if to say, "Finally, lady! *Now* you give me sneakers? I could have been walking months ago!"

There have been so many times in my life since when I've felt stuck in a corner like that little baby, red and blotchy and mad as hell. Each time my mom has always been there to say, "Just slow down, Lainey. You have to crawl before you walk." I hate when she says that. When I go silent on the other end of the line, she'll suck her teeth. "But noo-ooo. My baby girl just keeps trying to skip all that crawling mess."

She knows she raised a woman born to run.

By comparison, my mother is much more "go with the flow." She comes from a generation that taught Black women to take what you are given, to make do with what you got, not to rock the boat, not to go against the grain.

I have never been very good at any of that.

I ASKED TO BE ENROLLED in a pageant when I was three years old. While the rest of the toddlers in my category clung to their mothers' legs backstage, too shy to talk, right before our moment in the spotlight I tapped my mother's shin and told her I was going out there on my own. She says she didn't know whether to laugh or cry: "Here I was, getting fired by my three-year-old!" I walked out onto the stage, totally owning it. I planted my chubby brown legs, held the mic with both hands, and launched into an unsolicited origin story about "the ring on my finger that my daddy gave me." When I was finished, I blew the audience a kiss and exited stage left.

I felt excitement bigger than my tiny body could contain when they crowned me Tri-City Tot Princess. There is a picture of me from that day, wearing my crown and sash, beaming in my little white ruffly dress with matching socks that were poking out of black patent leather Mary Janes. My chin is thrust up in the air so high and my smile is so wide, you can't even see my squinty little eyes.

I was the only brown girl in that pageant. But no one tells a three-year-old that. I didn't know then that I had defied any expectations. I didn't know what kinds of people got to wear crowns. All I knew is that day, I was one of them. And you couldn't tell me nothin'.

"When a girl
is born,
a universe of
possibilities is
born within her."

CHAPTER 2

White Paper Family

As long as we are not ourselves,
we will try to be what other people are.
MALIDOMA PATRICE SOMÉ, *OF WATER AND THE SPIRIT*

The first time I realized race was a Thing, I was staring at a pile of magazines in preschool surrounded by a sea of pudgy White faces. We were all huddled together for our first official school assignment. The only brown kids there were me and Juan, the sweet Mexican kid who taught me how to tie my shoelaces. The teacher was instructing us to make collages that represented our families. All we had to do was dive into the large stack of magazines on the table, cut out pictures of people who resemble our family members, and paste them onto a sheet of paper. Easy enough. I have always loved a collaging moment—even way back then.

As I flipped through the pages, I saw smiling White ladies in pristine kitchens, cute White babies wearing Pull-Ups, handsome White men in tailored suits, White kids picnicking on Crayola-green grass. I had never heard anyone use terms like "representation" before; all I knew was no one on any of those magazine pages looked like me or my family. It reinforced what I had somehow already internalized: I was different. Other. An oddity living in a White world.

My mom continued to try to circumvent the lack of diversity at school by instituting her own informal cultural literacy program at home, doing whatever she could to ensure that her mixed kids were fluent in Black culture. She enrolled me in West African dance class and was adamant about my wearing my hair in braids. She made us elaborate soul food meals, and filled our household with *Ebony* and *Jet* magazines and literature that filled our minds with endless "Black facts" about inventors, engineers, astronauts, and dancers who looked like us. This was right around the time the first diversity boom hit the small screen and America entered into the golden age of Black sitcoms—*Family Matters, The Fresh Prince of Bel-Air, The Cosby Show, Martin, Living Single* all got heavy rotation in our living room throughout the early 1990s. Weekends were a total immersion—our Saturdays were spent at the Black hair salon and Sundays in the Black church.

Every Sunday, my mom, Eric, and I piled into our White Ford Taurus and journeyed approximately thirty minutes south on highway I-880 from a predominantly White world in Newark to the Black world inside Antioch Baptist Church in San Jose. My dad usually drove separately in his midnight blue El Camino because he needed an out if the hollering from the pulpit went on too long. And it always went on too long for his taste. He was raised in a much more time-oriented Irish Catholic church where no act of God required more than sixty minutes. My brother and I, on the other hand, had no choice but to stay with Mom to the end. We served as ushers and we sang in the children's choir.

For us, there was no escaping.

Bᴀᴄᴋ ɪɴ ᴛʜᴀᴛ ᴘʀᴇsᴄʜᴏᴏʟ classroom, though, while all the other kids were glue-sticking their little brains out, I was still slowly flipping through the pages, searching for any hint of myself or my mother or brother. Each page was teeming with White smiling faces, and visual cues that seemed to confirm it was better to be White than whatever color I was. At that age, when a teacher hands you a pair of scissors, a glue stick, and a stack of magazines filled with White people, and asks you to cut out pictures that look like your family, you do what anyone living in a hyper-White world would do—and what all of my classmates were doing—you cut out White people. And that's exactly what I did.

Picking a White dad was easy. There were so many to choose from! I could have a White businessman dad. A burly White hunter-looking dad. A White cartoon dad with a tool belt around his waist. A White smiley, mustached dad in a blue collared shirt. I went with the White modelesque cartoon dad in the slick business suit. He was holding a briefcase and seemed to be heading somewhere very important. (I'm pretty sure I found him in a Men's Wearhouse ad.) Of course, this man could not have been further off from my actual dad, who was still working as a carpenter then, coming home covered in sawdust.

Choosing a Black mom was harder. I saw very few, if any, women with skin the color of mahogany in those magazines. And if I did, none were as sophisticated or as regal as my mom. She woke up every morning at 5:00 A.M. to get dressed to the nines for her desk job, wearing silky blouses with strong shoulder pads, high-waisted pencil skirts, and heels with black tights. I couldn't find *her* anywhere in those pages.

In the paper depiction of my life, I cast her as a brunette soccer-mom type instead. It was just . . . easier. I decided to be a blond girl with long pigtails. And just when things started getting really fun, as I was deciding which freckled little boy would be my brother, one of the teacher's aides interrupted me. The jig was up. The adults in the room seemed concerned. I felt like I had been caught doing something wrong.

The TA slyly pulled out the sole Black magazine I hadn't touched and pointed to a Black girl inside. "Ohhh, she's pretty!" she said in that artificially high-pitched tone adults use when cooing at babies. Then she flipped to another Black girl who looked nothing like me. "Oh, what about her? She reminds me so much of you. Her hair is just like yours." She laughed awkwardly. I froze, ashamed.

I got the message: I was supposed to be cutting out brown people, but it all felt more complicated than that. Don't get me wrong, I loved my family just as they were, but adding a Black mom, a Black brother, a Black me to this White paper family I was constructing would have meant having to own that I was not like the rest of my classmates. And I really didn't want that. I wanted to belong. To me, belonging meant blending into my environment.

I know now that the teacher was trying to give me an out. To point me in the direction of who I really was. But the more she cooed and pointed at Black people, the more singled out I felt. It's like somehow my baby brain had already absorbed too much of the whitewashing in those pages to retreat now. So, I straight up ignored the poor woman and continued collaging my way into this temporary delusion of Whiteness.

Big mistake.

When I came home with my White paper family, it was as if my mom had been readying herself my whole life for this moment of reckoning: it was time to have the Race Conversation.

She was acutely aware of how the world could make little Black girls feel invisible. And she wasn't having any of that, not in her house. Not her girl. That was when she pulled out the assignment I'd just completed at school and launched into a full-blown intervention that contained a string of her famously cheesy one-liners, starting with:

"Houston, we have a problem!"

"We are going to redo this, Lainey," she finally said to me, in a gentle but serious tone. "This time Mommy's going to help you, okay?" She wasn't angry or even disappointed. This was a loving intervention. An early course correction, redirecting me to own my Blackness in a world that can make it hard to embrace.

The next thing I knew, my brother and I were sitting at the oak wood table in our dining room, rummaging through a stack of *Ebony* and *Essence* magazines filled with Black bodies.

Eric was visibly annoyed that he had somehow gotten roped into this thinly veiled race exercise turned arts-and-crafts project. He had better things to do at six years old. But when he so much as attempted to squirm out of his seat, my mom shot him the Look and said, "Boy, do you value your life?" This was never not a rhetorical question. Thinking back on it now, it all seems like some sort of satiric Dave Chappelle sketch on how to raise Black kids in White America.

With Mom as our spirit guide, this family project was actually sort of fun. The caramel-complected brother-sister duo I picked to represent Eric and Elaine in my new family collage came from a syrup advertisement. They looked happy and mischievous, just like us. I selected a slim, fashionable Black woman with dramatic eye shadow and a perfect Colgate smile to be my mom. She graciously allowed me to keep my suit-and-tie dad, even though he was as fictitious as the blond version of little Elaine.

When my mom finished admiring this reimagined—and much more realistic—family collage, she made me tape it to the wall right next to my bed. So, for the next five years, these were the first images I saw every morning and the last images I saw every night. She was serious about dismantling any misguided notions that I was or could ever be White. But more than anything, she wanted me to see pride in my Blackness. And she did everything in her power to make sure I did.

My MOM REFUSED TO buy me White dolls. Meanwhile, at my friends' houses, no one seemed bothered that all we ever played with were White dolls. In fact, it was viewed as the norm. I tried to ignore the tightness in my belly whenever my White friends came over and we were subsequently forced to play with Black dolls. Instead of Ken, the male counterpart to Barbie, we had to sneak into my brother's room to borrow his collectible M. C. Hammer doll to play the love interest.

I was probably seven years old when I *begged* my mom for this next-level ballerina doll that I saw on a commercial. This doll could turn out like a real ballerina and she came with a pink leotard, matching leg warmers, and her own barre. She was in demand and overpriced—but my mom dutifully searched multiple stores and stood in a long line to get her for me. And yet, when I unwrapped the gift on my birthday, my reaction was lukewarm.

I politely said, "Thank you, Mommy," and put the gift aside.

"Oh, that's all I get after all your mama went through to get you that thing? Uh-uh. What's the matter?"

I finally buckled. "It's just that—this isn't the one from the commercial."

This was code language for "I wanted the White one."

THE WANT-TO-BE-WHITE complex runs deep and started young for me. Only as an adult in quiet moments of reflection can I begin to see clearly the subconscious impact of White supremacy at work in the messages I was fed as a child. By centering and positioning Whiteness as superior, Whiteness as the norm, and everything else as a deviation, a racial hierarchy is reinforced. The subsequent microaggressions are as small as the fair "flesh-colored" Band-Aids we were handed in school (which were clearly designed for White people). Because Black and brown dolls were *never* front and center in advertisements (if they existed at all, they appeared as some sort of off-brand sidekick), and because I lived in a world that reflected this hierarchy I saw in the media, I grew up with an unspoken suspicion that the world would see me as second best, too.

The only magazines I saw with Black women on the cover were *Ebony* and *Essence*—and most supermarkets in my hometown didn't carry them in the checkout aisle. Even shopping for Black beauty products in convenience stores with my mom became an unintended lesson in what it means to be marginalized. So often we'd have to go searching beyond the well-lit general market beauty aisle and end up crouching into some small, poorly lit corner of far less favorable shelves for "our" hair care.

It was certainly a far cry from the outright oppression that my mother's family experienced in the Jim Crow South. Yet these messages were subtle but powerful reminders of a racist past that still has not been fully dismantled—and of a dominant American narrative in which our stories are primarily told through the White gaze.

I remember learning about slavery in school under especially awkward circumstances. I was lying on the cold floor of the classroom next to my classmates, our bodies packed tightly next to one other like sardines. We had been instructed to scoot our desks to the perimeter of the room while our teacher turned off all the lights and began playing the movie *Roots* on the small television above the whiteboard. We listened to terrified women screaming, babies crying, and waves crashing against a very creaky boat. The assignment was to just lie there imagining it was us on the slave ship. As the sole Black person in the room, it was all a bit alienating and I can't say it made me feel any more of a connection with my ancestors' harrowing journey to this country. I just kept wondering what everyone else was thinking—and if they were as traumatized as I was seeing LeVar Burton from *Reading Rainbow* getting whipped like that. But it felt too uncomfortable to ask.

OVER TIME, EXPERIENCES LIKE these all worked in concert to uproot some sense of the pride in my heritage that my mother worked so hard to instill. She kept on plotting and planting seeds anyway, making sure I learned a crucial lesson: when the world tells you to shrink, expand.

"When the world tells you to shrink, expand."

CHAPTER 3

Brown Girl Boss

Keep in mind always the present you are constructing.
It should be the future you want.

ALICE WALKER, *THE TEMPLE OF MY FAMILIAR*

Relentless. That's what we were: two relentless brown girl bosses.

Claudia Ortega's skin was roughly the same shade of caramel taffy as mine. She lived in a cul-de-sac exactly seven minutes away in a four-bedroom home tucked snugly between a smattering of fancier houses belonging to all the White girls we wanted to be friends with in fourth grade. I can still smell the fresh tortillas and Downy fabric softener inviting me inside. I spent more time at her house than my own in those days. Despite my efforts to blend into her family, my puffy plaits and the halo of frizz that swelled around my hairline in the heat were dead giveaways that I was definitely *not* an Ortega. Though it didn't stop me from pretending I was Mexican by association anyway.

On Saturday mornings we would race to share a seat at her family's dining-room table to sop up chorizo and ketchup using torn-off edges of her mother Teresa's famous homemade tortillas. We'd dance like Jennifer Lopez in *Selena*. I even picked up some Spanish curse words from her older siblings, whom we devised elaborate spy missions to eavesdrop on. We would crawl shamelessly beneath beds, hide in closets, press ourselves up against closed doors, cupping our ears with our tiny hands to listen in on forbidden conversations about family secrets, sex, and drugs. How else were we to uncover the mysteries of the world our mothers would never tell us about?

It was the early 1990s in our small Northern California town, where thick white blankets of fog sometimes covered our entire peninsula. And beneath that blanket, global history was being made just miles away. But little girls like us had little to do with the happenings in Silicon Valley— a place that sounded more like a ride at Disneyland than the hotbed of digital innovation it was becoming. The World Wide Web had just been invented and Nokia was about to debut the first "smartphone," which flipped open and was as big as our forearms. Dial-up internet and AOL Instant Messenger hadn't hit our households just yet.

Little did we know, we were in the final days of Life Before the Internet, when imaginations still roamed freely in backyards across America and Giga Pets were the only tiny mobile machines kids had developed compulsive, codependent relationships with. These were simpler times, when dopamine levels spiked at the sound of the ice cream man, Nintendo Super Mario Bros., and cassette tapes with parental advisory labels. In not much more than a decade's time, MySpace, Facebook, and Twitter would come along and change all of that forever. But we were just eight years old then, and focused on one thing and one thing only: handling our business.

I'M NOT EXACTLY SURE when our playdates turned from choreographing epic Barbie telenovelas in Claudia's bedroom to hustling like two real-life tween entrepreneurs, but soon we would have our very first full-service beauty salon up and running in her backyard, *and* an imaginary magazine under way. While our "businesses" were makeshift at best, the grind was very real. We were busy creating a world that we could not only be a part of, but a world we could run. For our magazine, we sketched high-fashion girls with severe eyebrows onto construction paper—then we'd industriously wrap our "pages" in Saran wrap "for the glossy feel." We built the salon with anything we could find lying around Claudia's house. Old sheets became airy walls between our massage and manicure stations. We even trawled door-to-door shamelessly asking neighbors for scrap cardboard to build our reception desk. Each slab of grease-stained cardboard became an investment in our vision.

We may not have been popular, but *dammit* if we weren't enterprising! Who knows—maybe it was all a warped, socially awkward tactic to lure in new playmates. A way to establish ourselves as worthy members of our (very White) community. If nothing else, we knew our salon was a way to make those girls in Claudia's cul-de-sac *see us*. We might even be able to make them our patrons.

And one by one, we did.

When our salon was finally ready, we went around the block again to announce the grand opening. We offered manicures, hair brushing, massages, makeup (secretly borrowed from her older sister's Caboodles). Terrin became our first loyal customer. She was the next-door neighbor who was a year younger than us and just looking for something to do. Then came Courtney and Cheyenne. Even Teresa, Claudia's mom, would show up every now and then between loads of dishes and laundry for a hand massage and a hair combing.

We didn't make a dime, but the thrill of our booming business was addictive. All Saturday long, Claudia and I ran around busily, relishing the role of boss ladies who had this adult thing on lock. During our obligatory "smoke breaks," we would slink around the corner of the house to light up fake cigarettes that we rolled with construction paper and stuffed with cotton balls. With each puff we'd gaze up at cartoon-shaped clouds that would shape-shift with every blink. Our counterfeit cigarettes managed to deliver a little buzz, sending us into loopy fits of laughter, flashing buckteeth that busted the "grown-ass woman" facade. Back then, that was what power was all about: faking it until you have enough to actually make your own rules. We could smoke if we wanted to—we were rounding out our first decade on Earth with our shit all kinds of together.

I may have been confused about my race and clumsy in navigating social circles, but it was clear even then that I wanted to be the boss. Long before I knew exactly what career path to pursue, I knew that I wanted to be *great*. Not mediocre. Not average. Anything but ordinary. I wanted to design my own extraordinary life—a big, colorful existence. There was no obvious path to success, though. I would have to make it up along the way.

At my actual home—the one my parents owned and forced me to come back to—I would stay up all night working on collages for my beloved photo albums. They were my most prized possessions. I made dedicated spreads for each of my friends using cut-out quotes or phrases that captured their essence, alongside pictures of our best memories together.

"Lainey, you better be getting ready for bed!" my mom would holler from the kitchen, breaking the hum of one of her church hymns.

"I am, Mom." I'd chirp, lying through my jacked-up teeth.

"Girl, I know you're not telling your mama no tales!" Even in her sarcasm, we both knew this was an active threat. I'd often retreat to my bed, where I would lie still and feign sleep until all the lights were off in the house. Then I'd reach for a flashlight to continue perfecting my work. I'd balance on furniture and nearly topple over in order to pull down my meticulously curated photo albums from the tall shelf in my closet where they were stored. To find the perfect touch, I'd dig furiously through the bloated gallon-size Ziploc bag filled with cut-out quotes, pictures, and colorful letters in interesting typefaces that I found in magazines like *YM*, *Seventeen*, and the Delia's catalogue that showed up every once in a while, like a gem hidden in junk mail. I didn't always see myself in those pages then, but I used them to create something of my own—something that reflected my world. And I couldn't sleep until my pages were *just* right.

I DIDN'T KNOW WHAT JOURNALISM was until many years later, but I have always loved stories—telling them and pulling really good ones out of other people.

During bathtime as a kid, I pretended to be both the interviewer and the VIP interviewee. Talking into the portable showerhead, surrounded by bubbles, I was Barbara freaking Walters. Other days I was playing Oprah Winfrey. And I only interviewed the best: Michael—both Jackson *and* Jordan. Whitney. Janet. Mariah. MLK. Elizabeth Taylor. Even Einstein. And we went *deep*. I got the untold secrets. The gems all of America only wished they knew about the biggest icons, dead or alive. When the roles would reverse and I was the one spilling the tea, there would be dramatic pauses and fake tears as I detailed near-death experiences, multiple divorces, groundbreaking medical discoveries, you name it.

APART FROM *THE OPRAH WINFREY SHOW*, which I watched religiously after school, one of my favorite TV shows as a kid was *Lifestyles of the Rich and Famous* with Robin Leach. I didn't see very many people of color on the show, but that didn't stop me from imagining myself in that rose-colored world. There were women with long, red nails; loads of gold rings; big, voluminous hair; dramatized eye makeup with bold eye shadow, and mascara on the top *and* the bottom lashes. They lived in big houses with winding staircases. They drove hot pink convertible Corvettes like my Barbies. They wore lots of silk and did everything in high heels. They were extravagant and glamorous and impossibly cool. I imagined myself living a life like that. And I gravitated toward characters who became references for the kind of woman I could be:

In my mind, she was Tracy Chambers in *Mahogany* but less tragic. Jacqueline Broyer in *Boomerang* but less ruthless. Whitley Gilbert from *A Different World* but less whiny. Hilary Banks on *The Fresh Prince of Bel-Air* but less ditzy. Clair Huxtable but without the law degree.

My real-life role model was my aunt Janet, who owned a hair salon called The Place 2 Be.

MY AUNT JANET was my mom's first friend in California. They met in their twenties and have been like sisters ever since. In my eyes, my aunt Janet has always been a boss and very much the heroine of her own big life. She drove an antique convertible Mercedes-Benz, vacationed in Jamaica, and carried cigarettes in her purse that she never let me see her smoke, which made her even more cool and mysterious to me. She had a big walk-in closet spilling over with silky blouses and lacy bras with cups that I could fit my whole head into. Whenever we visited her well-decorated apartment, which smelled like a garden of potpourri and incense, I would lock myself in her bathroom to ogle all the dazzling cosmetics and perfume that lined the shelves. There were fancy hand creams and body lotions and pristine bottles of mysterious potions that I would dab on, spritz, and delight in, thinking, "*This* is the life!"

Until I was old enough to build my own backyard salon, I spent the better part of my Saturdays throughout my childhood in my aunt Janet's real-life salon waiting for my mom to get her hair done, which quite literally took all day. I was never allowed to chemically straighten my hair, but on special occasions, like Easter Sunday or Picture Day, my mom let me get my hair "silked" (aka flat ironed) like Aaliyah.

But most days, I would just help sweep up hair off the floor while studying all the different variations of Black womanhood on display. Her clients came in every shade, shape, texture, and flavor of Black—from the palest freckled skin to the deepest, richest skin tones. Some came in for relaxers, others for braids or twists. One by one, I watched them transform, and I'd build dramatic story arcs for each of them in my head. I imagined their big lives and big jobs. I idolized these working women who strutted in and out of that salon with car keys in hand, always on the go.

The only other place I had ever seen Black women this glamorous was in the pages of my mom's *Essence* magazine, which I pulled out of the mailbox every month and pored over. I looked forward to the beauty and fashion spreads that depicted Black women as these exquisitely styled, sophisticated deities. Beyond that inspiration, I also learned things about navigating work (negotiating raises, dealing with office politics), managing money (401ks, IRAs), detecting health crises (mostly fibroids and diabetes), and maintaining relationships (cheating lovers, undercover brothers)—all stuff I probably should not have known at ten. But the point is, each issue felt like a celebration of a modern Black woman's life. It was exciting and nourishing. My favorite section of all was iconic editor-in-chief Susan L. Taylor's *In the Spirit* column. It was a soulful monthly meditation on moving through life's challenges with faith, integrity, courage, and joy. I hung on to every beautifully crafted sentence.

When I look back at my childhood, I see what a profound impact that magazine and those afternoons in my aunt's salon had on me. It's how I discovered the beauty and plurality of Black womanhood. Those were the counternarratives I needed to see myself and my own glorious possibilities reflected back at me.

My DAD WAS THE ONE who discovered my writing ability before anyone else. One morning in third grade, I found him stretched out on his favorite recliner in the living room reading one of my short stories. His hair was slicked back, still wet from his morning bath and a fresh douse of Aqua Net hairspray. His big blue eyes were bright and clear. Sheba, our black cat, was nibbling on dry kibble nearby; Blondie was purring in his lap. I was rubbing the sleep out of my eyes when he startled me with unexpected praise: "WOW-ee-zow-ee, Lainey! This is outta sight. You're a great writer, just like your grandma Pat and your ol' dad. You've got to keep at this, baby."

I beamed from ear to ear and curled up next to him.

"Deb, ya gotta come over here and read this. You won't believe it!"

And just like that, my favorite subject changed from math to English.

Until then, I hadn't ever considered that I could become a writer. Let alone a *great* writer. But those early affirmations, those moments of feeling seen—particularly by the man who created you—they matter so much to a little girl.

My DAD WAS A lead carpenter and the breadwinner of the family for more than two decades before a work-related back injury ended his career. Losing his mobility and a fundamental aspect of his identity as a provider had to be harder on him than any of us could ever know. But his most rewarding job of all—and arguably the hardest—became waking me up in the mornings throughout my childhood. Getting me to school on time was always an ordeal.

I could sleep through an earthquake, a volcanic eruption, possibly even the end of the world. I've damn near lost roommates, boyfriends, and jobs over my body's inexplicable disregard for alarm clocks. For many years, I was convinced that this compulsion to oversleep had to be some sort of disorder. To this day, I am embarrassed to admit that I still deeply struggle with get-yo-ass-up syndrome. At least back then, my dad was still down to be my human alarm clock.

When all other tactics failed to get the job done—tickling me, pulling the covers off of my virtually comatose body, shouting—my dad made up a wake-up song that he sang to me nearly every morning for sixteen years: "Lainey Flainey, give me your answer true. I'm half crazy over the likes of you." He'd saunter into my room and sit on the edge of my bed, tap, tap, tapping my tiny body to the beat until I finally woke up. Looking back, it was the most loving, patient act of parenting in the universe. Of course, at the time, it was simply annoying as hell.

"And we're off like a herd of turtles!" he'd say. Every. Single. Day. These sweet morning rituals carried on all throughout junior high and high school drop-offs.

If driving around in that old El Camino was his pride, having me and my brother along for the ride was his joy. After hitting play on his favorite Eric Clapton cassette tape, he'd tap, tap, tap to the beat on the steering wheel all the way to school. We'd all ignore the sound of his coffee mug rolling around on the floor in the backseat.

I'm not exactly sure how he occupied himself during the days after he went on disability leave from work. But I sensed that he had lost his way.

SOMETIMES BACK IN ELEMENTARY school, my brother and I would stand under the flagpole for hours waiting for dad to pick us up. All the other kids had gone home and all kinds of dramatic scenarios would play out in my mind. Had he died in a car accident? Had aliens abducted him? When Mrs. Dees, the school child-care provider who wasn't exactly known for being the nicest lady, would approach us with concern in her eyes and ask if we were "okay," I wondered if I'd somehow end up in her care permanently, a brown Orphan Annie.

Eventually his El Camino would swing into the empty parking lot and we'd run up to the door, relieved he hadn't forgotten us for good.

"Hey, buddy! Heya, Lainey! I'm sorry, you guys. Your dad just laid down for a little nap, and boy, I really wiped out this time."

It was around this time that we learned to detect the faint scent of Coors beer on his breath. I likened it to spoiled apple juice, sweetness gone sour.

We rarely spoke about it over the years, but my dad's drinking and depression quietly plagued our family since before I could remember. It was one reason I insisted on spending so much time at Claudia's house, and why I filled up my after-school schedule with extracurricular activities. I never questioned how much I meant to him, and I knew that he would do anything in his power to protect me and my brother. The problem was that he seemed powerless over his own demons—or "lesser angels," as my mom would say.

Long before his debilitating back injury put him out of work, the loss of his brother, who was his best friend, seemed to create in him a well of loneliness—a deep emptiness—that never fully went away. We all cope with trauma differently. My dad turned to alcohol to self-medicate.

But only when he thought we weren't looking.

He'd disappear into the shadows of the side yard or slip away to drink in the toolshed. He thought we didn't notice. But we always knew. Sometimes, we would even pour his beer down the drain and leave the tall Coors cans on the counter—our passive-aggressive way of letting him know that as invisible as he felt, we saw him. We just wished we never had to see him like *that*.

One particular bender is burned into my memory.

It was a Monday, which meant Dad had to play chauffeur because Mom had choir practice at church. I was running late for gymnastics and my dad was more out of it than usual—he could hardly keep his eyes open as he stumbled out to the car. I noticed a wet spot on his chest pocket. Folded inside was the check my mom had left on the oak wood table for him to deliver to my gym coach. He must have guzzled too quickly to notice the beer spilling onto his T-shirt.

I wasn't sure which was worse: the fear of dying on the way to practice, or my drunk dad handing my gymnastics coach a soggy, beer-soaked check with my last name on it. I didn't have any control over the outcome, so I held my breath and gripped the armrest the whole way there, praying that we would be okay.

For better or worse, we arrived. As I slipped out of the car and opened the gymnasium door, embers of shame and humiliation erupted into flames inside me. There we were, the dysfunctional dad and his ten-year-old daughter on display in front of the judgmental coaches I had been working so hard to please. My dad slurred and fumbled through the check drop-off. I picked up on the dismay in my coaches' stares, but I deflected, pretending everything was fine, smiling nervously, all the while clenching my jaw, wanting desperately to disappear.

It was hard enough feeling like the underdog as the only girl with braids and brown skin on my team. Now I had to carry my dad's shame around, too, like weights around my ankles. From that point on, I worked even harder for my coaches' approval. In some twisted way, it was as if I thought perfecting my performance could somehow undo the humiliation of that moment.

Looking back, I can see how all those early impulses to strive for perfection—from my photo album to the backyard business—were, at least in part, a reaction to the things I could not control in my world. Like my dad's drinking. That early inclination to overcompensate, to distract from my family's shortcomings, drove me to overachieve at anything I took on because, the way I saw it, I couldn't control my dad's behavior but at least I could control my own.

Over the years, his road to recovery was bumpy. But the truth is, it could have been worse. A lot worse. He was never a violent or angry drunk.

Just a clumsy one. And I always felt loved by him. Plus, the upside of having an alcoholic parent with Catholic guilt was at least we'd always know when he "fell off the wagon" because the kitchen would be spotless, the lawn would be mowed, and he'd be bathed and chopping up veggies for his famous "bachelor's stew" all by the time Mom came home from work. Overcompensating for his bad habit was part of his cycle. So were his heartfelt apologies whenever he got caught. Still, however harmless, each slip felt like a breach of trust, a broken promise to our family.

WHEN I LOOK BACK, I see a little girl running, pushing, working creatively to compensate for things that were beyond her control. For years, I felt like an imposter with a hidden flaw waiting to be found out. I worried that I might be stained, too, just like that check in my dad's pocket. So I worked harder to deny failure and shame a place in my life. I learned to excel by not looking at it. I ran away when I needed to. Full speed ahead. In the fast lane. Onward. Into new people, new places. I often fell into the potholes of perfectionism. No matter what, I got back up and positioned myself in the light.

But like a shadow, shame follows wherever you go.

Until you make peace with it.

Over time I've learned to accept and even appreciate this part of my story. What I discovered is that my dad is beautifully flawed just like the rest of us, and his struggles played an important role in making me who I am. And I've learned to love who I am. Even if certain parts were forged by fire. Sometimes the things that hurt the most propel you the farthest.

"I've learned to love who I am. Even if certain parts were forged by fire."

CHAPTER 4

Pretty or Butt Ugly

You really have to love yourself to get
anything done in this world.
LUCILLE BALL

In fifth grade I learned I wasn't one of the "beautiful people" after finding a balled-up piece of paper ranking the girls in our class from pretty to butt ugly. It was authored by a handful of bored boys who thought this would be a fun activity. I announced my discovery to the other girls through a chain of whispers that spread like wildfire. At lunchtime we all met up by the tetherball courts anxious to unfold the note, which in some twisted way felt like it held our fates. After reviewing the results, silence befell the group, each of us unsure what to do about the sinking feeling in our bellies. It was all so traumatizing that I can't even recall exactly where I landed in that ranking—but let's just say it wasn't pretty.

"Let's make a list ranking the boys," I announced.

I figured, if we could be treated merely as props to be assessed, picked up, put down, laughed about, and discarded, then maybe flinging the weight of judgment back onto them would show them just how shitty it felt. A feminist act? Not really. Though maybe not the worst idea in the world either.

For so much of our lives we are told what beauty is, what it looks like, who possesses it, who doesn't. We pretend to subscribe to the cliché that "beauty is in the eye of the beholder," but in reality, beauty so often feels like a self-selecting world of the haves and the have-nots. The definitions are restrictive and binary. You're either in or you're out. And the ones pushed to the margins are rarely given the pen to write ourselves and our own definitions in.

Little did I know, one day I would hold the proverbial pen, and I would use it to remind young girls of their power.

But it was only fifth grade, and writing a list to classify—and, okay, objectify—the boys was the best retaliation I could come up with back then. Who knows if they ever even read it.

This elementary school behavior became early evidence to me that there was a power imbalance at play between genders that none of us girls could yet articulate. It was as if that little piece of paper written by idiotic little boys had the power to dictate our self-worth. I learned that day just how sensitive young girls are to messages that tell you what to believe about yourself. I saw how we absorb other people's opinions about our bodies like a sponge sops up red wine after a spill. These early messages can tarnish the way we see ourselves and translate into limiting beliefs that stay with us for a lifetime.

The image of me and those poor girls huddled around that crumpled piece of paper, wincing, eager for the most superficial form of validation, still disturbs me. Though I suppose it isn't a far cry from the experience of participating in social media today. Every day we curl over our phones, endlessly scrolling, falling deep into comparison traps, searching for superficial forms of validation in likes, mentions, and follows.

I SPENT MY KINDERGARTEN THROUGH sixth-grade years feeling virtually invisible to boys. With the exception of that one time in third grade when Kevin Patrick chased me around the T-ball bench trying to kiss me, with two streams of dried snot running down his nose, your girl was getting no play.

I was smart, funny, athletic, and reasonably popular, but I didn't consider myself attractive compared to the other girls at school. Petite blond girls with straight teeth and bangs were the Thing at my school then. The closest I ever got to bangs was frizz that swelled along my hairline at recess; and perhaps because my baby teeth took an absurd amount of time to fall out, I ended up with a mouthful of jagged adult teeth that grew in on top of each other in strangely different sizes and shapes. The cool girls wore "designer" Union Bay leather jackets with puffy denim sleeves and crisp white K-Swiss sneakers. Meanwhile, my mom refused to pay that much for a jacket and shoes I'd outgrow in six months, so we shopped the knockoffs at Payless or the marked-down racks at Ross on layaway.

As a result of this seemingly widening gap between me and the beautiful people of Bunker Elementary, comparison crept in where complete confidence once lived. Self-doubt began to fester in the spaces that limitless possibility once occupied. A certain discomfort in my own skin ate away at that unabashed, "chin to the sky" self-assuredness I was born with. A slow but steady process of shrinking began. And you could see it play out in my hair.

IF YOU EVER WONDER how a teenage girl feels about herself, where she is in life, who she's trying to be, just look at what is going on with her hair. Especially if she has curly hair.

My personal journey of discovering, decoding, rejecting, accepting, and eventually embracing my natural hair reflected a larger arc in my winding road to self-acceptance.

I DIDN'T EVEN DISCOVER THAT I had naturally curly hair until the fifth grade, because my mom insisted on keeping it in braids throughout my childhood. We had a ritual: every Sunday night I'd grab the Pink Lotion, Sta-Sof-Fro, and the wide-tooth comb from underneath the bathroom sink, then plop down on a bean bag in between her legs, where I would watch TV, eventually falling asleep, while she designed intricate braided styles on my head. Whenever I would periodically wake up to squeal, she'd call me "tenderheaded" and swiftly pop me with the comb to remind me what actual pain felt like. Then she'd wrap my little head in a scarf and carry me to bed. My friends looked forward to seeing how I'd turn up to school on Mondays—no two styles were ever the same.

Once I was given agency over my own hairstyles, I remember looking into the mirror after showering one morning and noticing for the first time that I had CURLS. Springy little boingy curls that actually seemed pretty exceptional, particularly when they were sopping wet. I decided for picture day I would wear my hair down and curly—*exactly* like this. I naively assumed that drenching my hair in water was the key to maintaining this look. So at school, like clockwork, every thirty minutes I excused myself from class to dunk my whole head under the faucet in the girls' bathroom. Who cares that the back of my shirt was completely soaked—all I kept thinking was: "DO YOU SEE HOW CUTE MY HAIR LOOKS?!"

By junior high, I had moved on to plastering it with ultra-hold maximum-strength Dep gel and my dad's Vidal Sassoon hairspray, which gave my curls that crispy, crunchy, Top Ramen look I was going for. Like all the girls at my school, I liked to wear it in a half up/half down situation, with a little folded-over bun on top and two stick-straight antennas poking out in front. (Nineties kids know the look.) I didn't think to check the outrageous alcohol content of my products, which were no doubt drying out my strands to dust, but I was quick to check anyone who had the audacity to try to touch my hair. I don't know what it is about curly hair that makes it a magnet for other people's hands, but I constantly found myself swatting them away like flies. My friends already knew the deal: you do not touch Elaine's hair. That was the rule, and I had a zero-tolerance policy, because I very sincerely feared that it might erupt into a chalky explosion of frizz. I still maintain this rule today, but for different, more politicized reasons. (Cue: Solange.)

Over the years, my hair has played a big part in an ongoing experiment with my identity. As a teen, it was like a mirror reflecting to the world what was going on inside. I was never allowed to use chemical straighteners, but I spent years heat styling it into submission as a means of shrinking myself to fit into a narrower, neater version of what it meant to be "pretty" or "professional." There were times it became a part of a costume that allowed me to morph into other identities and ethnicities altogether when I wasn't comfortable in my own.

Having curly hair and light brown skin meant that I could blend in with Afro Latinos, East Africans, Indians, Polynesians, all depending on how I styled my hair. For me, being biracial was like being born with built-in ethnic camouflage that afforded me the ability to shape-shift with my surroundings. I went from a relatively preppy, predominantly White elementary school to a more diverse junior high school with a dense Mexican population—and my identity morphed right along with my environment.

BACK THEN, BRITNEY SPEARS was the biggest pop star in our world. And my best friend Brittney Mayer was the most beautiful girl in seventh grade. She was half Mexican, half White, and truly picture perfect, with a slight frame, a tiny upturned nose, and unnaturally long eyelashes. She wore bangs that barreled off her hairline in a perfect half circle, landing just above razor-thin, immaculately arched brows. Those "Brittney Mayer" bangs were often imitated but never duplicated—no one else could quite crack the code on her mastery of a curling iron.

Students at our junior high school were forced to abide by a mandatory dress code, but we indulged in what little creative control we had over our personal aesthetic. Each morning before school my dad waited outside in the car while Brittney and I consulted each other on our beauty looks: Liquid or pencil eyeliner? Curly or straight hair? Loose, sparkly eye shadow on our lids or glitter gel highlighter on our cheekbones? Self-expression in those days was limited to deciding what tiny, glittery butterfly hairclips to wear, which, by the way, we stole by the handful from Fashion 4 Less at the mall. (One time the store manager caught on and chased us into the parking lot—unbeknownst to my dad, who was the slowest getaway driver *ever*. We almost died of panic attacks in the backseat while he crept along at five miles an hour.)

Junior high was all about looking and acting as hard core as possible: Brown lip liner, severe eyebrows, puff coats, baggy overalls, crop tops, and—especially on special occasions—pin-straight hair. This was pre–blowout bars and pre–blowout bar budgets. To straighten each other's hair we resorted to a clothing iron as our go-to hot tool that smoothed away curly and wavy textures like wrinkles on a pair of slacks. We would each take turns folding our bodies across an ironing board to go at it. One time we accidentally burned off the bottom-right chunk of my hair—the entire section just sizzled right off.

It was sort of a given that whenever boys were around they wanted Brittney's attention, not mine. It never bothered me, except for that one winter ball in eighth grade when the final slow song of the night came on and I was the last one standing. One by one each of my friends got pulled away by boys—and I was left to roam the dimly lit gym alone. I darted across the floor, pretending to be on an important mission, but when I reached the bleachers to wait out the humiliation, I found myself sitting among a sad smattering of other students—which uncoincidentally included some of the only other Black girls in our school. I tried to play it off like it didn't matter, but my mom saw it all over me when I came home that night.

I ended up sobbing in her lap.

By the time I entered high school, which had an even more diverse student body, things got really confusing. With the exception of church, where boys somehow seemed off-limits, this was the first time I was immersed in a world with eligible Black guys my age. Suddenly I found myself turning heads—an entirely new experience for me. I had never felt attractive or desirable around the White guys I grew up with, then high school hits and, *boom,* all these Black dudes are checking for your girl! It was foreign and exciting—and honestly, it made me a little queasy. Just when I had gotten used to being overlooked by guys, this sudden surge of attention came with a certain male gaze that made me feel invisible in a brand-new way. I went from being the token Black girl in a sea of Whiteness to the new, "exotic," "light-skin-long-hair" chick.

I didn't have the language for things like "light-skin privilege" then and I hadn't yet learned about the paper bag test that had historically divided Black people into a virtual caste system based on the shade of brown skin they were born with. All I knew at the time was that I was uncomfortable with the premium that seemed to be placed on "mixed girls." In music videos all the "video vixens" had light skin and long hair, and the only mixed-race girls I encountered wore their light-skin-long-hair identity as a badge of superiority. I wanted nothing to do with any of those stereotypes.

Little did I know, I was on the eve of my next mini teenage identity crisis.

"For so much of our lives
we are told what beauty is,
what it looks like, who
possesses it, who
doesn't. . . .
And the ones pushed to the
margins are rarely given
the pen to write ourselves and
our own definitions in."

CHAPTER 5

Ride or Die Syndrome

When someone shows you who they are,
believe them the first time.
MAYA ANGELOU, VIA OPRAH,
VIA DEBRA WELTEROTH, MY MOM

A t fourteen, I was ready for love and everything that came with it. I wanted to walk around campus holding hands. I wanted someone to call me after school. I wanted to understand what love songs and rom-coms were all about. Most of all, I was ready to "get chose."

Enter First Love, the most beautiful boy I'd ever seen. I was in seventh grade when he made my heart stop as he crossed a grassy hill at Newark Junior High. First Love was in eighth grade, and he looked like the literal FaceFusion of Lil' Bow Wow and Trey Songz. Pretty boys with cornrows were very much my type then. From that moment on, every time I spotted him, time slowed down, my heart pounded, and my hands trembled.

I did not muster up the courage to speak to him for another two years.

By then, I was a freshman in high school and had joined the track team, where he was already a star. His 400-meter dash and signature cornrows had people all over the state talking. My mom, however, was unimpressed: "All I see is a big ol' ego packed into a little man's complex." She went on to share one of the best pieces of dating advice she learned from her first love: "Baby girl, a woman should never compete for space in the mirror with her man."

Like so much of our mothers' wisdom, her advice landed on deaf ears. I fell for him anyway.

Our romance brewed on the track after school. We started "officially" dating the spring of my freshman year, and those first three months were dreamy. We'd talk on the phone hours past our bedtime, even after my parents sent warning shots to hang up by way of firm pounds on the thin wall separating our bedrooms. We paged each other sweet nothings incessantly. (For those who remember pager code, extra credit if you can decode this: "143," "637.") He even made me a cassette tape with sides A and B filled with R&B and neo-soul slow jams: Maxwell. D'Angelo. Ginuwine. Avant. Carl Thomas. Jagged Edge. He told me each song expressed exactly how he felt about me. I memorized every lyric.

OUR FIRST KISS PLAYED out like a cheesy scene right out of the Black *Wonder Years*. First Love rode over to my house on his bike. We exchanged giddy smiles, awkward eye contact, and then our lips locked. The butterflies in my stomach went berserk as he rode off into the sunset. I sprinted into my house, snatching the cordless house phone off the wall charger like it was a 4x1 relay baton, speed-dialed one of my best friends midstride, and screamed into my pillow after collapsing onto my bed in disbelief. I had never known that specific brand of euphoria in my life. We waited three months to say "I love you," and from that moment on I was all in. Blissfully, naively, ALL IN.

"All in" meant I didn't mind that he repeatedly wore that same raggedy burgundy sweat suit to school, which was shredded at the knee and accessorized with a durag and house slippers. I thought it was attractive how little he cared about what other people might think of him. When he strolled into AP geometry late, pajama pants hanging below his tiny butt, chewing on a straw, chucking the deuce to the teacher, I'd shake my head, feigning disapproval, while smiling coyly. If he didn't show, I became his de facto spokesperson, suddenly responsible for explaining his whereabouts. It was one of my new wifey duties I took pride in, although frankly, most days I had few clues as to where he was.

As a relatively good girl who pretty much followed the rules, I was seen as a good influence on First Love; even his parents trusted me to help keep him focused on the right things. But inside, I secretly marveled at his ability to get away with anything. Sometimes he'd show up to class. Sometimes he wouldn't. But somehow he always did well on exam day. It was one of the great virtues of being a prized male student athlete with charisma, charm, and intellect to boot. The bad-boy mystique just added to his allure.

I keep all of my notebooks, and each one from high school is sprinkled with doodled hearts between our names. I even feted our hundred-day mark with a homemade cake (a treat no other man in my life has ever had the pleasure of receiving before or since). I begged my mom to show me how to bake and then snuck into his third-period class to decorate his desk with balloons, confetti, a card, and I even instructed his classmate to light the trick candles on the cake. He walked in (late as usual) to find a blazing fire hazard of puppy love melting all over his desk. We were only a hundred days in and I was already doing the absolute most.

First Love could be really sweet when he wanted to.

On my sixteenth birthday, he interrupted my choir class to usher in a massive bouquet of balloons. All eyes in the amphitheater landed on me.

They "aww"ed in unison, swooning as he stood in front of the class leading everyone in singing "Happy Birthday." Of course, he tacked on the hella Black Stevie Wonder rendition as an encore.

For Valentine's Day, First Love filled my bedroom with pink, white, and red heart-shaped balloons and arranged a family of teddy bears on my bed. They propped up a giant cardboard sign featuring a gang of glued-on Hallmark cards. He said he couldn't choose just one card to capture his feelings, so he wrote long, hilarious, heartwarming messages in all of them. (Clearly, he was pretty extra, too.)

But what I once perceived as passion felt much more mercurial post–honeymoon phase, when his mood swings became directed toward me. Between his infrequent grand gestures, he'd often pick fights, then ghost me. At track meets, he'd keep his distance. I told myself he just needed his space and I'd stay out of his way, pretending not to crave his attention.

On the bright side, his inconsistency taught me to cultivate a full life of my own, outside of any dependency on boyfriends. Between schoolwork, sports, student council, and my sister-friends, I invested my energy and focus on being number one in every other aspect of my life.

Yet no matter how good I got at impersonating a "chill girlfriend" with very, very few needs, First Love's aloof behavior started negatively affecting how I felt about myself. The more distant he became, the harder I clung to a false sense of confidence that I could guide us—guide him—back to a better place.

Once, after a particularly heated fight over the phone, I decided to hand-deliver a homemade meal to his job. I wanted to surprise him after his work shift but I didn't have my license yet, so I asked my best friend Tracy to drive me over to Lucky's, the local supermarket where First Love bagged groceries. We waited in the parking lot for hours while I replayed in my mind how the surprise would go down: The cold front between us would melt at the sight of me, his embrace would turn all the fighting into a distant memory, and we'd spend the rest of the evening making up during one of our cuddle marathons on his parents' couch. But those visions evaporated, right along with my dignity, when he finally emerged, accompanied by Zara, one of the cashiers who happened to be a nineteen-year-old college student—aka the Older Girl from Work he talked too much about.

The plate of food trembled in my sweaty palms as I braced myself for the moment when he would notice me standing in the parking lot. I stood up straighter and smiled sweetly, trying hard to mask the wave of envy coursing through my body. When our eyes met, without breaking his stride, he walked smooth past me. The boy even had the audacity to chuck me the deuce. As I watched him get into Zara's car, my heart exploded inside my chest, my cheeks began to burn. There I was, standing under the streetlights, humiliated, still holding his homemade meal.

To this day, I don't think I've ever cried the way I cried in Tracy's car that night.

"When someone shows you who they are, believe them. The first time."

Any time Auntie Oprah recited Mother Maya Angelou's greatest quote of all time on her show, my mother would respond emphatically from the kitchen, her voice rising above the sound of dishes clanking in the sink. "That's right! THE FIRST TIME." She even came up with her own Southern-style interpretation to counsel me: "If it walks like a duck, quacks like a duck, it's a duck." Applying these simple rules for character assessment helped me face the facts: First Love walked away from me like a jerk and deuced me in front of another girl like a jerk, so this must mean he was a straight-up jerk.

Yet somehow, despite this very precise logic, all the sage wisdom from our foremothers was quickly drowned out by the various auto-tuned ride-or-die chick anthems of the aughts. I didn't realize it then, but thanks to pop culture's objectification of women and the power imbalances reflected in the dysfunctional relationships surrounding me, I was being brainwashed into believing that women are often casualties of our own relationships. And that bending ourselves to make romance work is just part of the deal. No matter the song or movie or ill-fated anecdotes from my peers, the messages all seemed similarly detrimental for women:

Ride or die.

Hold your man down.

Deal with the drama and the crap and the pain.

Ride out the bumps.

'Til the wheels fall off.

As they say: relationships are hard. Right? Even my mom said you have to work at love. Plus, she chose to stay with my dad through all of his painful mistakes. Every day in my own household, I watched how loyalty and forgiveness functioned—even through dysfunction. These were my very first formative lessons in love.

And so, the harder it got in my own relationship, the harder I worked at it. Instead of walking away, I leaned in. I fought for it. I stuck it out. Because isn't that what you do for love?

Take a confused teenager's misinterpreted mom advice, mix with a steady rotation of raunchy rap videos that demean women and glorify bad boys, sprinkle in some romanticized clichés about love conquering all, and *boom*. You have the perfectly unhealthy recipe for how women lose themselves in shitty relationship dynamics. It's like an inborn disease of the mind and heart that gets passed down through generations, transcends age, and typically requires several rounds of heartbreaks, crushed self-esteem, and failed relationships to treat.

Adult me knows it should have been over that night. He didn't deserve that plate of cold food. Let alone my heart. But I was committed to the commitment—no matter what.

RIDE OR DIE SYNDROME

I WOKE UP THE NEXT day with a heavy heart. But I never broke up with him.

The grown Elaine wants to yell, "Leave him now! It will only get worse." But instead, teenage me would commit my first cardinal relationship mistake, one too many girls make.

"It hurts but he'll change," I thought.

I just have to ride out the bumps. Hold him down. Just like all the songs said. I was determined to make it work.

I had stupidly made myself available for reconciliation. Meanwhile, First Love continued ignoring me at school—this time leaving me feeling so small and lost that when the bell rang, instead of going to class, my body floated toward the parking lot.

I will never forget that day. It was beautiful outside. The perfect blue sky was wide open, watching me with its wispy clouds that went on seemingly forever.

My heart was breaking, but begging for a sign to hold on: "It gets better than this, right?"

Right then, I felt something within me affirmed—a deep, visceral knowing; perhaps it was a reminder of some agreement with the universe that no matter how small I felt in that crushing moment, I was destined for a love far greater.

"It gets better. There is more. Trust me," the clouds seemed to whisper.

From then on, the sky became my refuge. My coping mechanism. My own personal sign of hope pulling me higher when I was sure I was sinking.

AROUND THIS TIME, I'd noticed a nice boy with glasses at church, named Jonathan. He had a big, sweet smile and he sang next to me in the church choir (yes, I sang in the boys' section, thanks to the deep voice I inherited from my mother). He went to Bellarmine, the private all-boys school in Silicon Valley, twenty-five minutes away. The word around church was that he was studying to become a doctor. I thought he seemed so nice, but nice boys finished last in those days. We wouldn't exchange more than smiles and polite greetings for the next decade.

Meanwhile, per the mighty gospel of prefeminist era Beyoncé, my dating credo was basically: "If your status ain't hood, I ain't checking for you." Like many Destiny's Child fans in the early aughts, I, too, wanted a soldier. Back then, dating a bad boy "with street credibility" was every girl's relationship goal.

First Love was definitely not hard core by any stretch of the imagination. His dad worked in technology, and he was raised in a two-parent, blended family household in Newark. But he romanticized a bad-boy lifestyle—from the gunslinging video games he played obsessively, to the lies he told about growing up around actual gangsters in LA, to the music he bumped through his twelve-inch subwoofers—and he intentionally projected that image. It wasn't long before he'd start acting out that bad-boy fantasy with his best friend, who we'll call "J," a dark-skinned, lanky kid who was on his track team and lived in apartments around the corner from First Love's house.

I remember tagging along in the backseat for a few of their dubious post-track-practice adventures. I held my breath as First Love drove his beat-up Honda Accord like a race car. Scared we might crash, I pressed my back into the seat to brace myself. He'd leave the window all the way down as the chilly Bay Area wind violently whipped against my face. My safety and comfort weren't exactly priorities for First Love. I was lucky to be going along for their joyride.

I'd felt this before as a little girl in the car with my dad. I was scared, but when fear is familiar it keeps you holding on—and its grip works both ways.

"Babe, can you roll up the window?" I'd strain to project over Lil' Wayne from the backseat.

He ignored me.

"Babe, slow down."

He drove faster.

I still have so many questions for teenage me. First of all, girl: Your boyfriend should never scare you. Ever. Also, why. the. hell. was I in the backseat? PSA: If your boyfriend has you sitting in the backseat for anyone but his mother, he's not the one. Period. The end.

When we arrived at the dark cul-de-sac in the neighboring city of Fremont, First Love and "J" simultaneously got out of the car and opened the trunk as if it were a choreographed routine. Dark, shadowy figures approached. I squinted and tried to hear what was going on. Turns out these fools were selling weed. Conspicuously. To White kids in the suburbs. I rationalized it to myself as completely stupid but relatively harmless.

When First Love went off to college at Sacramento State University, his bad-boy act escalated, and so did his bad habits. But it took me a while to catch on.

FIRST LOVE VISITED ME from college during basketball season of my senior year. I was a cheerleader and spotted him from center court during my half-time performance. For the first time, I actually felt embarrassed at the sight of him. It was as if I were seeing him for the first time without rose-colored, love-drunk lenses. Cornrows were phasing out by then—even Alicia Keys had moved on. But there he was leaning against the gym wall, wearing the same old unkempt braids and beat-up house slippers. His beautiful, redbone complexion dulled. His pouty lips were now dry and discolored. Shadowy half circles had formed beneath his pretty brown eyes, and his gorgeously sculpted bone structure now seemed hollow. Up close, that skunky marijuana odor hung over him like the musky cloud of yesterday's hotbox.

Even with my attraction to First Love waning, I felt indebted to him, like I owed him my loyalty. I thought of the messages that had been drilled into me:

Ride or die.

Hold your man down.

Deal with the drama and the crap and the pain.

Ride out the bumps.

'Til the wheels fall off.

I was all in. Committed to the commitment. Even when it wasn't fun for me anymore. All because I didn't know how to let go.

At the time, I was a straight-A student, a varsity hurdler, a cheerleader, and in my second term as class president. (I ran my campaign on the corniest slogan: Don't Be Lame, Vote 4 Elaine. My God. I can't even type that with a straight face.) Point is: I was living a pretty squeaky-clean life in high school. But then on weekends I'd go visit First Love at his dark, dingy, off-campus apartment in Sacramento that reeked of weed, mold, and stale potato chips. My lungs still tighten when I think of my first night there—all I wanted to do was open a window and air the place out.

First Love had moved in with a wannabe rapper who sold weed and CDs from his car. There was only one bedroom, so the two nearly grown men would take turns sleeping on the floor. Even when their girlfriends were in town. We would roll out sleeping bags over stained carpet in a furniture-less dining room littered with empty soda cans, crumbs, and garbage. It was disgusting. I remember laying on that floor in that stupid sleeping bag thinking, "It's gotta get better than this."

First Love was going through a rocky transition into college, and though he wouldn't admit it, I knew he felt lost. By then, we had been together for three years and it felt impossible to leave him at what appeared to be his lowest point. So instead, I just existed at his lowest with him. I was trying to be his ride or die chick, trying to hold him down through the inevitable bumps in life. But his lifestyle choices made me more and more uneasy.

Still, I chose to stay by his side and I tried to steady myself: "It's just a phase. He'll grow out of this. He has so much potential."

Later on, I'd learn that First Love wasn't even actually going to school at the time. Instead, he and the lost boys of Sacramento spent their days driving around slanging CDs and weed. Weed was one thing, but the night one of them mentioned something about "moving rocks," it should have been over. (Had it not been for Jay-Z getting heavy rotation on the Top 40, I might not have even known what that slip of the tongue even meant.) Who knew if it was true or just bravado, but the fact that I never pressed the issue, that I chose to silence my concerns says more about me than it does him. Clearly, we were both drifting away from the couple I always dreamed we'd become.

Looking back, this *should* have been my deal breaker. But I kept hearing his parents' voices in my head: "Elaine's a good influence on him." I felt the pressure to keep him on track, even at the risk of him bringing us both down.

Before I met First Love, I had my sights set on going to Stanford University. But by the time college admissions rolled around, I felt too attached to him to envision darting out on my own path without him, so I did what any young, brainwashed, lovesick girl would do. The very thing I would later advise girls never to do. The one thing that, in my opinion, no parent should allow their daughters to do: after graduation, I followed my high school sweetheart to college. I never even applied to Stanford.

For many years, this decision has given me hot, chest-tightening pangs of regret. Not necessarily because of the state college I ended up at—but specifically because of my reason for choosing it. At the time, I convinced myself and my parents that it was the right decision for me, and that I was absolutely not doing it for First Love. "He's just a bonus!" I'd insist. Plus, the state system appealed to my parents' financial situation. We couldn't afford to fund a private or Ivy League tuition. I assured them that I had weighed all my options and that this was the right decision for me. But at seventeen years old, what did I know? As a high-achieving, minority, first-generation college applicant, I still can't fathom why a college counselor from my high school wouldn't have challenged me on this. There were plenty of scholarship opportunities available for someone like me.

———

By the time I joined First Love at college the following year, it was his last shot to get his act together. Since his parents had forced him to live on campus, I thought this meant we'd have a second chance at romantic strolls around school hand in hand, since he pretty much played me to the left all throughout high school. But to my dismay, that rudeboy behavior carried over into college. I felt like a convenient option at best. When he begged to borrow my car, I made him promise me that he wouldn't let anyone else drive it. Ten minutes after handing over my keys, I'd see his roommate in my car doing donuts in the parking lot.

Meanwhile, his anger issues were only getting worse.

Not long after matriculating into Sac State, I found myself in a heated argument with First Love, my back pressed up against a floor-to-ceiling window inside my dorm's stairwell. I don't remember why we were fighting, only that his veins and eyes bulged as we stood nose to nose, him yelling at the top of his lungs. In a fit of rage, to punctuate whatever point he was making, he balled up both fists and slammed them against the window behind my head. *Boom.* The window shattered, and the sound startled both of us into silence. Point made. The next thing we knew, his hands were covered in blood. I stood still, shaking, not knowing what to do. Panicked, he turned around and ran away to avoid getting caught.

After the incident, I sat alone on the floor outside my dorm room crying while replaying the scene, wondering: "How did I get here? I thought it would be better than this." I had never been hit in my life. Never witnessed violence in my home. And yet I didn't have the wherewithal to walk away even when I feared that's where we were headed. I was too ashamed to call home; typically I tell my mom everything—unless I'm not ready for what she'll say. So I kept the incident to myself.

———

During my freshman year of college, when I was back home with my parents for Christmas break, I got a collect call from the county jail. It was First Love. He was calling to inform me that he had gotten arrested. Several felony counts and a couple of misdemeanors later, he needed me to call his parents to tell them what happened.

The sound of clinking dishes in the kitchen sink stopped. My mom came over to fix her eyes on me while drying the last dish. Soon, my dad joined us on the couch with a concerned look on his face. We were all in disbelief. I jockeyed between his parents and mine, all of us piecing together answers. I spent the rest of the night staring at the ceiling, asking myself yet again, "It gets better than this, right?"

Over the next five and a half months, my life at college became even more bifurcated. I didn't want anyone to judge him. I didn't want anyone to judge me. So I hid his incarceration from everyone in my "new" life, even my dormmate Megan, who had quickly become my closest college friend.

No matter where I was or what I was doing, I made sure to be back in my dorm room at 8:00 sharp every night to accept his collect call. I bailed out on study groups, disappeared from house parties, turned down dinner trips to the cafeteria with friends, all because I didn't want him to feel abandoned. Those nightly collect calls were our only way of staying connected.

I have always been a terrible liar, and my own duplicity weighed heavily on me. But eventually, I got better at managing the duality of these two disparate identities: At school, I was the cheerful A student, an upbeat social butterfly who was eager to find my way and my tribe in a new environment.

But when it came to First Love, I was playing the steadfast ride or die chick whose allegiances were to a relationship that tugged me further and further away from the kind of college experience I wanted for myself, and from the woman I wanted to be.

On weekends, I'd take the ninety-minute drive to see him in jail, leaving my picture-perfect college life in the rearview window of my hatchback Mazda MX-3. It was so dinky, my mom called it the "jelly bean." It had leopard seat covers and it smelled of cheap vanilla, thanks to the yellow, tree-shaped air freshener I'd bought for ninety-nine cents at the gas station. Not gonna lie—the fact that it was stick shift and had a sunroof made me feel like a BOSS. I bought it with my own money when I was sixteen.

I never imagined that by eighteen, I'd be driving it to see my boyfriend in jail.

Nor could I have prepared for the humiliation and heartbreak of getting patted down in order to lay eyes on someone I had loved since I was fourteen.

We were supposed to be better than this.

I WAS IN THE LIBRARY sitting across from Rob Bell, my study mate from math class, one night when I finally got caught in my own lie:

Rob: "What'd you do this weekend?"

Me: "Oh, I went to visit my boyfriend."

Rob: "Where does he live?"

Me: "In Richmond."

Rob: "Oh, yeah?"

Me: "Yeah." Avoiding eye contact.

Rob: "I'm from Richmond, too. Where does he stay?"

Me: "Oh. Um. I don't remember the block. He just moved there."

He looked down at his textbook and started tapping his pencil, pretending to dive back into solving the math problem. Then his eyes darted back up at mine.

Rob: "What exit?"

Me: "What?" I let out a nervous laugh.

Rob: "Yeah, you go see him a lot there, right? You don't remember the exit?"

My mind raced. I couldn't think of any other exits in Richmond. Shit.

Me: "Um." Beat. "Atlas Road."

His small, squinty eyes felt like laser beams through me. I looked down at my lined notebook. The tapping of his pencil slowed. After a long, pregnant pause, he finally sliced the awkward tension with a question that left me exposed.

Rob: "Damn, E. How long he been in there?"

THERE WAS ONLY ONE destination that exit led to, and Rob knew all too well what it was. He did not judge me for knowing it, too. Instead, he confided in me about his dad's struggles with an opioid addiction that landed him in and out of jail throughout his childhood. He knew the guilt, the shame, the tug between life out here and life in there. That night in the library—letting go of the lies, seeing into each other's shadows—set us both free. I felt seen in ways that left me raw and relieved. I made him pinky promise not to repeat what I shared with him that night. He was too cool to kiss his thumb to seal the deal, but his eye contact let me know he wouldn't break my trust.

FIRST LOVE WAS ALREADY SLIPPING back into his old ways just months after getting out, and I was finally slipping out of the stronghold that he had on me since high school. After five and a half years together, I had officially and metaphorically ridden this thing until the wheels fell off; it was time to get out and run my own race in the other direction.

JUST DAYS AFTER WHAT was a surprisingly uneventful breakup for such a long-term relationship, I got into a car crash while driving home from work at golden hour. I was less than a mile from home, making a routine left turn, on my way to watch *America's Next Top Model* with Rob, and just as the most beautiful sunset caught my eye, a car came crashing into my passenger side at full speed. When I opened my eyes, I was across the street, shaken, my "jelly bean" totaled. But somehow I survived without a scratch on my body.

When Rob came to pick me up from the side of the road, I was rattled but grateful to be on the other side of a crash that could have claimed me. Grateful for another opportunity to get it right. Grateful for the lesson that life is too short to lose sight of where you're headed, to get distracted by anything that threatens to get in the way of where you're meant to go.

"If your boyfriend has you sitting in the backseat for anyone but his mother, he's not the one. Period. The end."

CHAPTER 6

Black Enough

The place in which I'll fit will not exist until I make it.

JAMES BALDWIN

irst Love and I broke up the summer after my sophomore year of college. I distinctly remember going into the bathroom and trying to cry—sitting on the cool tile floor waiting for the tears to come. When they did not, I knew it was really over. Truth is I had been over the relationship emotionally for quite some time. But our breakup invited a deeper reckoning.

Of all the life lessons that came along with First Love, perhaps one of the most pivotal was the foothold he gave me into the Black circle at my high school, and a certain permission to participate more fully in my Black identity. Maybe that is one of the reasons I stayed with him too long. Without First Love there as my liaison at the state college he chose, I would have to navigate my own entry into the Black social scene on campus. Now I would have to find my own identity outside of that relationship and in this new, much more segregated world I found myself in.

From then on, college became an awkward and profound exploration of my own Black experience. Those years would ultimately give me space to come into my own identity more fully. On my own terms. It was work only I could do. And in some ways, it was work I had to do for my own survival. Especially for a girl who had essentially chased a boy into college and got stuck there without him.

BECAUSE OF MY EARLY socialization in a majority White elementary school, I had inadvertently found myself folded neatly into the token Black friend slot. It was where I fit in, and for a very long time it was the only place I felt like I belonged. Like most Black folks in the 'burbs, I was often the only one: in my immediate friend group, in my classrooms, in Girl Scouts, at gymnastics, on my softball and volleyball teams. You learn to get used to being one of few brown bodies in White spaces. And I had gotten really good at it.

I was less practiced in Black spaces, and that discomfort gnawed at me; it was something I deeply wanted to overcome.

To be mixed race in America is to exist in a constant state of in-between. You have access to two worlds and are expected to be fluent in both, yet you never belong fully to either one. And as mixed kids know all too well, even in the in-between there is a spectrum. While First Love was biracial, like me, he was deemed more culturally "Black" than I was at the time. In high school, dating him was a bit like being handed an invitation to sit at what we will call the Black Table. Though because I was essentially First Love's plus-one, I was granted only temporary guest access, not full membership.

Let's discuss this Black Table phenomenon for a minute. Damn near every school with at least a handful of Black students has a Black Table. It is the area where the Black kids congregate on campus. Where minorities go to become part of the majority. Where outsiders become insiders. No code switching. No "inside voices." No one to remind you of the White Man's rules. At my school, you could go to play dominoes with reckless abandon like they do on the corners of Black neighborhoods across America. You might experience an impromptu freestyle battle. You could participate in an educated debate on the merits of Tupac versus Biggie's lyrical superiority. You could even get your hair braided at lunchtime—with beads! The Black Table is where you get to be among your people, to feel safe in your skin and inside your own self-made cultural cocoon. It is where you go to feel less alienated.

Until eventually the bell breaks up the jokes, dispatching each Black body back into the vortex of a mostly White high school. A space that often misunderstands and mislabels Black boys as troublemakers. A place where Black kids learn to work twice as hard for equal treatment, or to behave as tropes, performing for entertainment value, or perhaps worse, to escape into invisibility. A majority White classroom rarely fosters a true sense of belonging for Black kids in America. Which is why the Black Table is sacred. For those who are welcomed in, it might offer the only moments of reprieve in one's day.

It can also feel like an icy pit for anyone who is on the outside.

For me, entering Black spaces required bravely stepping outside my comfort zone—which at that time was represented by my own little cocoon of White and Mexican friends (and I knew better than to bring them along). Growing up, the Black girls generally gave me chilly stares, making me feel like an unwelcome intruder. There was always a tension I hated. A wall I struggled to penetrate. To be rejected this way by my own people was something I took personally. I wanted to say to them, "But I'm nice! I'm funny! I've got rhythm! I don't think I'm better than anybody! What do I gotta do?"

It reminded me of the summer my mom sent me and my brother off to the backwoods of Georgia to visit our relatives from her side of the family. My mom spent her childhood summers down South making memories with her favorite cousins along country roads, and in her grandmother's kitchen learning how to make soul food. She wanted us to have that experience, too. My brother and I protested, but we got shipped off anyway, mad as hell.

We stayed with my great-grandma Maggie and quickly made friends with our cousin Mark, who was around our age and lived in a trailer home across the street. He reminded me of Chris Tucker; he was tall, charismatic, a total jokester, and the only gateway to fun in the acres of dusty fields surrounding us.

One afternoon the three of us rode our bicycles to a neighbor's yard, where we discovered a trampoline. We jumped our hearts out on that thing. It was the first time that whole summer I felt happy and free. My hair was braided in singles that spread out like black noodles against the sunny blue sky. From midair I spotted two girls riding toward us on bicycles and I got excited, thinking, "*Finally*, girls I can play with!" It seemed like they might be coming over to join us.

Instead, they hollered from the dirt road: "Uhh-uhh, Mark! Why you hanging with that White girl?" They pointed in our direction, laughing.

My instinct was to laugh along. *White girl?* Where was she?

"Man, y'all need to shut the hell up! That's my cousin. She ain't no White girl!"

Mark's reaction confirmed that indeed the "White girl" they were pointing at was me. It stung.

I looked down at my scrawny, tanned limbs flailing in the wind, which were even more brown under the spell of the relentless country sun that summer. Still, I was considered high yellow to them, especially down South.

The feeling of otherness came at me and my brother from both sides.

Back home when I was playing in the pool with my younger White cousins, they would point at my legs underwater and ask me why I was "that color." On the flip side, as a preteen, my older Black cousin explained to me that the reason I had acne was because I had White in my blood, and that when White and Black mix, weird things happen to your DNA—you know, kind of like the deformities you see in the children of incest. Belonging is nuanced and in some ways fleeting for any teenager; but the longing for belonging is uniquely complicated as a biracial kid.

You exist at the divergence of two worlds that will never quite become one.

———

IN JUNIOR HIGH SCHOOL, I met my six lifelong best friends who, for all intents and purposes, are White. (Except for April, who would very much appreciate you knowing that despite her green eyes and light skin she is Puerto Rican and Mexican.) We nicknamed ourselves the Solid Six, and by the time we got our driver's licenses in high school, we'd all bought obnoxious matching bumper stickers that read "untouchables." At twenty-five, when they came to visit me in NYC, we all got tattoos on our right rib bones that read "Forever by my side." Half of us got it in Arabic and the other half chose Italian; an ode to that summer we spent a surreal forty-eight hours in Florence together. The sisterhood between Brittney, Tracy, Misti, Rachelle, April, and me is soul deep—nothing could ever come between us.

While race was rarely an issue we confronted directly, it confronted us at one fateful slumber party in eighth grade.

We were all wearing PJs and piled on Misti's bed, laughing hysterically, when the following exchange unfolded:

"Go get me some water!" one of them ordered playfully.

"What? No! What do I look like? Your NIGGER?" the other responded.

Time stopped. You could hear a pin drop. The illusion of sameness vanished. That ugly word divided us, cutting right through the thin veil of absolute trust and safety that bonded us. Race had suddenly entered the room. It seemed to corner me, and only me, breathing heavily in my face. I felt my face heat up with embarrassment. I wanted to escape my own skin.

My guilty friend looked at me in horror and began to wail, hysterically. She was horrified, embarrassed, and ashamed. She kept saying sorry over and over again. I don't even remember if I said a word. To witness one of my best friends hurl the N-word so carelessly devastated me. Yet strangely, I felt complicit—as if my stealthy ability to navigate Whiteness without ever disrupting it or challenging it had enabled her to see me apart from my

Blackness. It wasn't until that singular moment of betrayal that I felt like my race had become an inconvenient truth for us all.

I had gotten so damn good at *assimilating* that she almost forgot a Black person was even in the room. *Almost.*

It's a trippy thing to be lured into a false sense of inclusion only to have it violently snatched back. But that kind of shock can really happen only once.

I wonder now if all that time and energy my mom spent on immersing me in Black spaces growing up was to prepare me for times like that, when I'd need another world to turn to when this one no longer felt like home.

I forgave my friend for saying it, and the rest of my White friends for freezing up and not knowing what to do when it happened. This was, after all, a learning experience for each of us. And she was, like all of us, a person who was simply a product of her environment with a lot of growing into herself to do. I knew she had probably been exposed to that ugly word by way of her father's Louisiana upbringing. But I also knew her well enough to know she did not have a hateful heart. This was not someone who was anti-Black, nor someone who had ever—before or since—demonstrated a discriminatory mind-set. She was the friend who loved me so much that she would stay late, wake up early, or ditch class on a dime if I ever needed a partner in crime all throughout high school and beyond. She remains one of my closest friends to this day.

But the betrayal of a moment like that cannot ever be fully undone— because it transcended just our friendship and prepared me for a world that would inevitably see and respond to my race in similarly unpredictable ways. Part of getting comfortable with the discomfort of being the only brown body in White spaces is readying yourself for the next time a racist slur or an ignorant question might fly in your face without warning.

It created in me an urgency to seek out and to cultivate friendships out-side of the predominantly White bubble that was all I had ever known.

Joining the track team back in ninth grade gave me an important shot at breaking through this invisible cultural divide between me and the Black kids at school. Track and field was basically the athletic department's extension of the Black Table. It offered me a chance to acquaint myself with some of the Black girls without any reliance on First Love and his wishy-washy moods.

Sharee became my relay partner. Hadija ran the 100-meter and 300-meter hurdles like me. And I'm not exactly sure what Reina's event was, but she was renowned for braiding First Love's hair on the sidelines during meets. One day she invited both me and First Love over to her house and offered to braid our hair. It was basically like being handed my Black Card. Which is kind of a joke, but sadly, not really. Becoming cool with Reina and her sisters earned me entry into the exclusive Black bubble on campus. It felt fragile and precarious, and I tried very hard not to screw it up.

Reina lived off an exit in Oakland that White people avoided at all costs at the time. At her house, we drank Kool-Aid and ordered from the wing spot up the street. Joined by her sisters Mandie and Tia, we watched music videos on BET and taught ourselves the choreography in their living room (Ginuwine's "Pony" was a personal fave). It was the kind of cultural literacy program my mom could never enroll me in.

At our house, my dad insisted on serving us Minute Maid juice. Our go-to takeout was Chinese food from the Peach Garden. And in Newark, we didn't get BET as part of the standard cable plan. Up until then, my brother steadily filled our house with mostly punk-rock music or whatever rock bands he could binge-watch on MTV.

One weekend at Reina's, during one of our ten-plus-hour marathon hair-braiding kikis in Oakland, when I was in my Alicia Keys phase minus the beads, we came up with an idea to start a Black dance crew that would outdo the preppy cheerleaders and their vanilla halftime performances. (Never mind that I was one of those cheerleaders.) Thanks to the laws of right-place-right-time, I became one of the founding members of the Black Student Union's new dance group, because Mandie was the copresident of BSU, and, well, because she said so.

Joining them meant temporarily ditching my post on the cheer sideline. I proudly tore off my blue-and-gold cheer uniform. It was the high school sartorial equivalent of reverse code switching.

During football season at our biggest game against Logan, our rival high school, we took to the field in all-black uniforms, our ponytails poking out through caps inspired by Janet Jackson circa *Rhythm Nation*. We ran out onto the field and got into formation, adrenaline surging through our veins. The beat dropped and our bodies moved in imperfect synchronicity. We were nervous as hell, but natural rhythm and muscle memory worked its magic. Needless to say, we murdered it, and when we were finished the whole stadium erupted in applause. This never once happened after any of our cheer performances, ever.

"Wow, Lainey! You girls really showed those cheerleaders how it's done!" my dad raved afterward. He got such a thrill out of seeing his daughter out there with the Black dance team.

Of all my achievements in life, of all my track meets and talent shows, he will tell you that *this* was his proudest dad moment to date.

IF HIGH SCHOOL WAS about dipping my toe into a Black social life, college was about diving in head first. But I would, once again, find myself toggling between two worlds.

On college move-in day, while First Love was prowling the halls with his new roommate, meeting new people, I was sitting cross-legged inside my dorm room engaging in a deep, teary-eyed convo with my new roomie,

Megan. Our parents had just kissed us good-bye and left us to unload the
red wagons stacked with our belongings. Instead, we sat in the middle of
the floor and unpacked our life stories.

Megan was a bubbly White girl from a military family in Escalon, a
cow town near Modesto situated in the swath of American farmland between Sacramento and the San Francisco Bay Area. She looked like an
off-duty beauty queen: tanned, blond, and effortlessly pretty, with perfectly
symmetrical features. She had the tiniest, most perfect Barbie nose, which
I'd never seen on a real-life human. Her highlighted hair was thrown up in
a perky cheerleader ponytail and tied with a ribbon. We never spoke of it,
but I was pretty sure that I was going to be her first Black friend.

At first, part of me felt the pull to get out there and spread my social
seeds by meeting new people, different kinds of people—hopefully some
Black people. But all those inclinations faded away when Meggy's green
eyes welled up as she confided that her dad, who was very clearly her hero,
had just died of cancer two weeks prior. She melted into a puddle of tears in
my arms and we wouldn't emerge again from our dorm room until hours
later—by then we were burgeoning best friends. We quickly made friends
with Marcela and Heather, two transfer students who lived a few doors
down; they had been best friends since high school. They reminded me of
my Solid Six back in the Bay. The next thing I knew, we were all piling into
Meggy's car for our first family trip to Target.

But falling in friend love with Meggy and co. presented a precarious
inner struggle for me. I felt a real connection brewing with them, but
frankly, it was at odds with my master plan to make Black friends. I realize
how awkward that may sound, but it is what it was. Getting drawn in by the
grip of fragile friendships with White people was something I was weary of.
I could see the fork in the road up ahead. And I didn't want to get stuck in
the White lane again. My mom had always encouraged me to "go where it's
warm." But I didn't want to be trapped where it burned.

SACRAMENTO WAS MUCH MORE racially segregated than I expected. In high school there was the White Table and the Black Table; in college there was the White Party or the Black Party. When Marcela and Heather invited Meggy and me to our first college party, I found myself even more acutely caught between disparate worlds. This gravitational pull toward a White social bubble was all too familiar to me, and I was consciously resisting it this time around. But I didn't want to lose out on making new lifelong friends either. So I naively attempted to be a bridge between the segregated social scenes. My tactic: I invited Ashley, a Black girl I met in math class who I was interested in getting to know. I mean, *I couldn't be the token Black friend if there were two of us, right?*

I had barely made it past the front lawn of the party when a tall, heavyset White guy wearing a flannel shirt and a trucker hat came barreling toward me with a red cup in hand. His body charged right into mine as if I were invisible, until the collision caused his drink to spill.

"Excuse you," I said, rightfully annoyed.

"Watch where you're going, you fucking nigger!"

He spit the words out like a reflex, slapping me right in the face. I probably told him to fuck off. Or maybe I didn't. Maybe the words got stuck in my throat. All I remember is looking around for my friends, and seeing a cluster of White girls midsquat, ass cheeks out, peeing on the front lawn, drunk and laughing in the safety of their own world.

I couldn't blame them for getting that loose, but I knew I couldn't afford to behave that way. Not at a White party, not anywhere. Hell, I couldn't even walk across the very same lawn, totally sober, without the threat of being verbally accosted. I would have to tell my friends about the incident later and explain to them what that felt like. This is part of the uncomfortable responsibility that comes along with being the only one, the token Black friend.

But thankfully this time, I *wasn't* the only one.

"Let's get out of here," Ashley said, linking her arm in mine. When we locked eyes, I knew there was nothing for me to explain to her. She understood implicitly the impact of that moment, of that word. Having a Black friend there—even one I had only just met—was like having a safety net to catch me, someone who could absorb that pain with me. This unspoken sisterhood was a completely new dynamic for me.

Up until that moment, I had been looking at Blackness like it was a party I didn't get the invite to. Like it was a dance someone forgot to teach me. But that night I learned that as much as it is our shared history and a pride in our culture that connects us, being part of the Black experience is being bonded by the painful and sometimes violent experience of exclusion. All the time I'd spent thinking I had to maneuver out of the grip of Whiteness was just an illusion. You can never be stuck in a world you never belonged to.

NOTHING FORCES YOU TO CONFRONT your Blackness like walking into your first college party with White friends and being called a nigger before even making it through the front door. This experience confirmed for me what I already knew. What my parents had instilled in my brother and me since we were young: this world isn't always a safe place for Black bodies. And no matter how long my hair, how golden my skin, no matter what color my dad is, the world would always see me as Black.

Biraciality is a genetic fact, not a racial identity. Not yet, at least. Because as long as I was moving through a White world, I'd be seen as a Black woman—and treated accordingly.

"I had been looking at Blackness like it was a party I didn't get the invite to. Like it was a dance someone forgot to teach me. But that night I learned that as much as it is our shared history and a pride in our culture that connects us, being part of the Black experience is being bonded by the painful and sometimes violent experience of exclusion."

CHAPTER 7

I Am Not My Hair

As a black woman, the decision to love yourself
just as you are is a radical act.
BETHANEE EPIFANI J. BRYANT

In the fall semester of my second year of college, I enrolled in Introduction to Rhetorical Criticism, a course designed to critique and process the flood of messages in mass media. I'm not exactly sure who I expected to see when I walked into that classroom, but Dr. Michele Foss-Snowden was definitely not it. For starters, she looked too young to be a college professor. I'd guess she was around thirty years old. She was distractingly pretty and racially ambiguous, with long, curly hair the same texture as mine, except hers was dyed into this edgy, ombre look with cherry-red tips that matched her Lucite glasses. It was rare to have a teacher this youthful and cool-looking. I sat in the front row, intrigued.

Here was this young, beautiful woman who was also smart and held her own. I loved watching her command the room. The world tries to categorize women into binaries: pretty or smart, Black or White, young or old, smart or stylish. This professor represented the intersection of all of these things—and she was the first professional woman I ever saw myself in. I felt like I was getting a glimpse into my future self, the kind of woman I aspired to be.

I took the liberty of nicknaming her in my head: M. Foss.

ACCORDING TO THE SYLLABUS, rhetoric was defined as "artistically created persuasion that is aimed to shape hearts and minds on topics of social importance." Intro to Rhetorical Criticism, then, was designed to introduce techniques and strategies for analyzing these messages of persuasion.

On the first day of class, we were assigned a twenty-five-page paper that would explore the impact of messages embedded within a piece of cultural "text." The other faculty members (many of them old, White, and male) limited the assignment to analyzing speeches. But M. Foss preferred to show students how rhetoric operates in pop culture: films, music videos, ads, TV shows, music, etc. She invited us to choose any text across any medium, which we would then spend the semester studying in depth.

I chose the song "I Am Not My Hair," by India.Arie.

Before class wrapped, I highlighted M. Foss's office hours on the syllabus with a chunky yellow marker.

THE NEXT DAY, I showed up at her office door, wide-eyed, searching for clues about who this woman was.

She invited me in.

A quick scan of her bookshelf was illuminating. First, I saw framed photographs that seemed to resolve the racial ambiguity question. Pictures of her throwing up pyramid-shaped hand gestures with her line sisters revealed that she was part of the illustrious Black sorority Delta Sigma Theta.

Second, judging from the myriad books about race and culture on display, M. Foss seemed deeply interested in studying Black identity—and owning her own: *Who Is Black?* by F. James Davis, *Watching Race* by Herman Gray, *Enlightened Racism* by Sut Jhally and Justin Lewis, *Caucasia* by Danzy Senna. I wondered if she ever had the Race Conversation with her mom at the dinner table like I had or if her natural hair journey looked anything like mine.

Then I saw a smiling wedding photo of her with a handsome dark-skinned man, next to a tiny Stanford flag blowing in the AC—a reminder that I was indeed the silly girl who allowed some dude to derail me from applying to my dream college. It still made me wince, so I searched for another conversation starter.

That's when I noticed an adorable photo of her as a child with an older White man.

"Is that your dad?" Yeah, it was a loaded thing to blurt out, as if a new student inquiring about her professor's personal life wasn't completely weird and intrusive.

But she just laughed, as if she sensed where this was headed. "Uh. Yes, at least that's what I've been told."

"OH MY GOSH. Really? MY DAD'S WHITE, TOO!" I practically shrieked.

To understand my enthusiasm, you must understand this: it is pretty rare to meet a fellow member of the White Dad Club (I invented this umbrella term as an endearing way to classify those of us with minority moms and White dads, simply for the sake of making us feel less alien and more like part of some really awesome, really tiny tribe). My whole life I've been collecting a running list of any subtle distinctions that aim to capture the nuances of what it means to grow up with a White dad compared to a White mom. You can blame tribalism for my obsessive urge to classify the large swath of mixed-race people in America, which, by the way, is one of the fastest growing groups in the country. (Check the latest census: the number of multiracial children in this country is expected to triple by 2060.)

From my very informal and not at all scientific observations, I've found the White Mom Club to be much more common. It has always seemed, in some ways, like a remarkably different experience from mine altogether. I still find this topic endlessly fascinating. And I still get a little too excited whenever I meet a fellow member of the White Dad Club.

Now, hopefully you can see why I shelved all previously scheduled academic discussions with M. Foss and Went There instead. She was my professor, yes, but since she taught cultural criticism, I figured White dad comparisons were fair game.

The more we shared, the more we realized just how much we had in common: Our White dads both played guitar. They both wore Black Suede cologne. They both had kind blue eyes and squishy, warm hands we liked to hold. They both occasionally wore cowboy hats. And in less upbeat news, they also both liked to drink a little too much.

As a result, M. Foss and I had similar daddy issues, except she never got a chance to resolve hers because her dad passed away when she was in college.

"I was just around your age, actually, when I got the phone call," she revealed to me, her eyes becoming glassy. I resisted the urge to hug her. It was too soon.

Over time, though, during my sporadic office-hour visits, we built some semblance of a mentor-mentee relationship. I enjoyed asking M. Foss questions about her life, and she was always willing to share. She was an open book, providing so many answers I had been searching for—answers about race and identity, about family and forgiveness, about the world and where I fit into it.

Meeting M. Foss was like discovering a compass at a time in my life when I felt like I was wandering in the wilderness.

Apart from our glorious one-on-one talks, the work I did in M. Foss's classroom is what armed me with new tools to think critically about cultural messages in the media and a broader vocabulary to articulate how they impacted us. Through my semester-long deep dive into India.Arie's song "I Am Not My Hair," I learned new ways to see, synthesize, analyze, and express my take on the racial and gender disparities I was experiencing in more pronounced ways than ever before. It was both revelatory and prescient. I felt myself blossoming, not just as a student, but as a woman of color finding my voice.

For generations, we have been inundated with messages demanding that we view beauty and femininity through a Eurocentric lens. India.Arie's existence in pop culture challenged all of that. With her dark skin, dreadlocks, and headwraps, she emerged from the shadows of marginalization proudly representing Afrocentric beauty in mainstream media. Unlike the ordinary American pop star, her music had an empowering message that challenged racial stereotypes: "I am not my hair. I am not my skin. I am not your expectations." It was powerful and important work. Work that came to mean a lot to me personally, as these were themes I had wrestled with my whole life. It felt like a rallying cry to abandon the outdated notion that any of these superficial qualities define our value in the world.

Through the revelations I was having in M. Foss's class and the conversations that sprang from them, I began questioning and examining my own light-skin privilege as a biracial Black woman in America. I could see the ways in which I benefited from an inherently racist hierarchy that favored Eurocentric beauty standards. And I was beginning to understand the powerful role I could play in breaking some of that down, just by how I chose to show up in certain spaces. Choosing to own my Blackness as a biracial woman felt like a powerful response to a deeply racist world. I began igniting deeper conversations with people in my life around the topics of race and identity—even if it made some of them uncomfortable.

I had always loathed the superiority complex some mixed girls toted around like crowns. I could not stand it when Black girls pontificated about their trace percentages of Native American blood as a means of separating themselves from their own African lineage. Rather than heeding the urge to conform or shrink as a response to being "othered"—like I did at that sleepover with my White friends, and again at that college party—I saw the power in embracing all of what it means to be Black in America. This was precisely what my mom had been instilling in me since preschool. But it hadn't clicked until now.

From that empowered place, I began experimenting with new ways to use my voice in my world.

Natalie manuel and I met in one of our journalism classes. We were two big personalities who happened to love fashion and journalism, and we were both raised in the Black church and strong Christian households, so we gravitated toward each other right away. She felt like a kindred spirit. For our twenty-first birthdays, both in December, Natalie and I decided to throw a joint White party in a friend of a friend's off-campus apartment. We strung some old Christmas lights around their bare windows, arranged borrowed speakers in the corner of a sparsely decorated living room, and sent invites via group text instructing guests to bring a bottle. All we had to purchase was a package of red plastic party cups from Dollar Tree and our tiny white tube-top dresses we found at Forever 21 for nineteen dollars.

By midnight, the party was packed. A stream of frat boys and jocks came through in tall tees with brown paper bags in hand, flooding the kitchen counter with cheap liquor: Mad Dog 20/20, 40-ounce bottles of Olde English, and shots of Jose Cuervo. Sweaty bodies were swaying to 50 Cent; naturally, I was standing on a chair shouting "Go Shawty! It's your birthday!" By 2:00 A.M., people had moved on to the next party and those of us left behind either had too much to drink or were hoping to get lucky, or both.

A small coed group of us were packed like sardines onto one massive leather couch in the living room watching music videos and talking shit. I was annoyed because all the remaining male prospects seemed like dumb jocks to me. One football player in particular, named Tyson, was trying to get my attention. He seemed like the one decent guy in the group, but I was repelled by his corny lip-licking tactic, so I fixed my eyes on the television screen ahead and ignored him when he casually attempted to place his arm around me.

Since my breakup with First Love I had my guard up when it came to guys. My attitude was very: "Oh, you like me? Really? Why? You don't even know me. Boy, bye."

The truth is my reluctance to dip into the dating scene in Sacramento was bigger than my breakup.

I was going through my own awakening, and the work I was doing in M. Foss's class dovetailed with my own dating experiences. I was irked by the long-standing trend of Black men pursuing women with lighter skin. In a world that innately upholds White supremacy, this was not some random phenomenon; it was a symptom of conditioning. We were all conditioned to believe that lighter skin and straighter, longer hair was superior. I didn't want to be a part of perpetuating that myth. I could no longer ignore my skepticism about how colorism might inevitably inform why certain Black men were attracted to me. I wondered, "If my skin was darker, if my hair was shorter and more coarse, would these same guys be trying to talk to me?"

It seemed ripe for discussion. And M. Foss's classroom gave me the tools to start digging in.

That night at the party, when India.Arie's "I Am Not My Hair" music video came on the TV, I perked up.

"Ah! This is my soooooong." I hopped off the couch. "I *looove* India.Arie. She is so beautiful. She looks like such a queen in this video."

"Yo. That bitch is ugly," Tyson snickered and dapped his boy.

My head spun toward him and our eyes locked. "Ugly? Wow. What about her is ugly? I want you to break that down for me."

He took the bait: "She needs to do something with that nappy-ass hair."

I glanced around the room, taking mental snapshots of all these Black men nodding in agreement, laughing.

"Really? How would you describe your hair if you didn't shave it off?" I jabbed back.

"Yo, my shit nappy as fuck," he laughed. "Can't have my girl out here with hair nappier than mine."

"*Wowww.* Oh, so *that's* why all of you date White girls?" I couldn't help calling out the contradiction. I had never seen any of these dudes date a girl who was their own skin color. "How does it feel to hate yourself?"

"Damn! A nigga can't have a preference?" Tyson's friend chimed in, trying to back up his boy.

"Preference? Please. More like conditioning. If your personal preference is rooted in generations of systemic oppression, it is never really *just* a preference, homie."

"Nah. Everyone is entitled to their own preference, E.," Tyson dug in, holding firm that his consistent vote for light-skin chicks and White girls was pure, devoid of historical and societal influence.

"Okay, so all of y'all just happen to have the same preference as every rapper and major athlete and every other Black dude on campus? C'mon! Do you really think your 'preferences' aren't influenced at all by what you see on TV and in magazines? By what you've been *told* is beautiful and desirable and feminine?" I really wanted to unpack this. I didn't care if I sounded like I was nerding out.

"Nah, man. She just ugly as fuck," said one of the boneheads in the back.

"What's your mom look like?" I went for his jugular.

"*DAAAAAAAMNNNN!*" the whole room erupted in unison.

"I am deadass." I was pissed. "Show me a picture. Is her hair 'nappy'? Is her skin dark like yours? Is she ugly to you, too?"

"I don't even know why your light-skinned ass is getting so heated over this, anyway," someone retorted, clearly missing the entire point.

"Show me a girl you've ever dated who isn't light-skin-long-hair or Mexican or Asian or White with a big booty." I fixed my gaze back on Tyson, hoping he was willing to indulge me in a conversation that required some degree of consciousness.

"Damn, dawg, she just mad because she ain't got a big booty!" dude in the back added.

The room erupted in laughter.

For the record: Yes, I was and am still mad that I don't have a big booty, okay? But that wasn't the point.

I was mad because I was waking up to the ways in which society sets up Black people to hate ourselves. I was mad because so many of us are complicit in perpetuating this self-hating cycle of oppression, one designed to make us cling to Whiteness for validation. I was mad because of how insidiously racism works to keep us from claiming our beauty, our worthiness, our power. I was mad to see so many of us operating out of brokenness and shame.

I HAD ALREADY BEGUN a deeper process of questioning everything, including my place in the world, beyond the suffocating confines of my college life in Sacramento. It was as if the winds of excitement just sort of blew right over it like a wasteland. Nothing magical, nothing exciting ever seemed to happen there—at least not to me. Especially after my breakup. I needed an escape from the sleepy college town where my social life had become a bit like walking a tightrope between Black and White worlds. In some ways, I felt stuck in a place I didn't belong.

I knew there was more—more to see, more to explore, more to experience.

When your dreams are bigger than the places you find yourself in, sometimes you need to seek out your own reminders that there is more. And there is always more waiting for you on the other side of fear.

———

My aunt Janet's daughter, Chey, was a publicist at an entertainment PR firm in Los Angeles, and I begged her to hook me up with an internship during my winter intersession from school. When I landed the gig, Chey invited me to stay with her at her studio apartment in Koreatown. It was my first grown-up adventure. And it was thrilling.

Within days of my internship, I met a young female TV producer, one of Chey's friends, who said within moments of speaking with me: "Have you ever thought about doing TV?"

I had not. Well, not in a serious way, since I imagined those career paths were reserved for people with connections.

Then she said something that struck me: "You are so much bigger than you even know."

I didn't know what she meant or what prompted her to say that to me, but it seemed like a good omen and it left me feeling sparkly, like I had a good aura accompanying me on this trip.

The next day, her company sent me to cover a Warner Bros. musical showcase as an on-air reporter. My job was to interview Talib Kweli on camera. (My internal reaction when I got the call was basically Tom Hanks in that iconic scene from the movie *Big* where he's going ham on the super-sized keys of a piano.) I was nineteen years old, walking into a packed room of reporters with my camera crew and producer, feeling bossy, but I very quickly got my reality check: the producers warned me that with this many reporters in one room, "You only eat what you kill." Which meant, not everyone was getting the interview. Plus, Talib might not even show, and if he did, there was already a list of approved interviews. There was a pecking order on the entertainment-reporter circuit. We were just a local TV station, and I was a completely unknown entity.

And yet, I felt totally in my element. As soon as I heard everyone start shouting, "Talib, Talib!!" I cut through the crowd like a hot knife through butter. I walked right up to my subject, introduced myself, and calmly, without skipping a beat, whipped my head around to my crew and said, "Let's go." Lights. Camera. Action. I asked my questions in a conversational manner, as if the cameras weren't there, and as we closed out, Talib shook my hand and said, "Good to meet you."

Boom. I got my sound bites, my job there was done—and then he dipped. No one else got an interview that day.

My crew reacted uproariously: "Daaamn."

I felt it, too. The rush of finding out what you're good at is priceless. And having the opportunity to actually get paid for doing it is, well, the *dream*.

In LA, I felt electrified. Like there was actual magic coursing through my veins. I was finally waking up to my own possibilities, and to a deeper realization of the power of vision and faith—two of the most important tools I would need on my journey. For the first time, I understood that the bigness of my life would be determined not only by the bigness of my dreams, but also by my capacity to trust that there is a Higher Power who would always take those dreams and multiply them.

This was a reminder that there is a divine order, a divine flow to our lives. We don't need to have all the answers. But our job is to keep on dreaming and trusting enough to put one foot in front of the other.

To keep moving forward.

To keep pushing beyond whatever feels confining.

To keep searching for where the magic is.

To continue expanding, staying open to being stretched.

And allowing room to be completely awed by how much better it gets along the way.

"There is a divine order, a divine flow to our lives. We don't need to have all the answers. But our job is to keep on dreaming and trusting enough to put one foot in front of the other."

CHAPTER 8

A Different Kind of White

I realized that they weren't at all smarter than the rest of us.
They were simply emboldened, floating on an ancient
tide of superiority, buoyed by the fact that history had never
told them anything different.
MICHELLE OBAMA, *BECOMING*

L ife transitions are our biggest opportunities for growth. They push us to become the fierce heroes of our own stories. They pull us into new territories and ask us to become bigger, braver versions of ourselves.

Now, while all that might sound inspiring in an Instagram caption, it can be really, really scary to do in *real* life.

I wish people talked more openly about just how soul-wrenching transitions can be, and about the panic that floods your system when you're in the midst of one, whether it's a breakup, the loss of a loved one, a job change, or any other unceremonious ending or new beginning.

If you are in college reading this, I am sorry to be the one to break it to you, but brace yourself, because few life changes are as truly WTF-able as graduation. For me, it was one of the scariest moments of my entire life. No one and nothing can prepare you for what comes next.

But the silver lining with any transition is that the more we kick the doors open on hard truths, the braver we are walking through them.

THE FIRST COUPLE OF YEARS of college you feel like you have all the time in the world—to explore different majors, take up new hobbies (like partying), and maybe even fit in some naps. Then junior and senior year hits, and shit gets really real. During my junior year, I became laser focused on finding a summer internship that could open doors for me. I didn't know what I was looking for exactly, but I knew that I loved writing, storytelling, psychology, and style. I have also always had a strong eye for visuals. The world of media and advertising felt like the right place to start my Google search.

It was like winning the internship jackpot when I discovered the Multicultural Advertising Intern Program (MAIP), a gateway for students of color to land paid internships at top advertising agencies all over the world. For many young people of color, this program provides the only foothold into an industry we might otherwise be locked out of. The program also offers a rich network of media professionals who lead career workshops and host networking events.

After a rigorous application process, I was placed at Ogilvy & Mather, a major advertising company in New York City. My only reference for Manhattan at the time was the buddy-cop TV drama *New York Undercover*, starring Malik Yoba and Eddie Torres. It depicted the violent, gritty underbelly of New York, and that was certainly *not* part of my dream. But I knew this was an opportunity I could not pass up.

Once I arrived, I felt electrified by life in the Big Apple, which was teeming with impatient, fast-talking people like me. Always in a hurry to be somewhere, never wasting too much time on niceties. And there were so many places to explore. The fact that I could hop on the subway and at each stop pop up in the middle of an entirely different world was exhilarating. There was a new adventure around every corner and a million possibilities for different types of big lives that you could live there. I immediately connected with a handful of the other MAIPers who had come from a variety of backgrounds, all over the country; I relished any amount of time we got to spend together at MAIP functions, which mostly took place after work hours.

Unfortunately, as slick as the Ogilvy & Mather office was and as sexy as this global powerhouse brand would look on my résumé, it didn't quite come with the kind of big life I wanted. For a young, bubbly brown girl who enjoys fashion and meaningful human connection, working on menopause pharmaceutical campaigns wasn't exactly an ideal match. But I never would have known that had I not gone on the adventure in the first place. Remember this: Discovering what you *don't* want is just as important as finding out what you *do*.

THAT SUMMER IN New York City was also my first time encountering East Coast, Ivy League White kids, who I had nothing in common with except the internship itself, it seemed. Many of them had chilly demeanors and pin-straight, side-parted hair that hung like drapes on either side of their faces. I noticed lots of khakis and round-toe Tory Burch flats, and I overheard talk of vacations at family homes in the Hamptons. My fellow interns were, as I described to my mom over the phone, "a different kind of White"—nothing close to the mostly liberal, E-40-bumping, middle-class, urban dwellers I grew up with in the Bay Area's melting pot. Back home, I had grown used to being the only Black person in the room. But at least it seemed like we all subscribed to a similar culture, no matter what color our skin was. This internship was my first time encountering the social stratifications of class, and it was a complete culture shock.

While MAIP exists to create a pipeline of vibrant young multicultural talent into the advertising world, once I got there, I realized exactly why the program was so utterly necessary.

I found the corporate agency culture stiff and uninviting for someone like me. Whenever I was with the other Ogilvy interns, either brainstorming ideas or socializing at mixers, I noticed that no one made eye contact with me. And because no one was acknowledging me, I didn't talk much. And because I didn't talk, I felt like they thought I was stupid. It became a self-perpetuating cycle that I was too paralyzed by anxiety to break. I didn't yet have the tools to battle my own insecurities in order to find my voice and my place in that woefully unfamiliar space.

I felt more and more invisible by the day—like the best parts of me were being erased.

Throughout the three-month-long internship, I called home crying more than once. I was not a homesick person; I love my family, but I have never had any romanticized, nostalgic feelings about home. And I wasn't ever particularly shy. But that work environment made me second-guess myself and who I had always known myself to be. Part of it, I assume, was the naturally overwhelming experience of being the smallest fish in a really big pond. But there was also something else at play, something even more acute that I couldn't quite put words to.

"They don't even look at me," I told my mom on the phone one night, fighting back tears. "They treat me like I'm not even there."

In my intern group, Lily was the self-appointed leader. She was from Boston, and at least in my estimation she pretty much fit the archetype of a preppy, private-school-educated White girl to a T, complete with the side-parted hair and those Tory Burch flats. She seemed so self-assured, and all the other interns in our group hung on her every word. Lily possessed the kind of take-charge confidence that intimidated me. Yet somehow, by the end of the summer, I had earned her eye contact—and respect.

"One day," Lily announced on the last day of our internship, "when I'm the president of my company, I would totally hire you, Elaine."

It was intended as a compliment.

But coming from a peer in an internship program, it was outright insulting. "How do you know I won't be the one hiring you?" I imagined myself clapping back when I replayed the scene in my mind afterward. But after twelve weeks of atrophying into this smaller, unrecognizable version of myself in her presence, I simply shrugged off the comment with a quiet smile.

Back at the MAIP dorms late one night, I was confiding in Jay, a fellow MAIPer and aspiring film director. It turns out he was experiencing some of the same sense of entitlement and superiority complexes I had been contending with all summer at the office. We were commiserating about our internships and conspiring about ways to break into a different industry altogether. We both secretly wanted to pursue journalism.

As I was rethinking my life plan, I flashed back to the magazine journalism class I had taken the prior semester. On our very first day of school, the professor announced a challenge: "If you get published in a national magazine, you get an automatic A and never have to return to my class." I have always loved a challenge.

I worked two jobs throughout college, one of them an on-campus position where I made an important connection: a professor who was married to the editor-in-chief of *Figure*, a now-defunct fashion magazine for plus-size women. I asked him to hook me up with an email intro to send my meticulously crafted story pitch, and ended up getting assigned a two-hundred-word blurb about footwear. *Boom*. My first national byline came with an automatic A and a ditch-class pass.

With that newfound gap in my schedule, I started writing for *Figure*. My next published piece was a small sidebar in the style pages. As a staff writer and editor for the college newspaper, I kept myself busy with film reviews and local news reporting, and every once in a while I got to write about the burgeoning fashion scene in California's capital.

Sitting with Jay in that dorm, I realized that I was the most activated when I was up late writing on deadline, toiling over my stories.

"Maybe I need to go into magazine journalism," I announced, convinced that I might be encountering my very first career aha moment. I envisioned myself canvassing the offices of major magazines in NYC with my résumé and maybe even showing up to *Essence*'s headquarters, since I found out they were only a few blocks away from my internship.

"Hold up. *That's* not journalism," he said, laughing off my dream and dissing women's magazines as fluff.

It enraged me.

"Wait. What do you mean that is *not* journalism?" I retorted, prompting a debate that lasted longer than he was likely prepared for. I challenged every sexist point he made about how frivolous fashion writing was. I defended my stories like I was defending my honor. And in my estimation at least, I totally won that debate. Even though it was annoying to have to put up a case to begin with, I hadn't lit up like that in months. Winning that petty fight was the most alive and sparkly I had felt that entire summer.

It was a sign pointing me in the right direction.

"Discovering what you *don't* want is just as important as finding out what you *do*."

CHAPTER 9

The College Crisis

You are braver than you believe, stronger than you seem,
and smarter than you think.

WINNIE-THE-POOH, *POOH'S GRAND ADVENTURE:
THE SEARCH FOR CHRISTOPHER ROBIN*

hen I returned to college after my New York intern-
ship, I felt overwhelmed and intimidated. Not just
by East Coast White People and the extremely ill-
fitting advertising world. But by the *entire* world.
And the daunting notion of figuring out where I belonged in it.

After my encounter with Jay, I began to daydream more and more about
exploring magazine journalism. But I had no idea where to even begin looking for a job. And now I felt like I had wasted precious time that summer in
the wrong place.

At least I had another year left to figure it all out—or so I thought.

———

DURING FALL ENROLLMENT of senior year my academic adviser informed me that I had only one semester left, not two. I nearly peed my pants.

"WHAT? No way. This has to be some sort of mistake. My projected graduation date isn't until spring 2008."

"Nope. Because you packed in all your credits, you will be graduating ahead of schedule in December 2007." She delivered this information to me like it was a good thing. "Congratulations!"

For most people, this news might be reason to celebrate. But for me, it induced heart palpitations. The panic was bone deep.

I was going to graduate early, *by accident.* Seriously?! *WHO DOES THAT?*

I FELT AS IF I were peering off the edge of a cliff looking down into the big black abyss of my future. I knew I had to jump but had no idea where I might land. I didn't even know where to aim. But thanks to that internship in New York I did know that once I entered the workforce, I was inevitably going to spend more of my waking hours at my job than anywhere else for the rest of my life. So I'd better damn well *love* the work. I have always wanted a career that felt like less of a choice and more of a calling. But in order to heed the call, I had to quiet all the noise in my head. And the fear in my heart.

GROWING UP IN CHURCH, we were taught to trust that God has a plan for all of us. And I believed that. But there were no hard and fast hacks on exactly how to uncover that plan, except for the seemingly esoteric practices of prayer and faith.

This was the year I finally came to understand what that meant.

WITH ONLY ONE SEMESTER left, I used graduation as a deadline to figure out what the hell to do with my life. I quit the party scene, pulled away from shallow friendships that were taking me nowhere, prayed hard for clarity on my next move, and searched for signs that could point me in the direction of my destiny. I was embarrassed to admit it at the time, but I actually started looking forward to those Friday nights in—just me, myself, and Google, dreaming up the possibilities in candlelit solitude.

Trying to figure out how to pursue your passion in ninety days sounds like one of those bestselling self-help books or a viral TED Talk, but ultimately, in practice it was more like being lost in a dark room and not knowing if I'd ever find my way out. It required a deeper level of faith than I'd ever had to call upon.

I spent the next few months in a perpetually anxious state, searching, praying, and fasting from the frivolous things I used to waste my time on. But the deafening silence on the other end of my prayers tested the limits of my faith. Time was ticking, graduation was nearing, and I felt lost in the sauce.

While this period was scary as hell, I was certain even then that it was also absolutely necessary. It felt like it was all a part of a much larger self-discovery process. So I just kept praying, asking God for divine confirmation: "Send me a sign. Reveal to me why I am here. Make it so clear that there is no doubt in my mind of what I'm meant to do."

Then in a fit of anxiety, I interviewed for a life insurance adjuster job in San Francisco. You know, just in case I missed the sign.

THAT NOVEMBER, I CAME home for Thanksgiving and sequestered myself in my parents' study for hours Googling "magazine internships." I decided to get over my fear of rejection and just apply for the *Essence* internship that kept haunting me, making my heart race any time I thought about it.

Channeling my inner nine-year-old brown girl boss, I mocked-up an imaginary magazine using clips I'd written for my college newspaper and pictures I'd taken during my rookie modeling days in college. I included a deeply personal "letter from the editor" about how much *Essence* meant to me and wrote cover lines selling myself for the job. Using my dad's camcorder, I even shot an earnest home video pitching myself, with India.Arie playing in the background. My lip gloss was poppin'. But I hadn't quite mastered set design: the backdrop was my parents' janky bent blinds, a cluttered desk, and a very clunky printer. (Thank God this was pre-YouTube.)

None of this was required as part of the application, but I was determined to stand out. As a college senior, this was my last shot at qualifying for a summer internship like this one. So I went *hard* in the paint for this opportunity.

For my cover, I went with a retro, Billie Holiday–inspired rookie modeling photo of me grinning wide, my head tilted back, hands on my hips, elbows wide to create that perfect triangle of negative space. I had red glossy lips to match the big red flower pinned into my pompadour. The cover lines read: "How to Go After the Career of Your Dreams," "Exclusive: How This Writer/Model/College Student Plans to Make It to the Top." The cover story was titled "Elaine Welteroth on Why She's the One for the Job." I hit them with my very own, very *extra* interpretation of a magazine internship application.

While I worked manically in my parents' study, my mom set a sandwich next to me on the desk. She kept checking in every couple of hours:

"You still haven't taken a bite of that sandwich, Elaine."

"Okay, okay, I will. Thanks, Mom."

Two hours later.

"Lainey! You better take a break and eat that sandwich, girl."

Like clockwork, she'd be back again: "Lainey, really. You need to stand up and get away from that computer. Go get some fresh air. And eat that dern sandwich!"

"Mom, please! I'm trying to work. Don't you want me to get a job and a life so I can stop relying on you to feed me?" (Because who else can we unleash our inner drama queens on if not our own mothers?)

I *needed* to land this internship. By any means necessary.

I finished the application after midnight and leaned away from the computer screen. I was finally ready to finish off the sandwich my mom wouldn't stop harassing me about when I noticed a stack of her magazines on the couch. There on top was a cover image of Alicia Keys wearing a gorgeous red gown. Her silky hair was liberated from her signature cornrows and blowing in the wind (machine). I was transfixed.

I didn't even notice the name of the magazine, I just flipped straight to the cover story.

After reading the piece, my eyes were immediately drawn to the byline. The writer's name was Harriette Cole. This is going to sound like one of those hokey church testimonies, but intuitively I felt an instruction to look her up. The direction was so clear, so prescient.

In all the years I had spent devouring magazines, making collages for my photo albums (which in retrospect were every bit my first magazine prototypes), it never once crossed my mind to study who actually made these magazines I was obsessing over until now. These jobs just never seemed attainable for someone like me, with no connections in that glossy media world.

When I typed "Harriette Cole" into the search window, a slick headshot of a Black woman with a confident smile appeared on my parents' desktop computer screen. She looked like she was in her early forties. She had beautiful, milk chocolate skin, perfectly manicured brows with a high arch, and enviable dimples. She was wearing a sharp black blazer with a spiky Halle Berry pixie and silver hoops. As I read her bio I was riveted; my heart started pumping faster and harder, like I'd just found treasure in a wasteland.

After a stint on Capitol Hill, Harriette moved to New York City to pursue a magazine career. Her father was the first Black appellate judge on the Maryland Court of Appeals and would have loved nothing more than for her to follow in his footsteps by writing the law, but she had other plans. Instead, she spent the next eleven years working her way up the masthead at *Essence*, where she eventually became fashion director under the legendary Susan L. Taylor. Then she took the calculated leap to start her own production company, Harriette Cole Media, and went on to build her own creative business model. She became a bestselling author of multiple books and a longtime contributor to the *Today* show. She launched an XM Satellite Radio show and a nationally syndicated advice column. She also helped create and launch *Uptown*, an upscale lifestyle publication for affluent Black people. At the time I became aware of her, she was at *Ebony*, working as the creative director and, soon after, interim editor-in-chief (the first woman, by the way, to helm the magazine), charged with refreshing the iconic Black legacy title.

I was in awe: here was a Black woman who had seemingly cracked the code to building a thriving career across multiple media platforms and empowering women along the way just by being her authentic self. What I was drawn to most was not the magazines she worked for, but how successfully she had carved out a lane of her own in the media world at the intersection of style, spirituality, and Black culture. She was dedicated to helping Black women look, feel, live, and love better. But her work wasn't limited to one title or even one platform.

Harriette was well before her time—a "multi-hyphenate" before millennials made that a Thing. A personal brand before Instagram came along and made us all believe we had personal brands of our own to cultivate. In my eyes, she was a mini media mogul and an important voice in our community. A role model flying just under the radar.

In Harriette, I saw someone I could aspire to—someone I might even be able to connect with if I tried hard enough.

Just like that, after months of feeling lost on a dark, depressing path, it was as if a light bulb went on. If M. Foss helped me find my footing in college, now Harriette had emerged as my North Star, a shining example of how I wanted to navigate the media world. Her bio became a blueprint for my own career path. Magazines would come first, then TV, books, films, and beyond.

"This. Is. IT. *This* is what I'm going to do with my life."

What had been so foggy and unclear for so long had suddenly come into focus. I had my answer. And it came with an inexplicable, electrifying feeling. I looked up and thanked God.

This was my sign. I followed it.

And I never once looked back.

LATER THAT FALL, M. Foss invited me to join her on a trip to Chicago for an academic conference where she was presenting her work. She had also invited her favorite grad student Amánda, someone I had never even heard her mention before. I was flattered but also low-key jealous, like: "Wait, Amanda who? I thought I was your only student-friend-mentee situation?" My petty was showing.

M. Foss laughed and said, "You'll love her, trust me."

Despite my protest, Amanda and I crawled into our coach seats and flew to Chicago with M. Foss to bear witness to her—in all of her brilliant, curly-haired glory—tackling her presentation in front of a roomful of crusty, cordouroy-clad academics. Afterward, we ate the best deep-dish pizza Chicago has to offer. We got lost roaming the streets, and we laughed so hard we cried actual tears. It was the exact release I needed. But the real magic happened on the plane ride home.

High above the clouds, we huddled together and challenged each other to share one thing we really, *really* wanted. The thing we wanted so badly it was difficult to even say aloud. Growing up in church, they'd say, "Where two or more are gathered, so, too, is the Lord in your midst." Being suspended in the air with these two women, it felt like there was divinity among us.

M. Foss revealed that she and her husband had been trying, unsuccessfully, for years to become parents. When she cried, we cried with her.

Amanda opened up about how unhappy she was in her seemingly solid, long-term relationship. She described the kind of partnership she really wanted and how badly she desired to be married within a year and to start a family—a big family—with the right person. She was debating sticking it out or cutting it off to start over, but the idea of being single all over again was daunting. She felt like she was running out of time.

When it was my turn, I froze. Deep down I realized that I actually knew what I wanted, but I couldn't manage to say it out loud. They had to cajole me.

"Just *tell* us."

"It's so stupid," I said. "It's not realistic at all."

They kept coaxing until finally the words slipped right out of my mouth.

With my eyes closed, I took a deep breath and whispered, "I want to be the editor of a magazine. My dream is to work at *Essence*."

I immediately regretted saying it.

I knew how off it sounded. And that it'd never happen. I figured, at best, they would say something polite but dismissive like, "Oh, wouldn't that be cool?" And then fall into awkward silence. At worst, I expected a reality check: "Girl, that's one of the most competitive industries in the world. C'mon. I love you, but that ain't gonna happen."

Instead, in unison, they said: "DUH."

M. Foss proceeded to go *in*: "That is not a stretch—*at all*. I can *so* see you doing that, Elaine. You would make one *hell* of an editor."

Amanda chimed in with the kind of enthusiasm you can't fake: "Girl! Hell-ass-yes. Yes. Yes. Yes. I see this for you, E. This is *so* you. *Go for it*. I guarantee you'll get it."

I was stunned. "Really? Don't just say all of this to make me feel better!"

"Girl. If you don't get this application out, we are going to mail it for you," Amanda said.

These were women I trusted. Women I respected. Older, wiser women who knew things about the world I hadn't learned yet. And they believed I could do this.

I had braced myself for the worst, almost expecting them to laugh and completely shut down my delusions. But they didn't laugh at me. They didn't tell me I was crazy. That it would never happen. Instead, they affirmed me in the moment I needed it most.

I BELIEVE WE ALL HAVE CALLINGS. Purposes. Work that only we can do. It seems ridiculous now, but I came scarily close to never naming and claiming mine because I was so certain it sounded silly and impossible. I actually believed there was no way someone like me could ever land a job like that. Gripped by the paralysis of self-doubt, I nearly allowed fear to silence me, even in that safe space. But I'm so glad I didn't let fear win. Because it would have cut me off from what I needed most: encouragement.

The world doesn't prepare girls—especially little brown girls—to see the bigness of their dreams. It doesn't train us to embrace the expansiveness of our own possibilities. And small towns tend to reinforce small thinking. So seeing our full potential isn't work we can do alone. We need the other women in our tribe. Friends. Sisters. Mothers. Professors. When women affirm women, it unlocks our power. It gives us permission to shine brighter.

I am forever grateful for that fateful moment in the sky with these women who saw the bigness of the possibilities in front of me before I could see them for myself.

That conversation very literally changed the trajectory of my life.

I CAME BACK from Chicago buzzing.

It started on a simmer and then quickly became this bright flame inside of me. In my mind, I could start to see myself where I wanted to be—and it was thrilling.

Yet whenever anyone asked my least favorite question of all, "What are you going to do after college?" (and they'd always ask), I'd say, "I don't know."

Call it superstition, but I didn't want to jinx it. I have less to lose admitting all of this now, but back then, it was still a seed I needed to protect. I couldn't risk someone squishing it with a careless remark. Or tarnishing it by projecting their own fears onto it. It was too fragile.

Especially when, frankly, I still had no idea how I was going to fling myself into this terrifyingly big dream. I had no contacts in publishing. I knew no one who could even get me an email intro. If I was going to get there, I would need another act of God to make it happen.

I SENT OFF MY INTERNSHIP application to *Essence*, and while I waited for a reply, I turned my attention to connecting with Harriette Cole. Call it temporary insanity, but once I made up my mind that I needed to meet her, I would do whatever was necessary to make that happen. It wasn't quite creeper-level stalking. Okay, maybe it was.

I spent the next few weeks writing and perfecting my introduction letter to her. I proofread it so many times that I could recite it from memory. Eventually I snail-mailed it and emailed it, and after finding her office phone number, I called regularly just to see if she received it. The letter ended the same way I signed off over the phone every time I called: a professional but urgent request to speak with Harriette. All I needed was fifteen minutes.

I called so often I could practically hear Harriette's assistant Nubia Murray's eyes roll at the sheer sound of my voice:

"She still isn't available."

"No worries. Do you know when she will be available?" Maneuvering past her deadpan rejection actually became sort of entertaining.

"No." Shocker.

"Okay, well please do let her know that I would be happy to bring coffee by the office next week any time she's available."

"Didn't you say you live in California?" Nubia already knew my coordinates and probably had me on high-security watch.

"Yes."

"So what do you mean, bring her coffee?"

"Oh, I was thinking I could just fly out to bring coffee by next week. It's really no trouble at all. I'm happy to make it as easy for her as possible. All I'm hoping for is just fifteen minutes."

"That won't be necessary. Please do not fly to come to our office." Pregnant pause. "Let me see what I can do about setting up a *very quick* call at her convenience."

So you're saying there's a chance! Jim Carrey's infamous line from *Dumb and Dumber* is still an all-time fave, but I knew better than to let it rip even though it was going off in my head like an alarm.

"That would be wonderful," I responded, feigning decorum. "I really, really appreciate your help. I'll check back in soon."

"I'll email you if she can take your call. Good-bye." Click.

I was on cloud . . . 8.9. I was still holding my breath, hoping for confirmation that this informational interview was actually going to happen.

WITHIN DAYS, NUBIA EMAILED me with a scheduled time to speak with Harriette. It was December 19, 2007. I was graduating on December 21. This answer to my prayer came right in the nick of time.

I sat on the edge of my bed, readying myself for the call I felt like I'd waited a lifetime for. When the phone rang, I took a deep breath and asked God to help me be myself—I didn't want to screw this up.

"Hello, Harriette?"

Harriette had fifteen minutes blocked off for the call—but we talked for forty-five. She was every bit the polished sage I'd imagined her to be. I wrote down each word she said, making sure I captured every gem.

During our call, all my nerves went away—I was *on*. Sharp, clear, professional, and my passion came through, not as desperation, but as what it was: sincere conviction. I chose my words carefully as I articulated exactly what she meant to me, how passionate I was about entering into the business of magazine publishing. I asked smart questions, and I slipped in that working for her would be a dream come true, but also that if I never spoke to her again she had already changed my life. It was a lot to put on a lady who was probably just taking a quick call with a stranger in California between bites of Cobb salad at her desk. But I recognized that there were likely hundreds of girls reaching out to her for the very same thing. Guidance. Inspiration. Counsel. Encouragement. I felt lucky to be the one on the other end of that call.

As we were wrapping up, I said, "If there's ever an opportunity to work with you, please do keep me in mind. It would be an honor."

After I hung up, I let out a massive exhale in my empty room. I felt at peace and energized. I knew that I would likely never hear from her again, but having the chance to speak with her confirmed everything I felt inside about what I was meant to do.

WITH JUST A COUPLE days left before graduation, I was finally very clear about my goal: I wanted to land a paid magazine gig in New York City by June 1.

By any means necessary.

Plan A: Land the paid summer internship at *Essence.*

This was the dream.

Plan B: Pursue a summer internship at one of the other big publishing houses.

This seemed unlikely given that those spots at Hearst, Time Inc., and Condé Nast were rumored to be reserved for the Lilys and the Harvard grads of New York's tight-knit upper-crust circles. I had no one on the inside to call in a favor, nor did I even fully understand what nepotism was or how it worked.

Plan C: Get accepted into a top-tier journalism graduate school program.

Only a prestigious top-tier university or an Ivy League would do. I figured it would be redemptive after the whole following-my-high-school-sweetheart-to-state-college phase. Plus, I needed to make the best possible backdoor connections.

Plan D (contingent upon Plan C): Find a local editorial summer internship in San Francisco, then start my graduate program in the fall at whatever Ivy League school accepted me.

All of these plans required concrete action steps. I also still needed an actual job, because moving to New York City wasn't going to pay for itself. So I tacked on an immediate postgraduate game plan: Move back home with my parents to stack coins. Get as many jobs as possible. Grind every single day. Save ten thousand dollars and move to New York City by June 1.

THE DAY AFTER GRADUATION, I got a job working as a host and server at Nola, a restaurant near Stanford. The irony wasn't lost on me that I probably would have gone to that very restaurant as a customer if I had ever made it to my dream school. Instead, I was making minimum wage plus tips after graduating cum laude from a state college. It was humbling, but I was on a mission.

To supplement that work, I scoured all the usual career sites for writing positions, and found a posting via Craigslist (of all places) for a receptionist gig at a digital media start-up in San Francisco's swanky Embarcadero district. I applied and not only did I get the job, I even managed to drum up the audacity to negotiate that I could write my own online column from the front desk as long as I stayed on top of my primary admin duties.

Boom.

I wasn't home three days and I already had two jobs. The universe was clearly conspiring in my favor.

Monday through Friday I took BART to my desk job in San Francisco, while devoutly reading *The Alchemist* on my commute. After hours and on weekends I'd zoom across the Dumbarton Bridge to barely make it on time for my shift at the restaurant. I dropped drinks, I forgot orders, I couldn't memorize the menu, but I could hold great conversations with patrons and I smiled a lot, so I always managed to take home a respectable wad of greasy, crumb-lined tips.

I saved every penny.

WHEN I GOT A CALLBACK about the *Essence* internship, you would have thought I found a dead body by the sound of my scream. My plan was starting to come together. Things were happening!

When asked which editorial department I wanted to work in, I was too afraid to say straight up that I wanted the beauty and fashion spot because it was the most competitive. "I'd be grateful for any of the positions in any department," I said, hedging my bets. "If you gave me the janitor job, I'd take it as long as I got to work in that office this summer."

They laughed.

When I got the email confirming that I had been selected for the incoming 2008 intern class, I was practically levitating with joy. They offered me the role of editorial intern in the Work and Wealth department. It felt like that big expansive sky I had been looking up at for all these years finally opened up and made room for me in the clouds.

I WAS GOING TO NYC TO WORK AT MY DREAM MAGAZINE. MAMA, I MADE IT.

"When women affirm women, it unlocks our power. It gives us permission to shine brighter."

CHAPTER 10

Your Dreams Are Calling

It's time for you to move, realizing that the thing
you are seeking is also seeking you.

IYANLA VANZANT

I was exactly thirty days away from my big move to New York City for my dream summer internship when my cell phone rang. "Harriette Cole's office? This *must* be a butt dial," I thought. But even that would be an honor because it'd mean she saved my number.
"Hello?"

"Hello, Elaine. This is Harriette Cole."

"Oh! Hi! Harriette! What a pleasant surprise."

When I realized this was *not* a butt dial I lost all chill.

"My current assistant will be moving to Italy soon, so I am interviewing candidates and I thought of you."

I suddenly thought I was being punked by one of my friends.

"As I recall, you live in California, is that correct?" she went on.

"Yes, yes, I do," I stammered.

"Wonderful. Well, I have a shoot on Friday in LA and am looking for a local production assistant. The rate is two hundred and fifty dollars for the day if you're available," she proposed. "It would be good for us to meet in person anyway."

This was like that TV moment when the main character looks into the camera and screams.

"Absolutely! Yes. Of course. I'd be honored to be your production assistant," I said, zero clue as to what a production assistant even was. But I quickly got permission to take off from work to head down to Malibu to find out.

"Great," she said. "My team will send you the call sheet soon. I look forward to meeting you then."

Before we got off, I said, "I know you mentioned that there could be a potential job opportunity for me. I just wanted you to know that I've already accepted a summer internship at *Essence*."

"Ah." She snickered. "Congratulations. What department?"

"I'll be an editorial intern under the Work and Wealth editor," I replied tentatively.

"Work and Wealth?" She seemed puzzled.

The truth was I got placed in that department not because I was a money whiz, but because I wasn't brave enough to ask for what I *really* wanted. Which was the fashion and beauty spot. But who was I to be picky when I just needed the chance to get my pinky toe through the door? I could worry about climbing my way to the top later. My mom always said, "Beggars can't be choosers." I had just landed a dream internship at one of my favorite magazines. That was good enough for me. I babbled off a much more professional version of this to Harriette.

"May I give you one piece of advice?" she offered.

"Of course. Please," I said.

"If you know what you want, ask for it. And be specific. You might just get it."

Damn. She was right. I wasn't even working for this woman yet and she was already getting my life together. Then she hit me with more persuasive career advice:

"Listen, I worked at *Essence* for eleven years. I am very familiar with the environment and what you would be doing there. Let me tell you a bit about what you would be doing with me." The confidence in her voice was convincing. "In my office, you would be supporting me on all things fashion and beauty, including covers. Our HQ is in Chicago, so my assistant and I are the only editorial team members based in the New York office. At a place like *Essence*, you would be one of many in a sea of interns."

I was both spellbound, and now officially torn.

But first, I had to get to Malibu.

WHEN I RECEIVED the call sheet for the shoot, the first line jumped off my screen: "Serena Williams cover, August 2008."

HARRIETTE DID NOT TELL ME THIS WAS A COVER SHOOT.

Dreams I hadn't even dreamed yet were already coming true.

I quickly packed my overnight bag after work and tossed it into my emerald green, sun-bleached Honda Accord coupe. When I closed the trunk, I looked up and saw my mom under the porch light locking the front door. She had on her windbreaker and her "mom hat" with a scarf underneath, her purse hanging from her forearm, and a Saran-wrapped plate of food in her hand.

"Mom, what are you doing?"

"You thought I was going to let my baby girl drive all the way down to LA by herself in the midnight hour?" She marched over to my car with a wink. "You need your rest for tomorrow, missy."

"Mom! No way. Please, I will be fine!" I pleaded.

She ignored me.

"Seriously, don't you have to work tomorrow?"

"Girl, scoot on over." She shook her head and kissed my cheek. "Let the mama be the mama, will you?"

I started crying right there in the driveway. Here I was beginning my journey into adulthood, a journey I was determined to figure out alone. But being an adult doesn't always mean you have to do it *all* alone.

I shifted into the passenger seat, and she handed me a hot plate of catfish and cabbage that she had prepared for the road trip. Not realizing how hungry I was, I gobbled it up before we even made it onto the freeway.

"Mmm-hmmm, what happened to 'Mom! I'm not hungry,'" she teased. That woman always enjoys getting a rise out of me. "That's my daughter all right. You still have the appetite of a football player when you want to. Now, go ahead and recline that chair back, Lainey. You need your rest."

I slept nearly all six hours of the drive. When I woke up, we were winding through a spooky basin on highway I-5 that's all sharp turns and thick fog. My mom was leaning forward, grasping the steering wheel with white knuckles. I knew she was nervous because she was squinting and breathing like she was in Lamaze class. I offered to take over.

"Don't be silly, girl," she responded without taking her eyes off the road ahead.

I know my mom like the back of my hand—and she does *not* like driving long distances, let alone at night. This act was nothing but love.

I dozed back off feeling immensely lucky—yes, to have a shot at this magazine job, but even luckier to have a mother like mine.

WE SPENT THE NIGHT on my cousin Chey's floor—three grown women sharing a blow-up mattress. The next morning, I woke up early to drive down to Malibu. The ride along the Pacific Coast Highway was breathtaking. I had spent my entire life in California and had never seen this unbelievably beautiful part of the state. *This* was the California you see on TV.

When I arrived—to a gorgeous, gated mansion right on the ocean—I parked my car and took a deep breath. There was no trace of nervousness or fear in my body. I was *ready*. I felt like I was living the Black Lauren Conrad *dream*.

Just then Harriette called to say, "I'm running a little late, so go ahead and get things going." She offered no clear direction except, "Do not talk to the celebrity."

As I walked down the driveway to set, I did a double take at the first person I saw.

"Marcia Hamilton!?"

Back in the day, Marcia was one of the best hairstylists in my aunt Janet's salon in the Bay. She did my and First Love's hair for our junior and senior prom. She once transformed me into a ratchet princess with hot-pink-striped bangs for a hair show in San Jose before she took off to become a big-time Hollywood hairstylist. I heard she was Jada Pinkett Smith's go-to; I didn't know she was working with Serena Williams, too.

"Elaine! Oh, my God, what are you doing here?" she said, her arms swung open wide for a hug.

"I'm the production assistant today," I said proudly. "How random is this!?"

It was a good omen.

I quickly filled her in on my postgrad plans. She was so excited for me, and pulled me over to meet Serena.

"Hey, how are you? Nice to meet you," Serena said, flashing that warm, world-famous Serena smile I'd seen from the tennis court on TV. On the outside, I played it totally cool as Marcia shared our backstory. Inside, I was practically having an out-of-body experience.

Harriette's instructions rang in my head: "Don't talk to the celebrity." Here I was already breaking the only rule my new boss had given me. But the truth was, *I* did not talk to her, she talked to *me*. Marcia helped break the ice, giving me instant cred with the crew. It all felt quite kismet. God was really showing out.

By the time Harriette arrived, everything was under control and I had established a good rapport with everyone on set.

When the shoot kicked off, Serena was posing in the shallow end of the infinity pool overlooking stunning views of the Pacific. I was standing behind Harriette looking into the monitor, doing this dance of auditioning for the role, wanting to prove that I could add value, but also trying to be respectful of the boundaries. I fell back and waited for my moment.

I watched the monitor carefully, knowing we had more flattering suits for Serena's body on the rack. It was killing me. I finally leaned in close to Harriette and whispered, "I think she would look incredible in the blue swimsuit."

I now know interns and production assistants do not belong behind the monitor at shoots. Interns don't make styling calls. Interns basically don't speak unless spoken to on set—especially when it is their first day. But Harriette did not tell me to go away or to be quiet. Instead, she paused. Long enough to make me regret my very existence. Then she said, "Serena, let's try you in the blue swimsuit next."

Harriette was my first example of a female boss who elevated everybody around her. She was early evidence that a truly confident leader stands in her power without using it to make others feel small. She ran the show with integrity, grace, kindness, and class.

Serena changed into the blue suit. And I knew, in at least one small way, my voice mattered that day.

Oh, and that swimsuit? It made it onto the cover.

THE DIFFERENCES BETWEEN the girl on set that day and the girl who showed up every day to my internship at the ad agency in New York City were stark. At Ogilvy & Mather, I was never sure what to say or do, or even how to dress in that environment. I felt small, miserable, and out of place, like my light had dimmed, like I had lost my voice. That wasn't the self-assured woman I knew I was meant to be.

Yet that day in Malibu, I was standing on the other side of fear, and my whole vibe said: "I got this." I felt sharp, funny, and BIG. Like I was actually glowing. I carried a sense of belonging in my own skin.

When I looked back on my life, that girl had always been there—telling her stories on that pageant stage, running her own little talk show from the bathtub, loving on her best friends with outfit advice, brown girl bossing in the backyard. I felt like that big bright light the name card in my Easter egg basket described all those years ago. Yet somehow I was never quite able to be that girl at work. Not until this moment.

I realized that if we aren't vigilant, we can move through our entire lives feeling smaller than we actually are—by playing it safe, by unconsciously giving away our power, by dimming our radiance, by not recognizing there is *always* so much more waiting for us on the other side of fear.

But when we *are* brave enough—to go there, to grab what we want, to tap into who we are—*damn*, it feels so good.

As we were nearing the end of the shoot, Dudley, the director of photography, gestured for me to join him and Harriette on a grassy hill where they seemed to be discussing business:

"So when are you coming out to New York, kid?" he deadpanned.

I looked at Harriette. She was smiling and nodding.

"What do you mean?"

"You are hired. That's what he means. We'll start with a summer internship. And then we will go from there."

"Oh, my God. This is—incredible. Thank you. But, wait—Harriette, I told you about my *Essence* internship."

Dudley scoffed. Harriette shook her head as if I were a very amusing, silly girl.

"You don't understand; I told them I would be their janitor! How do I go back and be like, 'Ha! Just kidding, I'm not coming after all.'?"

Harriette and Dudley laughed, but they weren't backing down.

"How much are they paying you?" she asked.

"Ten dollars an hour," I said.

"Great. We'll match that." She continued. "I can tell you that at *Essence* you won't have the opportunity to see and do the things that you just did today for years."

Harriette was luring me. And it was working.

CALLING *ESSENCE* TO TURN down my dream internship was the hardest call I had ever made.

My contact was curt and condescending. "You're going to *Ebony*? Ha. Yeah, okay. Good luck."

My friends had similar responses: Marcia and Chey both crumpled their noses and said, "Why would you work at *Ebony*? Instead of *Essence*? Girl, are you crazy?"

Essence was the sexier choice at the time. It was the only major magazine for stylish Black women. *Ebony* was like your auntie and uncle's magazine. It was older and, well, dustier. But I decided not to chase the sexy—or what sounded sexy to other people. I felt a higher calling, a tug inside me telling me to work alongside Harriette. I had to trust that.

I had heard church people testify about miracles "on the other side of prayer." But until your prayers are answered in a miraculous way, you reserve room for doubt. There's always a chance this faith thing is all made up. *But finding Harriette?* That was nothing but a *God thing*. The opportunity in Malibu was a *God thing*. And now this door opening in front of me was a

God thing. It was all connected. For the first time in my life, my prayers had been answered in a tangible, undeniable way. There was no longer a doubt in my mind that *this* was God's plan for me. And I was good placing my bets on that.

Whenever friends or family felt the need to fling their fear onto my future, I would just tell them, "This is between me and God."

My COLLEGE FRIEND NATALIE landed an internship at CBS in New York City, which serendipitously meant we got the chance to be roommates in Brooklyn in a summer sublet I found on Craigslist. Neither of us had ever heard of East Williamsburg, but we naively assumed it must be the eastern part of Williamsburg, a hip, up-and-coming neighborhood we'd heard about. "I'm sure it will be fine, Mom!" I assured her as I packed my bags. It was the year Bush rendered a tax break, so I used the extra money to buy my mom a round-trip ticket to help us move into our new spot, sight unseen.

When we landed in muggy New York on May 31, 2008, the black-car driver knew from how much we smiled that we weren't real New Yorkers.

"East Williamsburg?" The driver chuckled. "Ah. You must mean Bushwick." He seemed amused by my stupidity. "No such thing as East Williamsburg."

I was too excited to worry. We handed him my new address on a piece of paper, loaded in our luggage, then piled into the backseat. The closer we got, the more I chanted, Biggie-style: "Where Brooklyn at! Where Brooklyn at!"

But as we drove deeper and deeper into Brooklyn, the streets whizzing outside our windows started to look more and more rough. When the driver stopped the car, my mom's eyes grew wide with concern. "Is there a problem, sir?"

The driver threw up his hands. "This is the address you gave me." Then he offered protectively in a thick Spanish accent, "Miss, this isn't a neighborhood I would feel comfortable leaving my daughter in either. Not this neighborhood."

"Lawd Jesus." My mom shook her head dramatically. By then I was in full-blown panic, too.

The apartment was located off the J/M/Z line at the Myrtle/Broadway stop, a twenty-five-minute train ride away from Manhattan, but to the uninitiated, this particular block in Bushwick looked mad suspect. Now, of course, I recognize it as any other classically New York block, but back then we were used to pristine streets and clean, spacious suburban neighborhoods with freshly cut green grass. All of my and Natalie's naive California-girl dreams of a New York fantasy life shattered on that littered sidewalk.

"Lawd Jesus," my mom kept on, like a broken record, as we scanned our new surroundings.

Back in the summer of 2008, "East Williamsburg" was a newly invented term gentrifiers were using to rebrand this slice of Bushwick, the mostly Dominican neighborhood where boarded-up buildings were covered in graffiti. Bare-chested men walked around blasting loud music from portable speakers and potbellied uncles in tank tops chilled curbside on couches. The stray dogs and cats that roamed the streets had nicknames. The fire hydrant was a spontaneous community fountain enjoyed by all the neighborhood kids.

As we stood there, two White girls in their early twenties with artful tattoos emerged from the front gate of our new apartment building wearing high-waisted booty shorts and miniature hipster bangs. These were the people we were renting the apartment from, and they were quick to assure my mother that the neighborhood was "*Tooootally* fine."

Feeling bamboozled by the Craigslist ad, all I kept thinking was, "Holy shit, what have I done?"

As soon as we walked through the gate, we saw a smattering of friendly art-school kids hanging out in fold-up chairs on the concrete foyer drinking beer. They all craned their necks to greet us with peace signs, like: "Hey, what's up?"

"Look! We already made friends," I said to my mom, mostly in an attempt to let myself off the hook.

Once we got into the apartment, my mom let us know how she really felt: "First of all, those girls need to put some pants on. I don't know where they think they are, but this ain't no place to be walking around dressed like that."

Eventually, she let up. We were adults now and this was our decision that we would have to live with.

"Well, ladies, y'all are the ones with one-way tickets." She giggled facetiously, making it clear that the decision whether to stay or go was on us. "Remember I already have my round-trip ticket back home." Before my mom left, she cosponsored our first Target (we pronounced it "Tar-jay") run on Atlantic Avenue, where we scooped up blow-up mattresses, cheap dishware, and wicker living-room furniture. She helped set us up and then she was off, back to California.

As soon as the front door shut behind her, Natalie and I crawled out onto the fire escape with a pack of Black & Milds, feeling in charge of our lives in our new neighborhood, which was, in fact, totally safe. *Ish*. I thought of me and Claudia Ortega in her backyard. It was that same feeling. We were, finally, *almost* grown. Two brown girl bosses turned working women in New York City.

"If we aren't vigilant, we can move through our entire lives feeling smaller than we actually are—by playing it safe, by unconsciously giving away our power, by dimming our radiance, by not recognizing there is *always* so much more waiting for us on the other side of fear. But when we *are* brave enough—to go there, to grab what we want, to tap into who we are—*damn*, it feels so good."

CHAPTER 11

Started from the Bottom

If they don't give you a seat at the table, bring a folding chair.

SHIRLEY CHISHOLM, FIRST BLACK WOMAN
ELECTED TO CONGRESS

On my first day of work I bounced out of bed. I pulled on my favorite top, a sheer black turtleneck with flouncy details on the shoulders, and a pencil skirt that puffed out around the hips, accentuating my slight frame. I grabbed the devotional my mom left on my makeshift wicker nightstand and then headed out for my fifty-one-minute commute to the office. I had butterflies in my stomach the whole way in. It took three trains to get to the world-famous Rockefeller Center stop, and I had to walk underground for what felt like a half mile in heels (I hadn't yet learned the art of packing flats). By the time I reached the lobby, I was sweating but too undeniably stoked to care. I was living *the dream.*

To my surprise, there was no fancy marquee sign on the door. And once I got inside, the dingy carpets, walls, and desks made for a space that felt like the set of an office drama from the late 1970s. The "fashion closet" at

Ebony was a spare storage room piled high with office supplies and beauty products spilling out of torn shopping bags. There were no racks overflowing with designer clothing. No in-house beauty or fashion team. This was nothing like the illustrious offices I'd seen on *Sex and the City* or *The Devil Wears Prada*.

But it wasn't just the office decor or the dysfunctional organization system that did not live up to my fantasies—I could whip that beauty closet together in no time, and I was happy to schlep with the best of them. No, it was bigger than all that. Two things occurred to me that very first day: in the world of media there is a hierarchy, and as an intern at *Ebony*, I was at the very bottom of it.

In many ways, working at *Ebony* was like a haunting metaphor for what it meant to be Black in America.

The traditional business model for the magazine industry relies on advertising dollars. *Ebony* proved to be a hard sell for most marketers who were focused on reaching the general population, not niche "urban" audiences—even if our demographic did over-index on spending in their category. Without the gravitas of founder John H. Johnson, who for more than fifty years cultivated powerful business relationships that ensured the company's profitability, it was an ongoing struggle for the sales team to convince big advertisers to view this Black-owned legacy Black magazine as a worthy investment, especially in an economic climate that was slipping into the steepest recession since the Great Depression. The "multicultural" budgets were always smaller and more scarce. As a result, *Ebony* was grossly underresourced as a business, marginalized on newsstands, and barely staying afloat.

There was also a perception issue within the industry. I learned quickly that Black titles are not always regarded with equal respect; especially in the fashion and beauty space, we were commonly treated as second or even third tier. (To this day, it is still considered an industry norm that the "more important" magazines get preferential treatment.) We felt it in interactions with other steely editors and recalcitrant publicists who would suddenly light up in the presence of another assistant editor from *Vogue* or *W.* We didn't have the same access to the designer clothes, the parties, or the shows that so many of the other magazines did. Whether it was sample requests or interview requests, we were very clearly on the bottom of the pile. At the time, it seemed to me that we existed in what felt like a dark, dusty corner of the publishing world.

In its heyday in the 1960s and '70s, Johnson Publishing Company was the epicenter of Black culture. The Black husband-and-wife founders, John and Eunice Johnson, were media moguls and icons in their own right. Together, they owned *Ebony;* the weekly news digest *Jet;* and their own cosmetics line, Fashion Fair, which spun off into a traveling fashion show franchise that did more than just introduce unadulterated glamour to thirty Black cities a year all over the United States—it poured more than 50 million charitable dollars back into these communities. Launched during the civil rights movement, Fashion Fair, Eunice Johnson's brainchild, was uniquely responsible for putting Black designers and models like Stephen Burrows and Pat Cleveland on the map.

No one in history had done more for the Black fashion community than Eunice Johnson in those days—she was the OG Black girl magic legend. But her story routinely goes untold. When European fashion houses wouldn't loan to her magazines, she flew to Paris and purchased couture in cash, then paraded it around on Black bodies on runways she built in Black communities. She showcased couture from the most esteemed designers of the time, from Yves Saint Laurent to Oscar de la Renta. Eunice Johnson, and *Ebony*, were our people's introduction to capital-F Fashion.

Back then, Johnson Publishing was thriving, giving a voice to the Black community, breaking the biggest stories on Black stars, and carving out a proud place to see ourselves and our rich cultural legacy centered.

But the *Ebony* empire had fallen from relevance since those days.

Harriette's job was to rebuild it.

This was such an important undertaking, and I believed in Harriette's vision—and yet there I was, knee-deep in an avalanche of at-home relaxer kits and manila folders spilling out of torn boxes, thinking of the uphill climb ahead. "Shit. Maybe Marcia and Chey were right. Maybe I shouldn't have turned down *Essence* for *this*," I thought. At the time, *Essence* was owned by Time Inc., a large, respected (White) media conglomerate. As a result, they had more resources. *Ebony*, by comparison, was more of a mom-and-pop shop. I imagined my contemporaries in proper, luxurious fashion closets and wondered if I had made the biggest mistake of my career by taking the "unsexy" route to success.

That first dose of career FOMO hits hard. Despite Harriette's warm greeting and the immense privilege of having an office desk I could call my own in New York City, a few hours into my internship I was crying in the bathroom stall. I kept reminding myself that this was all part of God's plan. But I worried, still, that I might get stuck there, pigeonholed in this seemingly grim corner of the publishing world.

By noon on day one I knew already, deep down, that I had to start dreaming up a bigger dream. Not just for myself, but for *us*, a people deserving of representation in all of our glory. I wanted to help bridge the divide between the lack of representation I saw in mainstream publishing and the excellence of our culture, our beauty, and our icons. I could already tell that crossing over would not be easy, but as I sopped up my tears, I set my sights on making my way into Condé Nast one day, the most prestigious international publishing house of all, home to *Vogue*, *Vanity Fair*, and *Glamour*.

I admit, I never imagined myself at any of those titles before. I had only ever flipped through *Vogue* for fleeting moments of a fantasy, like everyone else, but I never saw myself on those pages or thought the magazine was for me. Now from my new vantage point, I vowed to myself that if I could make it this far into a world that was once only a dream to me—even if it was the very lowest rung—then surely I could aspire to chart my own path to the pinnacle of it.

I nicknamed it the Condé castle, and I was determined to make it there someday. Okay, maybe not to *Vogue*, but I imagined there *had* to be a way in on the ground floor at one of the other titles under the storied publisher's umbrella.

Maybe it was the dogged spirit that comes from growing up desperate to get out of a small town that pushed me to always reach higher. Or maybe it was, at least in part, a millennial's delusional confidence. I had at least a sliver of lived experience to stand on that proved where there's a will, there must be a way.

But first, I still had much to learn—and I was ready to do the work to get there.

That night, back home in Bushwick, I pulled out the stack of magazines I had lugged from my bedroom in California and made a vision board with cutouts of words that inspired me and images of the most fabulous Black women I could find—*my superheroes:* Beyoncé on her rock-star shit wearing an embellished leopard leotard, swinging her blond strands; Lauryn Hill in a rare sleek-bob-and-blunt-bangs moment, snipped from the pages of *Essence*.

In the very center of the collage was the cover shot from the most recent September issue of *Ebony*. It was peak Black Girl Glamour, featuring all the most iconic divas: Tyra, Iman, Alek, and Kimora. Every shade of brown skin glistening. This was "the new *Ebony*"—Harriette's *Ebony*, and it reminded me of why I wanted to work for her in the first place. On the plane to New York, I had pored over that issue cover to cover. Harriette's fingerprints were all over it. I also swooned over the autobiographical feature story from legendary *Vogue* editor André Leon Talley captured in those pages (until then, I had no idea he had started his career at *Ebony*, too).

America was at the precipice of electing our country's first Black president and *Ebony* seemed well positioned to reclaim its rightful place in the sun. That evening, I began to see a place in the clouds for me again. But I knew I'd have to carve it out for myself. Day by day. Page by page. One story at a time. One Herculean effort after the next. All on a shoestring budget.

So I buckled down. I stopped feeling sorry for myself, and I decided that I was going to do what my ancestors have done through *much* more harrowing circumstances than navigating a career come up in media—I was going to do the best I could with what I had.

Two weeks into my internship at *Ebony*, I found myself on set with MICHELLE OBAMA for her September 2008 issue cover shoot. It was just months before her husband's historic win. Harriette was right: this was turning out to be one of those rare career opportunities after all, rich with experiences I'd *never* get elsewhere, especially not during my first month in the game. (It felt like poetic justice seeing *Essence* shooting in the studio across from ours, knowing that *Ebony* had been the magazine to snag a shoot with the most high-profile Black woman in America—thanks to the publication's founding family's deep Chicago roots.)

That very morning, Mrs. Obama's face was seen by the world on the cover of *The New York Times* next to a headline that read: AFTER ATTACKS, MICHELLE OBAMA LOOKS FOR A NEW INTRODUCTION. Nevertheless, she practically floated into the studio, the perfect picture of grace on heels. (Manolos, by the way.)

While mainstream media was busy crafting snide attacks that perpetuated a false Angry Black Female narrative, Mrs. Obama looked into the eyes of every single person on set that day, making each one of us feel like the most important person in the room. She greeted us with warm smiles and firm handshakes, seemingly unbothered by all the fuss swirling in cyberspace about her persona and her outfit. She had just set the internet ablaze after appearing on *The View* in a $148 White House Black Market dress, which subsequently sold out overnight. For our shoot, she insisted that she wear her own clothes in order to keep the focus on her message. She borrowed nothing. By taking control over her wardrobe, she was reclaiming control over her own narrative.

What sticks out in my mind the most is that the soon-to-be-First Lady of the United States rolled up to the set of one of her first solo American covers with eight of her best friends from Chicago in tow.

My job that day? To look after Mrs. Obama's homegirls.

Prior to their arrival, I arranged eight fold-up chairs in perfect formation along the sideline of the shoot. I triple-checked arrival times, prepped snacks, and printed eight extra copies of the call sheet, just in case.

We were putting Michelle Obama on the cover of the only Black-owned national magazine just before the historic 2008 presidential election. Playing even a small role in this seminal moment in American history was an indescribable honor. I was so proud to be a part of it in any minuscule way, even if the highlight of my contribution that day was reaching deep into my purse to procure a tampon for one of Mrs. Obama's best friends in the ladies' room.

OUR FIRST BLACK First Lady would soon grace many magazine covers—magazines like *Vogue* and *Elle*, which rarely featured Black women then, let alone had them as cover girls. But before any of them, *Ebony* was telling her story and galvanizing our community in time for the most historic presidential election in American history. A win that would not have happened without the Black vote.

Yet even Black people often predicted *Ebony's* extinction: "Why do we even need Black magazines anymore anyway?" Some considered this a progressive mind-set during a uniquely progressive time—after all, we were getting our first Black president! The ultimate symbol of our equality!—but these were still the early days of an era ill-defined as "postracial America," a fallacy too many bought into.

This wouldn't be the first or last time in my career that I would find myself in a position to prove the impossible. Under those circumstances I learned that being underestimated can be one of the greatest motivators.

For thirteen hours straight on my first Fourth of July in New York City, I was holed up in my muggy, AC-less apartment in Bushwick, feverishly transcribing Harriette's twelve unforgettable interviews for that cover story. Illegal fireworks popped off outside my window and sweat dripped from my brow as I archived Black woman wisdom from *the* Michelle Obama; her mother, Marian Robinson; and the powerhouse that is Valerie Jarrett. My job wasn't sexy, but it was rewarding.

I knew then that I was right where I was supposed to be—and that I was playing the long game.

I QUICKLY BECAME PART OF the *Ebony* family, starting with Carolyn Coleman, who was Harriette's outbound executive assistant and the first Afropunk-rocker I'd ever met, apart from my brother. She wore bantu knots and a septum ring to the office. Carolyn was in her final few months in the role, preparing to leave her nine-to-five in order to pursue a music career overseas. Sharon, the kind but meddling office manager from Trinidad, sucked her teeth whenever her three teenage daughters ran amuck in the hallways after school. Then there was Idris, a beautiful, chatty gay man in his early fifties who would pop up at my desk with his well-moisturized curls, a crisp checkered shirt, and a complementary pocket square just to chitchat. "Oh, aren't you cute today?" he'd say in his syrupy Jersey accent. I loved his vibe, and the wild stories he'd tell me about industry nights from back in the day. Craig Robinson was a big, boisterous, bald, charismatic bro-tha from New Jersey who nicknamed me PB&J. That was his way of teasing me for showing up every day with a stockpile of peanut butter and jelly sand-wiches wrapped in foil—my breakfast, lunch, and dinner. I'd stack them on my desk at 9:00 A.M. and work my way down, one by one, like PB&J Jenga, until the end of the night. I was always still there nibbling and typing well after the rest of the colorful cast of characters cleared out of the office.

According to the employment paperwork I signed, my summer intern-ship term was June 1 to August 31, 2008. But summer came and went. No one ever said anything to me about leaving, so I didn't. I just kept coming in, and somehow I kept getting paid . . . September 1, October 1, November 1.

One day I got ballsy and decided to change the title in my email signa-ture from Editorial Intern to Production Assistant. *Boom,* just like that: I got my first promotion, albeit fraudulent. With my new job title, I started to take on more responsibility, too. I had already whipped the beauty closet into shape, so I was on to bigger things, like call sheets and fashion credits, and I even started writing for the beauty and style section. They had been relying on freelance support to produce those pages, but since I was in-house and willing to take on more, they slowly but surely shifted that work onto my plate. I pitched ideas during editorial meetings, I organized shoots, I called in and curated beauty products for stories I wrote. Soon the editors in Chicago were referring to me as the production assistant, too.

My master plan was working.

By this time, Carolyn had departed her post to chase her musical dreams in Italy and I had assumed the bulk of her administrative responsibilities assisting Harriette. I saw this as my opportunity to initiate a conversation with Harriette about a permanent position and a raise—a raise for a job I technically didn't even have.

I played hardball, too. I was making ten dollars an hour. I asked for twenty. They came back with twelve. I kept a straight face and said, "I'll have to take the night to think about this."

It was an extremely bold move, especially during such dire economic times—the crash of 2008 directly impacted all magazines, including ours. Not to mention I was just an entry-level hire who had extended her own welcome. *(PLEASE NOTE THE ABSOLUTELY INSANE AUDACITY OF A MILLENNIAL IN HER TWENTIES.)*

The recession was in full swing and people in publishing—as well as in practically every other industry—were losing their jobs left and right. Rumor had it that, for the first time, not a single editorial intern was hired at Time Inc. that summer. Which meant, had I taken that *Essence* internship after all, I would have inevitably been shipped back to California in August and dumped into the shipwreck of other recent grads desperate to find work. Choosing *Ebony*, the decidedly less sexy option, ultimately saved me from the unemployment line.

And here I was risking all that to make a few more dollars an hour.

After praying about it, I trusted my instincts and decided to go bold or go home: I called Harriette to explain that I simply could not see doing this job at their proposed rate with the rapidly rising cost of living in New York City. I politely asked if the company would reconsider their position, and as a bargaining tactic, I refrained from work the next day to apply pressure to the negotiation. This was by far the boldest move I made in my nonexistent career. And I certainly do not recommend this tactic.

I could hardly sleep that night. My mind raced the entire next day: Had I just made a huge mistake? Would Harriette fire me on the spot the next day? Who could know? I was just twenty-one and trying to make it in a world I hardly understood.

The next morning, I was terrified to walk into Harriette's office.

"Good morning," I said timidly, holding her venti hazelnut misto, light on the milk.

Without looking up from her computer, she said, "Have a seat."

I was shook. My body quivered as I lowered myself onto her taupe leather couch. When she finally lifted her eyes from the keyboard, she glared at me.

"Elaine, what you did yesterday . . ."

When her nose flared, my jaw clenched and my throat tightened into a knot. She was speaking in a tone I did not recognize. All I kept thinking was: "This is bad. This is bad. Yep. You screwed this up."

"What you did yesterday was very risky, and I would not have advised going about it the way you did," she went on. "But it was smart. And I am proud of you for asking for what you believe you deserve."

This was taking an unexpected turn.

"When you didn't come in yesterday, I called the Chicago office and I told them I can't do my job without support. I went to bat for you," she said in a steady, even tone. "We are going back and forth on numbers, and there are no guarantees that . . ."

The phone rang, so I stepped out, pretending to give her privacy while trying to listen from my desk. A few short moments later I was called back into her office. She had a grin on her face.

"Well. That was the Chicago office calling with approval on bumping you up to twenty dollars an hour," she said.

In my head, I jumped up and down like Oprah had just given me a car. But in real life, I tried my best to maintain my composure. Except I can't count how many times "Oh, my God. Thank you, Harriette" spilled out of my mouth.

I walked into the office that morning certain I had gambled away my job. Yet, in some twist of fate, I managed to double my income overnight in the middle of the recession for a job I didn't even technically have in the first place.

WITH MY NEWLY SECURED ROLE, I made sure Harriette never once regretted going to bat for me. Every problem was an opportunity to be seized. When I felt strongly that *Ebony* deserved an invite to a Fashion Week event, I'd chase it. When we needed a beauty and style department, I became it, single-handedly. When there was a feature story I thought we should report on, I wrote it. When a Black film was premiering in New York City, I'd cover it. When a system was broken, I'd try to fix it. When I thought that we should be cultivating a stronger social and digital footprint, I'd create it. When I saw other media brands backstage at fashion shows with video crews, I'd wheel and deal so that we had one, too.

And whenever Harriette said, "There's no budget for that," as she often did, I found a way to make it happen anyway. Within a year, I was *formally* promoted to beauty and style editor.

After some needling, I convinced my friend Luke Burke, who was a producer at MTV, to entice his camera crew to shoot videos for *Ebony* during New York Fashion Week. For free. I hustled for access to the top shows and harassed beauty publicists for backstage credentials so that we could have a shot at capturing coveted designer interviews. On good faith, Luke's crew trailed me backstage to Carolina Herrera, Donna Karan, Derek Lam, and more. The highlight that season: snagging a memorable interview with *the* Oscar de la Renta.

We had not been approved for a designer interview with Mr. de la Renta, but in my mind, "no" was just the beginning of a negotiation.

Harriette always told me every notable editor has a signature look and that my big, curly hair would be mine. So I wore my hair down and let my curls bang—hoping it'd give me something to be remembered by. In an attempt to channel my style idol, Michelle Obama, I wore a sleek, black-on-black look: a shin-grazing, faux leather A-line skirt with a long-sleeved bodysuit. I swiped on the best shade of red lipstick I could find in the beauty closet and hopped in a cab, hoping—praying—to get this interview.

When I saw Mr. de la Renta in person backstage, he was as tall and as grand as I'd imagined, and he seemed to be wrapping up his final interview. This was it: something told me to just go for it. I approached Erika Bear-

man, his widely respected publicist and gatekeeper, who was known ador-
ingly at the time by fans online as @OscarPRGirl. She was just as gorgeous
in person as she was on the internet: she had big blue eyes and long raven
hair that spilled down her back like a Disney princess. In her staggering
six-inch heels, she towered over the rest of us mere mortals. I was intimidated but I sucked it up and flashed a smile, hoping to disarm her:

"Hi, how are you? I know we are not on the list for an interview, but I
wanted to quickly introduce myself. My name is Elaine Welteroth. I am the
new beauty and style editor at *Ebony* magazine. I know Mrs. Eunice Johnson and Mr. de la Renta have a long history, and I was hoping, if there is any
way possible, that I might be able to sneak a quick moment with him on
camera?"

Her head began to shake "no" before I had even finished my earnest,
long-winded pitch.

"I'm so sorry, but unfortunately this is his last interview and we are
about to start the show," she responded politely.

Just then I caught Mr. de la Renta's eye and he *actually* smiled back. It
gave me the boost of confidence I needed to look back into her crazy-big
eyes for one final plea: "I totally understand. If there is *any way* you might
be able to make an exception, we would be super quick—just one question."

She glanced at him and then back at me: "Let me see what I can do." She
was actually considering my request.

The next thing I knew, I was being ushered over to meet Oscar. He was
warm and gentlemanly, with a distinctive glimmer in his eye. There was a
rarefied air around him, confirming that I was indeed in the midst of one of
the greats—right up there with Harry Belafonte. As we greeted each other,
I subtly waved down my video crew. It reminded me of the time I gracefully
bulldozed my way into my very first on-camera interview with Talib Kweli.

It was go time.

During our spontaneous interview, Oscar spoke about the importance of diversity in fashion, and reflected on his roots in the Dominican Republic, where, he said in his distinctive Spanish accent, "we come in all shades of brown."

He and Mrs. Eunice Johnson had developed a friendship over the years; he had great respect for her boldness and elegance, and he was one of the few high-fashion designers who supported her mission by sending his clothing down the Ebony Fashion Fair runways. He recognized what *Ebony* meant to Black women and made a point to say how proud he was to have Black women walking his runways. And thankfully, my pro bono crew was there to capture it all on camera.

During our interview, I felt seen, and perhaps in some small way, that I was carrying the torch for Mrs. Johnson's legacy—one that was so much bigger than me. It left me with an indescribable high and a deep sense of validation that the work we were doing was worth it.

I WAS BEGINNING TO SEE the fruits of my labors blooming into a respectable career path. I finally felt like I was carving out a lane and a name for myself in this dizzying, fast-paced world, one that was spinning even faster in the dawn of digital media. It felt good to represent for a brand I believed in, even if we were the underdogs. And if nothing else, at awkward fashion events, people were starting to recognize my hair.

It had been roughly two years since I landed in the editorial trenches of New York City, and in those two years together, Harriette and I had gotten relatively close for a boss and her protégée. By then, I had moved to Harlem, twenty blocks from Harriette, so sometimes she would offer me a ride home after work in her black car. During those late-night car rides, I got rare glimpses into the mind of a woman I revered. I learned what a female executive, and a workingwoman at forty-eight, worries about. Surprisingly, her anxieties weren't all that dissimilar from the kind of things that kept twenty-three-year-olds like me up at night: our unknowable futures, our changing bodies, our uncertain wealth propositions, the state of the world, and securing our place in it. But I also learned that when you're at the top, you have different concerns to contend with, too, like P&Ls, and mortgages, and high-profile haters, and the threat of getting knocked off your throne.

Still, nothing prepared me for the day when Harriette unceremoniously asked me to help her clean out her office:

"I'm getting fired tomorrow," she announced in a calm, matter-of-fact tone. My mind didn't immediately compute the meaning of her words.

"What?" I laughed, thinking she must be joking.

"Come, help me pack up."

She wasn't joking.

The next morning, I was on a conference call with the Chicago office for our weekly editorial meeting, which Harriette typically ran remotely, when I spotted the CEO walk Harriette into a nearby conference room. The CEO was based in Chicago and rarely made an appearance at the New York office. Something was definitely up.

Moments later, an unfamiliar female voice on the other end of the conference line began excitedly introducing herself as the new editor-in-chief. Just then, the big boss came gliding around the corner, followed by Harriette, who flashed a forced smile at me while holding her index finger up to her neck like an imaginary knife. It was the signal: She was out. Just like that.

Harriette's clear vision and hard work taught me the power and possibility of transforming a media brand. Working up close to her, I watched how she made notable strides to put *Ebony* back on the map in a meaningful, contemporary way. Prior to her leadership, the magazine had not produced original covers or fashion shoots in years. During her tenure, the brand won awards for the new design of the magazine, and the *Today* show showcased *Ebony* covers almost every month. She put Alicia Keys on the cover in that red gown, which caught the attention of even me, a then nineteen-year-old college student who was certainly not checking for *Ebony* back then. During our time together, there was a body-positive Serena Williams cover, a historic Michelle Obama cover, a curly-haired Beyoncé cover, and even the most elusive, inimitable cover get of all: Prince. *Ebony* landed the first exclusive interview with President Obama after he was elected, and we produced the last shoot and interview with Michael Jackson before he died. These issues weren't necessarily selling better than other magazines on the steadily declining newsstand in 2010, but they were arguably refreshing the brand's image and rebuilding equity for a sleepy title that had long fallen from relevance.

Harriette was hired to help reenergize the brand and was clearly succeeding at building buzz when the plug was pulled. Somehow, it wasn't enough.

There were theories floating around—mainly that she refused to move her family to Chicago for the job—but whatever led to Harriette's unexpected departure from *Ebony*, it left an indelible impression on me. My takeaway was clear: in business, no matter how much value you bring, you will always be disposable.

By then, Harriette was so revered in the industry that when she was pushed out of the *Ebony* empire, Prince himself immediately hired her to travel the country with him to document his first American tour in years.

Growing up, whenever I'd present anything to my mother as "unfair," she'd quickly clap back: "Guess what else ain't fair? *Life*."

It always seemed so harsh, like such an incomplete examination of the facts at hand. Eventually, I'd come to see her frustrating response as a training ground, preparing me for a truly unfair world, where the facts frequently get twisted or overlooked. She was teaching me that the world wouldn't always see things the way I saw them. She wanted me to know I wouldn't always have a say in the matter either—"That's just the way it goes, princess," she'd say. Her message to me was clear:

"Falling down is inevitable. It's the getting back up that's on you."

The point was to become unbreakable. My mother's words were the warning shot that fairness, justice, and security are not guaranteed to any of us. No matter how hard we work. Especially for women of color.

Harriette's story served as a stark reminder of my own master plan: the magazine industry was just a first stop—not a place you stay forever. Take it as far as you can, and when the time comes, jump. And by then, be ready to fly.

WITHOUT HARRIETTE THERE TO guide me, I had to learn the hard way not to discuss my age at work. This lesson landed hardest during my first fancy business lunch. It was commonplace for editors to go for meals and drinks with publicists and brand execs in order to build advantageous relationships that you could leverage for the magazine—or your next job move. I was a junior editor at *Ebony* when I was invited to my first lunch meeting by an important executive at a global beauty company. We went to BG, an upscale eatery on the seventh floor of Bergdorf Goodman, the ritzy uptown retailer, overlooking Central Park. When my lunch date arrived with a fresh, bouncy blowout and Birkin bag, I was surprised and somewhat relieved that she was Black—there were so few Black beauty execs in the business. We got on well. The small talk flowed surprisingly easily, until all of a sudden her body language turned cold.

It must have been an oldie-but-goodie song reference I was unfamiliar with that triggered her suspicious line of questioning: What year had I graduated from college? And how long had I been at *Ebony*? Eventually, she came right out and asked, "How old are you?"

"Twenty-three," I said as I nibbled my overpriced appetizer.

That was when she reached for her BlackBerry, mumbled something about a fire back at the office, and then left me with the bill.

I was making twenty dollars an hour, even less if you accounted for the fact that I had no health insurance and twenty to forty hours of weekly overtime I wasn't at liberty to bill for. No corporate expense account. And now here I was, stuck with a hundred-dollar lunch bill.

In business, time is money, and it became clear this exec didn't think a twenty-three year old was a worthy investment of either. That experience burned through more than just my bank account; it was etched into my mind as a reminder to guard my age as if my job depended on it—because one day it just might.

From that day on, I never *ever* discussed my age. With anyone. Even as the years went on and I moved up the ranks, my age remained a mystery to my team.

People like that exec had always just assumed I was older, which typically worked to my advantage professionally. It was hard enough gaining respect as one of the few Black women hoping to climb the editorial ranks. I worried if people knew how young I was, it might chip away at the credibility and authority I would earn over time. I carefully dodged the question whenever it came up at beauty events or around the office, sometimes going to great lengths to avoid being "found out." True story: By the time I was senior enough to have my own assistant, I'd insist on booking my own travel so I wouldn't have to reveal my DOB.

Age, I'd learn, is a precarious issue for women in any industry. You want to be in the game long enough to be revered, but you also never want to be considered "too old." On the beauty editor event circuit, I could sense veteran editors becoming paranoid about potentially aging out and losing relevance in the digital era. On the flip side, seniority still mattered in those days, so young editors like me had to be careful not to get labeled "too young" either.

ONE UPSIDE TO LIFE at *Ebony* in those unsettling days after Harriette's departure was the arrival of the new CEO, Desiree Rogers. Previously, Desiree was the notoriously glamorous social secretary for the Obama administration. The first black person to occupy that role. She was so impressive and well-dressed that, in her White House days, Anna Wintour had taken a keen interest in her and even invited Desiree to sit beside her at Fashion Week.

Desiree brought with her a cache that *Ebony* could benefit from. As the beauty and style editor, I benefited from it, too. I went from begging for invitations to fashion shows to sitting front row beside Desiree at Jason Wu, one of the hottest New York designers (he had recently dressed Michelle Obama).

That was my first front row moment, and thanks to Desiree's star power, it was photographed in *The New York Times* in an optimistic profile story about her new role at *Ebony*. In the piece, Anna Wintour was quoted praising her—"Desiree is a rock star"—an endorsement that goes a long way in the fashion world. They also printed Pulitzer Prize–winning fashion writer and critic Robin Givhan's tweet observing us at Jason Wu: "When was the last time *Ebony* had a front row seat at NY fash week? When did hell last freeze over?"

"Falling down is inevitable. It's the getting back up that's on you."

CHAPTER 12

Are You My Husband?

The best worst news—no one is going to come and save you.

KATE DEARING, TV WRITER

We spend so much of our twenties searching. For ourselves. For our soul mates. For success. For the illusion of security.

In some unconscious way, our relationship to people, things, and titles can become a projection of how we want to be seen in the world, especially when we are still forming our own identities.

Twenty-three was a particularly tricky year for me—as it is for many of us. While I was busy kicking ass and taking names in my career, I was still very much expecting to be saved from the rest of my life by some modern version of Prince Charming.

At least once in every chance encounter with a reasonably eligible bachelor the question floated through my mind: "Are you my husband?" Admittedly, it was a pretty obnoxious and exhausting way to move through the world. But such is life at twenty-three.

M. Foss had advised me once to treat dating like gardening instead. Plant the most promising seeds. Water them all. Taste what each has to offer. And when you find one that produces fruit you could eat every single day, give a little more love to it and start pruning the rest.

Thankfully, I had women like her and my mom in my life who were there to remind me that *dating is a process*. One that is inevitably unpredictable, often disappointing, and sometimes painful. But the important thing to remember is that it's *your* garden. Nothing good can grow if you don't nourish your own soil. And only you can decide when to stop feeding dead things.

Since I married my career early, it left very little time for developing my "green thumb," so to speak. Still, I managed to keep a modest garden variety of guys around. My tactic for weeding out the bad seeds: celibacy. I know I probably sound like a prude, but after all that I had invested in First Love, my new rule was: I won't even kiss a man until I know he is worth my time.

As you can imagine, most of my plants wilted quickly. And the rest required significant pruning:

There was Green-eyed Model/Actor/Broke Dude, who lied as well as he kissed. That one time he showed up to my door with groceries to make dinner? *Swoon!* The time he asked me to pick up my own toilet paper on my way to visit him at his friend's apartment where he was crashing on the couch? *Boy, bye!*

Millionaire Money Bags, aka Wannabe Sugar Daddy, an older dude who drove a Rolls-Royce, put me up in fancy hotels, took me on a shopping spree, and left two hundred dollars on the nightstand after our first kiss. That man made me feel like Pretty Woman, but only in the "big mistake" sort of way. Needless to say, he never made it past first base.

Blasian Twin, who forgot we had already exchanged numbers and handed me his phone to input my number (again), when I discovered that he had previously saved me as "Elaine—No Sex." I swiftly deleted my own contact card.

Self-Hating Business School Student, who gave a shameless dissertation over dinner on why he would never date or have a child with a dark-skinned woman—as if this was some sort of compliment to me. I roasted him so hard I lost my appetite and left him right there at the table before our food even arrived.

Problematic Black Doctor, who told me at a restaurant in Harlem that I'd be a better woman after a "good beatdown" in the desert where no one could hear my mouth. He said he was just kidding. I practically ran home.

Fashion F-Boy, who was a little *too* close to his best friend/roommate/business partner for my taste and used words like "serving" to judge my outfits as inferior. We went to parties together and liked to philosophize about life, so I kept him around probably longer than I should have, considering how condescending he could be at times.

Then, a few nights before my twenty-third birthday, just as things were slowing to a halt with Fashion F-Boy, I met a man I was certain would be my Future Husband.

My friend Namik invited all of us to a house party at this fancy high-rise building in Midtown West. The apartment was stunning—floor-to-ceiling windows overlooking twinkling views of the Hudson River. The lights were out and it felt romantic inside. All my friends were there by the time I arrived after a late night at the office. Within seconds I noticed a handsome, well-dressed man with a bald head and a fit body. I learned he was the host of the party, a Harvard Business School graduate and newbie investment banker, which, to a magazine editor making twenty dollars an hour in New York City, was the most literal translation of a Disney prince. I watched him closely as he milled about his impeccable apartment, making sure everyone's drinks were refreshed. He seemed well-mannered and worldly. "He could totally be my Future Husband," I remember thinking before we even exchanged words.

When our eyes eventually locked, it was as if no one else was in the room. He approached me at the end of the night to ask for my number, and instead of pulling out his phone, he memorized it on the spot.

My friend Andrea witnessed the whole sappy thing. "Dude has gaaaaaame. He was smooth with it, too!"

The elevator doors had barely shut when my friends—the ultimate hype squad—erupted in cheers:

"Yasssssss, girl! You just met your husband!"

"Oh, my God. You guys are crazy!" I said, but inside I was beaming.

"Y'all should have seen the way he asked for her phone number," Andrea continued. "He memorized that shit! Who even does that?"

They went on; I rolled my eyes, blushing. I was bracing myself for a false alarm, but secretly hoping he'd call.

"He's a banker and he's fine! If you don't want him, hand me that phone, sis. I'll wait for that call!" someone in the elevator hollered.

We all laughed.

Before I reached home—*ping*—there was his text:

"Make it home safely?"

After a couple days of texting, the ball was in my court, so I decided to invite him—along with the rest of my prospective husbands—to my birthday party. Why not? It seemed like an exciting, modern idea at first. May the best man win! There was just one small issue: Fashion F-Boy had organized this party for me as a last-ditch effort to crawl out of the doghouse. It was too little, too late for us, but I was broke and twenty-two and I wasn't about to turn down a dinner party held in my honor at Spur Tree, the trendy, top-shelf Jamaican spot on the Lower East Side.

The party was in full swing by the time I realized that juggling two dates was like playing with fire, and someone—inevitably me—would get burned. I was half hoping Future Husband wouldn't show. But in case he did, I put my closest friend, Brooke, in charge of being a human buffer between boys.

Just when the narrow, dimly lit room thinned out, in walked Future Husband, briefcase in hand, a long trench coat on, a Black version of the paper dad I'd cut out for my family collage as a little girl all those years ago—aka the total opposite of my actual dad. He also seemed nothing like my erratic First Love, except that he was fine as hell and he took my breath away on sight. He came off as the steady, refined, responsible type; he held a high-paying finance job and wore custom suits with Prada shoes. If I was the Black Carrie Bradshaw, he could be my Big.

I nudged Brooke into action while I played it cool, sprinkling my attention around the room, trying not to seem suspiciously partial to any one plant in this very, very small plot.

Unfortunately, by the end of the evening, Brooke bailed on me, and I ended up in a cab with *both* F-Boy and Future Husband. Things went from bad to worse when F-Boy held the taxi door open for me and, instead, in came Future Husband with a casual tap of the shoulder and a "thanks, man" as he scooted in close next to me in the backseat. Clearly, Future Husband was stunting.

You could cut the tension with a knife in that car ride. We didn't make it to the next spot before F-Boy went off on me (honestly, who could blame him?), and my immature shenanigans were exposed right in front of Future Husband.

At that moment, it became glaringly clear that, according to M. Foss's dating metaphor, I was a terribly inexperienced "gardener."

I apologized to everyone, hailed my own cab home, and cried all the way uptown. When I called Brooke to ask her why she ditched me—and to accuse her of being a bad friend in a moment of self-inflicted drama—she shouted back, "You are messy, Elaine," and swiftly hung up on me.

Twenty-three was off to a horrendous start.

I had my shit together at work, but my personal life was in shambles: My best friend and I were in our first fight. And I had ruined not one, but two romantic prospects.

Then Future Husband texted me. I was afraid to look and braced myself for a message calling me out.

Instead, his text read: "Hot cocoa?"

WHEN MY CAB PULLED up to his building, Future Husband was waiting for me outside in brutal 19-degree weather, holding a bouquet of flowers with leather gloves. As he whisked me inside, the doorman waved and called me by name: "Happy birthday, Elaine!" This man might as well have invited me into a magical kingdom far away from the harsh elements, and my "mess." Inside, it smelled like an actual gingerbread house, with gourmet hot cocoa bubbling on the stove. Meshell Ndegeocello played softly from surround-sound speakers as he served me a mug with mini puffs of marshmallow bouncing excitedly like buoys along the rim. A panoramic skyline watched us as we talked all night, feet-to-feet on his sofa.

"I could get used to this," I thought as we both drifted off to sleep.

WE FOUND OURSELVES FALLING for each other during that romantic spell between Christmas and New Year's, the only extended break of the year for workaholics. We spent the next seven snowy days and snuggly nights holed up in his apartment, a romantic bubble in the sky, swapping life stories, ordering in obscene amounts of empanadas, and dancing to Fela Kuti in our socks—but we didn't even so much as kiss on the cheek.

I was still trying to hold out as long as possible on physical affection in order to weed out the guys who were too impatient to wait for me. It was simultaneously my most grown-up and most innocent courtship. Still, things moved *fast*. By New Year's Eve we were cohosting an intimate dinner party for our friends, toasting new beginnings high above a sparkly skyline. We kissed for the first time at midnight. In mid-January he gave me keys to his apartment, and by Valentine's Day there were diamond earrings waiting for me on the bed after work.

"Diamonds?!" I was stoked. No one except my great-aunt had ever given me diamonds. I was only eleven then and they were tiny hand-me-down studs that I cherished—until, of course, I lost them. But a *man* buying me diamonds? This was a big deal. They were a pair of large platinum, diamond-encrusted hoops. Truth be told, I wasn't big on diamond hoops. But one can overlook that when they are *real* DIAMONDS. It was such a generous gift that I didn't exactly know how to react, so I did what I saw women do on-screen whenever they were presented with grand romantic gestures: I squealed, I oohed, I aahed, I thanked him repeatedly, I ogled them in disbelief.

The next day, I noticed he was distant. When I pressed him, he said he was disappointed by my reaction to his gift.

"How was I supposed to respond?" I asked, genuinely confused. His face was frozen in an unfamiliar chilly stare. I didn't try them on, he pointed out in a hostile tone. He went on about how he had designed them himself, and how deflating my response was for him.

I was shook. I wondered how I could have gotten this so wrong; I felt confused about what exactly he was expecting from me in return after his romantic, over-the-top gift. Was I really supposed to read his mind? Maybe this was a mismatched love language thing? Why hadn't women's magazines prepared me for this? I had been flying high off our new love and his grand gesture meant a lot to me, but his overreaction to my underreaction pricked my confidence. Like a wilting balloon, the romance and sparkle of that special moment came leaking out, and I scrambled to find the hole that needed patching.

I really wanted this to work. I wanted him to be The One. So, I apologized and bought him a card explaining that I was committed to getting it right next time.

Looking back now, I realize we need to learn as women to trust that bad feeling the first time, and not try to will it away.

FUTURE HUSBAND AND I were equally consumed by our respective careers. It wasn't unusual to send nightly check-in texts from our offices around midnight:

"Still there?"

"Still here."

"Probably going to be another hour."

"Me too. Maybe an hour and a half."

"Cool."

However many hours later on his way home sometimes, he'd swoop me up in the black town car his company paid for, a nice perk. If love was about balance sheets, on paper this was a rather idyllic match for two ambitious people climbing the corporate ladder. Looking back now on those days, I think we both enjoyed how little effort our relationship required in the fleeting moments outside of work.

But acclimating to each other's social circles would take some adjusting: it turns out Black people from Harvard Business School—aka Bougie Blacks, as I appropriately nicknamed his crew—were like East Coast White People, on steroids. I had never encountered Black people—especially Black women—who convincingly behaved like they were better and smarter than everyone. During outings with his colleagues, I felt embarrassed for being intimidated. Surely I would have confronted this archetype much sooner and presumably acquired a bit of an air of my own had I gone to an Ivy or a private school. (Damn you, First Love!)

If First Love was my gateway into the Black Table in high school and the Black Party at state college, Future Husband was my foray into the world of the Black Elite: a world of Jack and Jill traditions and Martha's Vineyard vacations. It was so different from where I'd come from. This was corporate America's next generation of Black executives: high-ranking, alpha Black females with phenomenal blowouts and a stellar bag-and-shoe game; code-switching Black men who "the old Kanye" on *The College Dropout* famously referred to as having the ability to "add up all the change in your purse very fast." (Disclaimer: Bougie Blacks may not fully appreciate this Kanye reference.) This high-performing, type A+ Bougie Black network seemed to take themselves, their impressive job titles, their posh vacations, and their fancy zip codes *very* seriously.

In time, I'd recognize that our sheer proximity in conjoining social circles as well as my own proclivity for high achievement made us more similar than I realized at first. What I initially perceived as intellectual airs, I came to see as learned survival tactics, puffed-up shells that disguised parts of themselves that might otherwise appear just as unworthy as I felt in their company back then. It became clear to me that they were responding to pressure, whether consciously or unconsciously, to reflect the characteristics of the wealthy White world they were emulating. The world we all competed in every day. I'd eventually learn the necessity of wearing those same masks at different points in my own career.

I had entered their world on Future Husband's arm with a pasted-on smile and a chip on my shoulder. But I realized early on that I did have one powerful tool to circumvent my own insecurities and their perceived superiority: I worked in fashion. If it was a game of spades, I had my trump card.

Future Husband and I presented beautifully at stuffy dinner parties: the steely businessman and his bubbly fashion editor girlfriend. I was at least eight to ten years younger than everyone in the room, but I worked hard to hold my own in conversations, hoping to come across believably as a peer—in age, education, and status.

This was long before I learned the power of showing up in spaces without the burden of veneers.

It was clear to me that Future Husband and I had cultivated very different kinds of Black social circles in New York City. I lived in Harlem, worked for a Black magazine, and joined a predominantly Black church, First Corinthian Baptist Church. Like Future Husband's network, my friends were all well-educated and ambitious, too, but I was a magnet drawn more to their warmth, their sincerity, and their soulfulness than to any of their accolades.

As my mom would say, my friends and I were down-home people. At our house parties, we did the wobble, drank rum punch, and engaged regularly in spirited arguments about current events—not excluding politics, but somehow there were always healthier servings of celebrity gossip. We all had master's degrees in Beyoncé. I felt very grateful to have found my New York City tribe early:

There was Brooke, my favorite southern belle from Kentucky, and a proud Howard alum, who became my instant bestie after meeting at a book club in Brooklyn on my very first weekend in New York City. I nicknamed her the Mayor of Harlem because somehow everybody in the neighborhood and their mama seemed to know her by name—from local shopkeepers to whoever happened to be dining at the next table. All she had to do was flash her deep dimples or bat those curly eyelashes of hers, and the girl could get anything she wanted. But she did not suffer fools gladly—as evidenced on my twenty-third birthday, the night I met Future Husband.

Then there was Offy, my well-read Ghanian roommate who was studying public health at NYU. Living with her for more than five years cemented a lifelong sisterhood, and it served as a rich cultural exchange for both of us. Offy was my first direct connection to the motherland—she still spoke her native tongue, and proudly indoctrinated us with all the reasons Ghanaian jollof was indeed the greatest jollof rice of all (Nigerians would hotly debate these sentiments). There was much about African American culture, history, and racial politics in America she didn't quite understand. But she'd learn—because we'd teach her.

The final addition to our foursome was Chloe, a DC transplant who quickly became my first biracial best friend when she moved in with Brooke after ending a bad relationship. While our backgrounds couldn't have been more different, we had much more in common than just our curly hair and caramel complexions. It was her relentless optimism, empathy, ambition, and diligence that I immediately related to. Chloe is a feeler and a doer—someone who dreams up goals and chases them until they are her reality. She was raised in the Congo and now worked in the nonprofit space. Because of her international upbringing, she inherited a wide-eyed way of seeing the world, and herself as a global citizen. One Christmas she lured me to Africa, where we spent the holidays traveling across Ethiopia and Rwanda and got our hair braided in a hut.

Stephanie was the whip-smart human rights lawyer in training with Midwest manners. Namik, my initial connection to First Husband, was an impressive Yale graduate turned ad executive, a lifelong vegan who looked like an actual life-size Black Barbie.

Then there were the guys in our crew: Kentay, Joshua, Andre, and Michael—the private equity banker from Texas, the L'Oréal marketer from LA, the Marvel technical artist from Brooklyn, and the ad exec who could sing like Beyoncé.

But the more swept up I was getting in Future Husband, the less time I was spending with my people. I was starting to feel untethered and disconnected from my crew; over time, I felt myself becoming a duller, flatter version of me.

This was around the same time that Harriette left *Ebony*. As is the case when anyone inherits a new boss, the pressure was on to prove myself all over again. Harriette encouraged me to stay at least until I got the title promotion I deserved, so that I'd fare better in the job market. I followed her advice. Fortunately, for doing the job of an entire department solo, I eventually succeeded in securing a title promotion (which came with a salary that was less than I was making hourly, but at least I got health benefits). I decided it was as good a time as any to start interviewing aggressively for a new job.

But no matter how much I accomplished at *Ebony*, like going from the minors to the major leagues, I knew making the leap from a Black title like *Ebony* to a larger, prestigious general market magazine would be *hard*— next to impossible.

What I didn't realize at the time was that I was interviewing for my own relationship, too.

FUTURE HUSBAND TOOK ME shopping for "interview shoes" at Bergdorf's. He sat back on the sofa watching me parade around, trying on heels, and silently slipped his credit card to the customer service lady with a wink. I walked out with my first pair of Louboutins; they were vanilla nude patent leather, and six inches tall with a modest platform. I could tell it made him feel like a man to wield his money and intercede on my behalf in this way. It felt unnatural to me, but I played right into it like a lapdog, grateful for his affection, performing for his approval, eager to please him with overt displays of my gratitude. The memory makes me cringe now—but back then it was like living out the ultimate *Sex and the City* scene. This was what women are taught to want.

We are also conditioned to seek financial security and a sense of stability in a husband. After facing some measure of financial insecurity growing up and feeling hindered by the unpredictable behavior of the men in my life,

I wanted to be taken care of by a man in a way I had not ever experienced firsthand before.

I already had everything I needed to be the breadwinner of my own life—but I didn't know it yet.

A few months later, Future Husband accepted a big job offer in Connecticut and earned a swift promotion to chief of staff to the CEO of a Fortune Global 100 company. We were suddenly thrust into a long-distance relationship. And at twenty-four, I was thrust into the role of CEO-Wife-in-Training.

"Could you ever host my CEO and our leadership team at our home?" Future Husband asked me out of the blue one Sunday afternoon.

It felt formal, like an interview question. Something in me wanted to have the right answer.

"Of course. I mean, I could figure it out," I fumbled through my response, trying to play it off as if the stakes weren't as high as they felt. "I would probably just order in a nice spread. But sure, yes, I could definitely entertain them."

The seemingly innocuous challenges kept coming: insidious tests of my intelligence. Of my homemaking ability. Of my sophistication

"Do you consider yourself an intellectual?"

"Who would you say are your smartest friends?"

"Why don't you ever notice the things I like to eat and fill your fridge with them before I visit you?"

It always felt bigger than just his questions, though—he was digging into something deeper about the type of woman I was, assessing whether I could be a worthy partner in his life. He emailed me a story about the best indicators for a man's success, whether in the boardroom or on the football field. The number one indicator was the wife he chose. I felt like I was being groomed and evaluated for a supporting character role in this much bigger life he was pursuing, but somehow I wasn't quite measuring up.

This was around the time Future Husband decided to take his mother and a female coworker to a big event at the UN. He came to town for it but never even brought up the idea of taking me. Whatever his reason, it served to amplify the voice in my head telling me I wasn't good enough for him. It seemed that in theory he was drawn to the sparkly girl with her own ambitions, a big personality, and equally oversized curly hair. But in practice maybe what he needed was a more conservative woman content to stay home in khakis and round-toe flats forever, a stalwart who existed to prop him and his big ego up. For him, I wore the flats, I put on the khakis, I learned to cook, but I was not the woman whose singular goal in life was to live up to his trophy-wife expectations.

Pause: If you *ever* find yourself walking on eggshells and contorting yourself into ill-fitting ensembles just to prove yourself in a relationship, *run*. Fast. And do not look back. He ain't The One.

But of course, I fell face-first into the trap of his mind games. I traded my signature red lipstick for the sheer gloss he preferred. I absorbed his painful jabs at my self-esteem without sticking up for myself because I assumed I was just being too sensitive. I ignored the ways in which I felt smaller in his presence because at least he made me feel a semblance of safety that I hadn't known before. He was offering me the kind of life I always thought I wanted. So I took the bait and invested myself in making it work. Slowly, I disappeared into the woman *he* wanted me to be.

MEANWHILE, A CHAMELEON-LIKE EFFECT was taking hold of me in my professional life, too. I stepped into those tan Loubs, slicked my hair back into a tight bun, and cranked up my interview game. I went all over town hunting down every entry-to-mid-level writer-editor job opening I could find at every magazine on the newsstand—from *Harper's Bazaar* to *Good Housekeeping*, and everything in between. I was willing to be and do whatever it took to get the job.

Working at *Ebony*, a Black magazine, had started to seem like a scarlet letter in interviews with White hiring managers. Pinched inside nearly every rejection notice was the term "overqualified." It seemed contradictory—wouldn't they want someone capable of rising above the call of duty? I couldn't help but see through the coded language. The impressive list of achievements and responsibilities on my résumé were deemed secondary to the washed-up "urban" brand I worked for. Ultimately, crossing over to mainstream media was proving more difficult than I had imagined. My fears of being pigeonholed in Black media were being legitimized with every closed door. But I kept knocking anyway, pulling all-nighters on edit tests and hustling even harder at work to beef up my clip book—producing up to twenty-five pages an issue.

One fateful afternoon, though, the doors at Condé castle finally cracked opened.

Holly Siegel was one of the few beauty editors who actually talked to me at the smug industry events beauty editors attended multiple times a week. She was the beauty director at *Nylon*, the indie youth-culture mag for alt-fashion kids and emo teens, which rendered her a fellow underdog of sorts in snobbish beauty editor circles. When Holly worked her way into the senior beauty editor seat at *Glamour*, she pulled up a proverbial chair for me at the Condé table—via Gchat:

"Yo. They're interviewing for the beauty writer spot over here. Want it?"

Holly was a Brooklyn-born, blond Jewish chick with a rebellious spirit that I admired. Her downtown, punk sensibilities made her indisputably cooler than everyone else in the otherwise uptight office. Plus, she was a talented writer who could outwit everyone if she wanted to, so she mostly got away with having a little bit of an attitude. This new job was a cakewalk for her, compared to *Nylon*, where she wore every hat in the beauty department like I had at *Ebony*.

I typed back: "Hell yesss!"

After a year of interviewing, you lose the ability to play coy.

Within seconds, she shot me the edit test—just like that. No HR vetting. No awkward first meeting with higher-ups. I took the test and was invited back to meet the executive editors. I prayed hard that they wouldn't avert their eyes when I walked in, that they'd actually see *me*, believe in my talent, take a bet on my potential, and not get tripped up on the title of the magazine I worked for. Determined to land this job, I scraped my curls back into that slick bun, slipped on my Interview Shoes, and went in with my preppy vibes blazing.

When I got the beauty editor job, you would have thought God herself snatched my wig the way I praise-danced in my apartment. This was a major turning point in my career. It was a step down in responsibility, but a step up in pay and prestige.

I underestimated what it'd mean to the legions of Black women in media who rarely saw one of us make that kind of leap from a place like *Ebony* to *Glamour.* I'd hear over and over that my hire meant something to them, too.

I MIGHT HAVE MOVED ONLY eight blocks south of my old satellite office in Rockefeller Center to Condé's legendary glass building in the epicenter of Times Square, but these were two completely different worlds—and the culture shock was significant.

I went from working independently in an all-Black, understaffed office where I held down all the beauty and style pages on my own to being plopped into a teeming pit of mostly White, well-dressed editors at *Glamour,* where there were entire departments dedicated to fulfilling each task. At *Ebony,* I learned to be scrappy; I sourced my own photos, called in my own products for stories, and generally fulfilled whatever grunt work was required to get my stories done well. Much to the dismay of the art director, sometimes I'd even mock up my own pages using Word Art—the poor man's Photoshop—just to inspire innovation for the design. At *Glamour,* there were five full-time roles in the beauty department alone, plus interns who managed the product closet, which was the size of my first apartment in Brooklyn.

Top editors frequently lamented Manhattan's arduous private preschool application process, and the assistant staff was comprised mostly of girls in their twenties who lived on the Upper East Side and would "weekend" in the Hamptons. Cubicle chitchat revolved around the cheeky ways in which they were conspiring to get their boyfriends to propose. I soon learned the term "Engagement Chicken," *Glamour*'s famous recipe that allegedly prompted men to get down on one knee. If you were aching for a ring, you should try it. It seemed like a problematic premise for a magazine promoting feminism, but who was I to ask questions like that. I was just doing my best to learn the ropes. And I was still hoping to just fit in—in my personal life and at work. Assimilating became my M.O. for survival in spaces I wasn't yet convinced I belonged in.

The *Glamour* staff was perfectly nice to me and I felt supported by the leadership there. Early on, I was even handed opportunities to represent the brand on TV. Throughout my time at the magazine, I banked a number of successful morning-show appearances, which were helpful in slowly making a name for myself. I managed the beauty makeover pages, worked my way up to bigger shoots, and took on longer beauty feature stories.

The role of an editor is to look at the whole landscape and to carve out stories from an interesting perspective with your reader in mind. Because my introduction to the editorial world came through the lens of celebrating Black beauty and Black culture, I had to learn how to interpret beauty for a primarily White audience. *Glamour* was the perfect training ground for me to study how to approach beauty editorials from a mainstream perspective. Educating myself on speaking the language of beauty across cultures proved to be instrumental in my career. In order to do my job well, I routinely had to put myself in someone else's shoes; I had to understand things about beauty that would never pertain to my own experience—from the art of self-tanning to how to make limp hair more voluminous.

Though it was immediately clear to me that it didn't exactly work the same the other way around. Many White editors are only ever expected to speak the language of their own culture. I worked alongside White beauty editors—bona fide "beauty experts"—who went their entire, illustrious careers without ever learning the ins and outs of chemical relaxers, and could not confidently help a woman of color pick the right foundation shade in department-store lighting.

Until landing at *Glamour*, I didn't fully appreciate the ways in which my training at *Ebony* had uniquely equipped me with the tools to succeed in this much larger slice of the editorial world. Not just because of the dogged work ethic it required to wear multiple hats around the clock for years. Once I was immersed in the trenches at *Glamour* I could see more clearly the value of my outsider perspective. *Ebony* wasn't just some "black hole," so to speak, that I had to dig my way out of. No way. My *Ebony* years laid the foundation of my career. They positioned me not only to stand out but also to stand firm in what I believed in. It made me the editor I would become. I walked away from that experience owning my unabashed pride in celebrating Black people in all shapes, shades, and colors through my work. But finding my voice and my confidence in a predominantly White office to pitch stories that pushed the envelope, that tackled issues that mattered to my community, and that challenged the status quo—that would take more time to cultivate.

AT *GLAMOUR*, I REPORTED to Felicia Milewicz, the flame-haired grande dame beauty director whose response to most of our story pitches was simply: "Fabulous, my darlings." Her thick Eastern European accent made her every move seem all the more grand. She'd stroll in around eleven in the morning in Chanel flats, flashing a signature toothy grin that lit up our corner of the office, and then dip out around four in the afternoon, leaving the bulk of the work to us worker bees. We weren't salty about it, though. She put in her time and had earned her spot as a beloved beauty industry veteran. She was the last of her kind.

For junior editors, there was a mandatory late-night work culture that I was naturally accustomed to from my *Ebony* days. While senior editors left early for glossy beauty events—sometimes chartered helicopters were involved—I typically held down the fort for the beauty department. Most of my team bonding went down after hours with the art department, a diverse team even then. The lot of editors, writers, and editorial assistants was less so.

There were times I couldn't help but feel a bit like a token Black hire. Rajni Jacques was the only other Black editor on staff at the time. She worked in the fashion department and is Haitian American, with long, straight hair, tomboy style, and a rich, chocolate complexion; she was much more reserved than me and we look nothing alike. Yet during routine editor meetings at "the wall" where the magazine pages were pinned up, we got mistaken for each other more than once. I was either blending right in or disappearing again.

While I was excelling at work, I was conscious of how my race, age, and working-class background all contributed to this feeling of "otherness" that seemed to trail me like a shadow in these new, rarefied spaces I was being welcomed into. And no matter how well I appeared to be assimilating, inside I struggled with feeling like an imposter.

I AM STILL CONVINCED THAT I never would have gotten the gig if it weren't for Holly Siegel reaching out to me. She was my unlikely ally.

By seven months in, Holly quit *Glamour* for a "grown-up" copy job at

Sephora in San Francisco. When Holly left, I was subsequently promoted to senior beauty editor, aka the window seat in the beauty pod, where I got the chance to prove my chops in larger editorial meetings. The more I pushed myself out of my shell, the more I felt the support of the leadership at *Glamour*.

It was a pretty sweet gig for a twenty-four-year-old Black girl who thought she'd never make it out of *Ebony*.

Years later, Holly told me she left because she had had enough of bucking up against a system that played skinny-pretty-White-girl politics. In her mind, I was a part of that hierarchy, too—the skinny part, at least. She recognized my hard work and qualifications, but at times she noticed the ways in which I enjoyed some measure of "pretty privilege" in an industry that extols rail-thin beauty. Especially at the dawn of the editor-as-influencer era. In those days, magazines, especially beauty departments, were known to hire for two seemingly disparate tracks: you were either the "show pony" or the "work horse." While I can imagine that being relegated to one or the other would feel limiting, to earn my keep I was always expected to be both. But at five feet, three inches with freckles and boobs, Holly wondered whether the magazine truly saw her value. Since I was the one plucked for media training and morning show segments, despite her seniority, she started to feel insecure about her looks and even uncertain about her future at *Glamour*.

I never saw it that way then, but learning her perspective made me even more empathetic to the ways in which so many of us—Black, White, young, old, rich, poor, and everything in between—are plagued with a comparison complex. At various times in our lives, we all struggle with feeling good enough, pretty enough, skinny enough, worthy enough, as we are.

"Nothing good can grow if you don't nourish your own soil."

CHAPTER 13

When It All Falls Down

There is nothing stronger than a broken
woman who has rebuilt herself.

HANNAH GADSBY, *NANETTE*

From the outside, my life looked perfect. By twenty-four I had landed a handsome banker boyfriend, a great job, a growing social media following.

People commented on my Facebook pictures (Instagram wasn't as popular yet):

Wow, girl, you have the dream job!

What a beautiful power couple!

You're so lucky!

But the veneer began to crack.

The warm, adoring gaze Future Husband had mastered in public and on social media quickly became cold and critical in private. His "evaluation" of me and my "performance" as his partner intensified over time. With every critique, I began shrinking and feeling more uninteresting—not sophisticated or smart enough for him. No matter what I did or didn't do, it was never good enough.

There was a series of small moments that chipped away at my self-esteem, but one fight in particular stands out:

I was in his Connecticut kitchen whipping up some Valentine's Day recipe I found on the back page of *Glamour*'s February "Love" issue (I kid you not); pots were boiling on three different burners as I was slicing organic baby cherry tomatoes. I felt like I was finally nailing this Hallie Homemaker thing. Not only cooking, but doing this man's laundry, too. (Please note I was doing for him things I had never done for myself, let alone any other man.) Then—*boom*—the laundry dryer buzzer went off, and the fantasy I was creating vanished as he came around the corner holding a single heather-grey sock. He looked upset. As he brought it closer to my face, he said, through clenched teeth, "I told you *not* to mix any colors with my whites."

I was taken aback by how stern he was.

"This is *not* white," he continued.

My heart started pounding. He seemed pissed.

"I didn't realize . . . it looked white," I stammered. "There is no light in the laundry area." Looking back, I am so ashamed that I even felt the need to explain myself, but his tone made me nervous.

He continued on, badgering me for my mistake in a condescending tone.

That's when I felt my mom's voice rise up from somewhere deep inside of me. "Don't you let him talk to you that way, Elaine. I didn't raise you without a backbone."

The alchemy of the room shifted as her strength suddenly emerged from me.

"Who do you think you're talking to?" I shot back, straightening my spine. "Do not speak to me like I'm your housekeeper. I was just trying to help you."

I don't know how long it'd been since I heard my own voice. I had been working so hard to please him that I hadn't realized I'd been practically holding my breath for months.

He looked stunned—I had never spoken back to him.

I stormed out of the kitchen fighting back tears.

It wasn't until then that I recognized the slippery slope we were on. If I kept allowing him to intimidate me, if I kept on shape-shifting to appease him, what would come next? Where was this all headed? I flashed back to First Love smashing the window behind me in college, and I cried on the Metro-North from Connecticut all the way back to Manhattan for work that next morning.

Growing up, girls are warned about the kind of abuse that leaves bruises and scars behind. But the cyclical mistreatment I was experiencing was invisible—it wasn't what people wrote magazine articles about or went on morning shows to discuss. And so I kept covering up how awful I was feeling inside, assuming this was what people meant when they said relationships were hard.

Not long after the laundry incident, I went on a business trip to Paris and then straight to Georgia to celebrate Mother's Day with four generations of our matriarchs—my great-grandmother, my grandmother, and my mom. That's when Future Husband suddenly stopped responding to my texts. I felt simultaneously uneasy and disappointed in myself for giving him the power to rattle me to my core, particularly during this precious slice of family time.

The day I returned home, he broke up with me over the phone, without a clear reason.

I was heartbroken. Looking back, I recognize what I felt more than anything was confused and completely powerless. I could think of a million reasons why I should break up with him—not the other way around. My ego was bruised, yes. But ever since I was a kid watching *MacGyver* with my dad, I have always hated unsolved mysteries. You couldn't pluck me off my dad's chest until the episode was over and I could rest knowing who the bad guy was. As a kid, my dad was always impressed by my ability to identify the TV bad guy early; it was harder to do in real life, especially once love was involved.

Something was missing from our story—and it gnawed at me. I spent the whole summer consumed with trying to figure out what went wrong and how I could fix whatever was broken between us.

Clearly, your girl couldn't catch a clue.

What I know now is that when we derive our worth from the relationships in our lives—the intimate ones, the social circles we belong to, the companies we work for—we give away our power and become dependent upon external validation. When that is taken away, our sense of value, and identity, goes with it.

I became determined to win back the warmth of his love because on some level I actually believed I wasn't enough on my own without him. I wanted the life that looked picture perfect, and I felt like I needed him in it to complete that portrait for me—even if it didn't always feel good inside. I wanted to find my way back into his light more than I wanted to find the light inside me—the light he had dimmed.

I KNEW I WOULD SEE Future Husband at our mutual dear friends' upcoming wedding, which was being held at an actual castle in New Jersey. I went all out to get his attention: I straightened my hair. I managed to get a designer to loan me the very same lavender, jewel-encrusted dress Rihanna wore to the Grammys that year. I hired somebody to do my makeup, and I paid $175 for a black car from Manhattan. I was doing the absolute most.

Brooke's parents were in town from Kentucky, and on my way out the door, her sweet, adorable dad cheered me on: "Ain't no way a man could see you in that dress and not want you back, sweetie."

At the time, I appreciated the vote of confidence, but in retrospect, what I needed more than encouragement was a sanity check. But no. Off to the castle I went to win back my prince.

When I arrived, guests were being seated and violins were playing. As I made my way to my seat, I felt my stilettos sinking into the wet lawn. I struggled to look elegant balancing a champagne flute in one hand while holding up the dramatic train on my dress with the other, hoping no one would notice me walking in late. Just as heads began to turn, I tripped on my train. As I regained my balance, I saw him out of the corner of my eye. A mix of excitement and panic shot through my body like a lightning bolt.

After the ceremony, I spotted him walking toward me. It felt like time slowed down, and everything went on mute. I thought, "This is the moment." I imagined him apologizing for the way he had treated me, telling me that he had been thinking about me, that he made the biggest mistake of his life letting me go. He'd say, "I love you. I miss you. Let's try this again." I perked up and smiled, ready to receive him, when instead, he passed right by me with a nod as he made his way into the dining room.

There I was again, in tenth grade, in the middle of the parking lot waiting for First Love with a plate of food in my sweaty palms. But this time, I was grownish and wearing a gown, in a castle, with makeup and hair I paid for.

I was mortified. Instead of calling it quits on my plan right then and there, I decided that the only way to get through the night without letting his cruelty win was to tear up the dance floor. I wasn't leaving until I sweated this good press out. I could feel the other men's eyes in the room on me, like, "Damn, who's that?" I ate it up and worked the room. Inside, I was destroyed.

Toward the end of the night, I made a couple of new girlfriends on the dance floor who kindly offered to give me a ride back to New York with them. As we walked toward the car, I was in knots.

"I have to go find him," I finally blurted out.

I shared my sappy unrequited love story with these new friends. We all took a vote on what I should do, and the jury was split.

On one side there were the "Hell naws," who said: "I would *never* go back up in there chasing a man. Do you see *yourself*? He should be coming to look for *you.*"

On the other were the hopeless romantics still fizzy from too much champagne to encourage me to use good judgment.

I was with the latter crew. So off I went up the stairs, back into the castle, searching for my Future Husband. *God, I must have looked so pitiful.*

Ten minutes later, on the long, deflating walk back down those stairs alone, I wilted like a flower well past its bloom.

"Did you find him?" my new girlfriends asked as I crawled back into the car.

"No."

"It's okay. Fuck him, girl!" the woman in the front seat shouted, reprising Martin Lawrence's stand-up *Runteldat.* "You got your 'fuck 'em, girl' dress on!"

"That's right! Fuck 'em, girl!" another one joined in, chanting from the backseat.

We all laughed.

I found out later that while I was chasing him, he was chasing one of the bridesmaids. It was a ratchet Shakespearean tragedy. Only less poetic.

What a waste. Of two whole years. Of my dignity, which I had clearly lost somewhere on the winding stairs inside that castle. Of that good press, which I successfully sweated out on the dance floor while seeking the attention of a man who used to love me.

To add insult to injury, I called him afterward and we met up to talk it out the very next day, in the rain at the fountain in Columbus Circle. As my mother would say, I just couldn't let a sleeping dog lie.

Perhaps one lesson to glean from this tragic tale is that an iron-willed woman can do anything she puts her mind to. If only I'd learned sooner to wield my powers more selectively in my personal life. We got back together; I got what I wanted.

ONCE FUTURE HUSBAND AND I were on the mend, I worked hard to convince everyone in my life to accept him again. It was so much work, but I thought it was worth it for the man that I was going to be with forever. Meanwhile, everyone who loved me was practically silent-screaming "Screw him!" from the sidelines. The loudest among them? My mother. But during our debate, I used her advice as my defense: She told me once that the reason she and my dad stayed together this long was because neither of them ever wanted to end it *at the same time*. Someone had to be willing to fight for the relationship.

I decided that I was willing to fight.

FOR MY TWENTY-FIFTH BIRTHDAY THAT YEAR Future Husband surprised me with a multitiered diamond ring. He slipped it onto my finger and promised to "never take me for granted again." To "respect, honor, and adore me forever," he said. It was the ring before "the Ring," if you will. I believed him, with every bone in my body. I knew then that all the pain had been worth it. He was The One.

When my roommate, Offy, saw my new sparkly accessory, she looked right at him and said, "The ring is pretty, but if you hurt her again, we are all going to hurt you."

He laughed off my play-baby-sister's death threats and said, "never."
They pinky-promised.

THINGS WERE LOOKING UP for me: I had fought my way back into the arms of
the man I was going to marry. I had broken out of a punishing corner of Black
media and into the fabled ivory towers at Condé Nast, where I was steadily
climbing the ranks. I was finally earning a respectable wage—with benefits.

I decided to throw a big blowout birthday party to celebrate this new
chapter of life, inviting all the people I'd met over my first few years in New
York City. My girlfriend who worked in event marketing planned out all the
details, including dress code. The guys had to wear bow ties. Ladies had to
wear red lipstick. It was very *Glamour* magazine. She hired a fortune-teller
who, instead of reading your palm, read your fate via the imprint of your lips
after you kissed a napkin with red lipstick on. It was all so extra, yet so
perfectly fitting for that stage of our lives.

I wore my hair tied up in an elegant bun with a powder-pink strapless
empire-waist gown that I found for three hundred dollars at French Connection, and I got my makeup done by my dear friend Sir John, who made
me feel and look like royalty—eventually he went on to do makeup for
Queen B herself. All my friends were there. Everyone looked beautiful dancing under an actual disco ball. It was the messy, magical *Sex and the City*
dream come true.

My friend Andrea posted a photo of Future Husband and me on her blog
with a write-up from that night. (He later asked me to have her take it down
because it was causing some sort of problem for him at work.) In the photo,
we were sprawled out on a couch, I was lying in his arms, and we were
looking at each other like some cheesy impromptu engagement photo. It all
seemed so idyllic.

At twenty-five, my career and love life—*finally*—felt on track. I had just been promoted to senior beauty editor at *Glamour* and was waiting for my handsome and successful Future Husband to propose.

And then I got the email that changed everything.

IT WAS 8:37 A.M. and I was still on the plane, just touching down after a weekend of celebrating my promotion in Chicago, where Future Husband had moved for a new job.

When I checked my email it wasn't just the eerie subject line—"Your Loving Boyfriend"—that gave me pause; it was the seemingly fake account it came from: Future Husband's first and last name at hotmail.com. This was early 2012; hardly anyone used Hotmail anymore. I had to wipe my eyes to make sure I was reading this right.

The message began: "We have not met before but you should pay close attention to what I am about to write."

My spine straightened.

The poorly written email referred to me as "Glamour Girl" and mysteriously welcomed me back from my weekend away in Chicago. I wondered if this was some kind of stalker. Then it quickly announced an affair Future Husband was having with another woman. (Ironically enough, the sender referred to this other woman as "Becky." This was pre-*Lemonade* and no, you cannot make this stuff up.) The content was almost too graphic and too hurtful to believe, but I found myself pausing to reflect on the disturbing timeline it laid out, which not only spelled out the affair in explicit detail—when they met, how often they hooked up, painful things he told "Becky" about me—but it also contained information about a secret pregnancy. The alleged abortion happened the same month he had broken up with me.

There it was. Finally. The piece of our story I had been missing. Reading those words felt like a punch in the gut that left me nauseous.

The brutal email continued on, stating that the affair continued post–promise ring.

It described Future Husband's relationship with "Becky" as "very emotional and passionate." He had allegedly taken her house shopping the same summer we had broken up, and apparently sent her flowers the same week I helped him move into his new apartment in Chicago when we were back together.

The email also revealed how "Becky" discovered that he was living a double life: Remember that blog post my friend Andrea posted on Twitter with our picture from my twenty-fifth birthday party? The one he had asked me to take down, claiming that it wasn't boding well for him in his conservative, corporate office to have one of my friends put his personal life on the internet? Go figure.

The email signed off: "I am sorry you had to find out this way but he has several skeletons in his past."

Just then, as the seat-belt light went off and everyone stood up to collect their carry-ons, my knees buckled beneath me. It was as if the air had been knocked out of my lungs.

As soon as I could collect myself, I called him and pleaded with him to be honest. To be decent. To not make a fool of me. If there was any truth to any of this, I deserved to know.

He, of course, denied it vehemently, swearing on every family member he loved, "dead or alive."

I didn't know what to do. But I knew in my heart that I had given this relationship every ounce of me—more than it probably deserved—and if any of this were true, it would be the end. Before I could walk away for good, I needed to know for sure, without a shadow of a doubt, that this wasn't just some insidious prank from someone following us online (a thought he planted in my mind). Yet, once this level of doubt is introduced into a relationship, it festers like poison in a wound. I pressed him as if I were a skilled attorney out for blood. He continued to deny it. So I decided to wait out the verdict, trusting a God who promises that what's done in the dark will come to light. I prayed for the truth to reveal itself and to set us both free.

I was afraid that if I shared any of this information prematurely with anyone who knew us, it would only exacerbate my doubts.

I told no one.

I put on my makeup and walked into work—it was my first day in my new role—and I pretended that everything was fine.

A COUPLE OF WEEKS LATER, I was up early one morning when my roommate, Offy, came darting out of her bedroom at 5:00 A.M. like a bat out of hell. She said that she had something to tell me, and her eyes were already starting to tear up. I sat down at the kitchen table to brace myself:

"Did you receive some weird email two weeks ago?" she asked.

"Here we go," I thought. My heart began pumping wildly. Before any semblance of emotion could take hold, I felt some sort of spiritual armor drop down, readying me for battle, blocking any tears. There was no time to cry. I prayed for the truth; there was no time like the present to accept it with open arms.

She explained that she had been alerted about Future Husband's affair through some twisted chain of telephone operator: it turns out he was cheating on me with his coworker, a fellow corporate executive who blurted the details of the affair to her mentee (sloppy). That mentee then looked me up on Facebook and found that we had one friend in common. That one friend happened to be a mutual friend of Offy's. Offy held on to the news for weeks, dismissing it as just hearsay, drama I didn't need to be bothered with. When that route didn't work, someone then devised the alias email tactic to spill the tea to me directly. I felt like I was living in some dramatic spiral from a Zane novel. Except this was my real life.

According to all these messengers, the Other Woman was now ready to come forward. She wanted to speak with me directly.

Auntie Oprah says our only obligation is to listen for life's whispers. And when you don't listen to the whisper, it becomes a roar. This particular roar was deafening.

I had been introduced to the Other Woman before at Future Husband's work events and heard him mention her name on more than a handful of occasions. There was that time she made him his very own special pot of Jamaican oxtails at the company potluck at her home. And the time she ended up at that big UN event that he brought his mother to instead of me. One time I even raised a red flag, inquiring if there was any attraction there, on either side—a question he seemed repulsed by, as he described her to me as "desperate," "overweight," "lonely," and someone he would "never find remotely attractive." From that point on, I never thought twice that there was anything going on.

Throughout everything we had been through, I had made many concessions. Sure, he could be self-serious and stoic, and at times his icy stare was enough to make me quiver. Sometimes I'd even slip away to cry in the bathroom because something about being with him had a crushing effect on my self-esteem. But I still found a way to believe that the good outweighed the bad: He was dependable and doting and generous and thoughtful and seemingly the most trustworthy man I had ever loved. He made me feel like our life together would be safe and steady. And I genuinely believed he loved me the best way he knew how. But what I placed the highest premium on was that he would never cheat.

I was wrong.

Finding out just how wrong I was became one of the most heart-wrenching and humiliating defeats of my life.

WHEN IT ALL FALLS DOWN

THAT MORNING I CALLED out sick from work and I booked a round-trip flight to Chicago that would give me just enough time to confront him in person and be back at my desk on time for work the next morning. I ignored Future Husband's repeated calls on the other line while I transcribed every word the Other Woman said to me over the phone about their relationship on the side, as well as all the other middle people who had involved themselves in this mess. When he couldn't reach me, he hacked my email and found the notes I had been taking—he knew he had been caught. After spending five excruciating hours waiting at the airport due to weather-related delays, I was forced to give up on my mission to confront him in person and I headed home instead. But first, I finally allowed myself to cry in the rain.

Over FaceTime that night, his eyes grew cold and his blank expression did not convey an ounce of remorse. It was chilling the way he watched me weep without so much as blinking. Eventually he cracked and we both hit our lowest points ever. He managed to manipulate me into worrying about his state of mind more than my own, and I am not proud to admit it took a couple of months to finally extricate myself from that relationship. I desperately wanted to be free from the tightening grip he had on my heart. But somehow I still felt compelled to protect his image, so I refused to tell anyone what we were going through, except Offy, who watched it all play out in front of her. I avoided my friends and family because I knew they would be able to sense my sadness. Then one day my mom called in the middle of one of our many tearful, drawn-out conversations. She had been trying me for days. This time, I clicked over.

"Lainey, are you okay?"

"I'm fine," I said, fighting back tears.

My mom was not buying it.

"Elaine, I have waited long enough. You are going to tell me, today, what the hell is going on."

What is it about moms who can sense and prick the very thing you are trying to conceal. I couldn't hold it anymore. I burst into sobs.

"It's okay, baby. Please just tell me what's wrong."

I couldn't even get the words out. All I could do was cry.

Finally I whispered, "He cheated on me."

She booked the next flight to New York.

When she arrived, I told her *everything*. After I finished, she sat up straight, and she said in her deep, baritone voice:

"Elaine, look at me. You will *never* call that man again. You understand me? *Never.* I don't care what time of the night it is, if it's two A.M., three A.M., if you are hurting, you call your mother. Or you call one of your friends who love you. But this is not love."

She leaned in for a response and held my chin between her thumb and index finger: "Look at me, Lainey. Do you understand me? We love you and *we* got you. But he doesn't get another second of your time."

And just like that, all the back-and-forth was over. I never called him again. He never called me either. No emails. No texts. Nothing. A three-year relationship with a man I thought I'd marry was done.

To this day, I don't know what it was exactly about the clarity of her instruction in that moment that did it for me, but I was finally set free. I even let out a little laugh. Not only was I free, for the first time in my life I felt unbreakable. I was ready to walk away from the biggest heartbreak of my twenties knowing, for sure, that I had the resolve and the resilience to bounce back from *anything*. I knew I would be okay—more than okay, I knew that I was more than enough on my own, without someone who made me feel smaller than I am.

And I never once looked back.

There's a Patois proverb that Ex–Future Husband used to say all the time: "What's for ya, cyan be un-for-ya." (English translation: "What is for you, can't be un–for you.) This was his way of saying, in essence, what is meant to be will be.

What I find deeply comforting about this old Jamaican wisdom is that the inverse is also true: What is *not* for you can never be for you. No amount of sheer will or work, no amount of bending or shape-shifting will make it so. No act or effort, no apology, no amount of therapy or prayer or repetition, no self-help, no distraction, no matter how hard you try, you can never force anything that isn't meant to be.

And so after Future Husband and I broke up, instead of fighting to "fix" it, I focused my energy instead on reclaiming what I had lost in the collision of our lives. The parts of my identity I had given up to fit into his: The voice I buried. The confidence that had been squandered away. The baggy boyfriend jeans and red lipstick I traded out for khakis and pearls.

This breakup was different than any other. I wasn't just brokenhearted; I felt my heart breaking open. A light inside was shining through me again. Letting go of that relationship meant getting myself back so that I could become the woman I always wanted to be.

"What's done
in the dark
will come to
light."

CHAPTER 14

A Seat at the Table

You can, you should, and if you're brave
enough to start, *you will.*
STEPHEN KING, *ON WRITING*

Not long after the breakup, I got another life-changing email. Except this one felt like a reward for finally, fully letting go of what was never meant for me—and making room for what was.

"*OMG. YOU GUYS! GUESS WHO JUST HIT ME UP TO GRAB COFFEE?*" I typed furiously in a group chat to my girl-friends.

"EVA FREAKING CHEN!!"

Eva Chen was the beauty and health director of *Teen Vogue* at the time, and she was pretty much unanimously considered the darling of new media. She embodied a new kind of magazine editor, one who embraced social media and stood at the forefront of the changes that were sweeping the industry. She was among the first to post #OOTD's (outfits of the day) and celeb selfies on this new thing called Instagram as part of her job. She even branded her own hashtag, #evachenpose, which was steadily gaining traction while the rest of the industry still thought of social media as a silly hobby at best, and a career distraction at worst.

Eva was equal parts smart and stylish with a refreshingly sunny disposition. She was savvy enough to glide confidently into fashion's most exclusive social circles with an unpretentious ease, garnering admiration from the new guard and respect from the old guard—a tricky line for anyone in the sometimes catty circus of fashion media to walk.

The next day, Eva and I met up in the Condé Nast office lobby, which resembles a futuristic spaceship. Her long legs poked out of a printed designer skirt that she had styled with a simple T-shirt. A thick cotton headband restrained floppy bangs that were resisting the grow-out phase. The opposite of try-hard: her style was youthful and fresh, but still Fashion with a capital F. She always managed to strike the perfect casual-chic balance that said: "I have nice things, but I'm not trying to impress you."

In a quiet corner of a nearby coffee shop, she told me, in confidence, that she was leaving *Teen Vogue* and was suggesting people to fill her role. She wondered if I would be interested.

"Honestly, I think you'd be perfect for it," she said.

Her vote of confidence meant more than she knew. Here I was, still processing my breakup, and Eva Chen was approaching me about the most coveted job in the industry. Flattered would be an understatement. But I was also instantly conflicted because of my recent promotion at *Glamour*.

We scooped up our drinks from the barista and started our speed-walk back to the office.

"Wow. I'm so honored that you would even think of me for this, Eva," I said, trying to keep up with her as we traversed an endless maze of tourists in Times Square. "Would it be okay if I thought about it overnight?"

"Of course. Email me tomorrow?"

Believe it or not, it was a hard decision for me; there was a recession going on, and jobs were hard enough to come by. Black girls were certainly not getting hired by the dozens at Condé Nast, let alone promoted. What if I applied and I didn't get it? My top editors at *Glamour* would find out and might think I was some entitled, opportunistic millennial who didn't appreciate my—very rare—promotion. I wasn't about to bite the hand that fed me. Plus, it was a big job. Was I really ready to run a whole department? Sure, I'd done it at *Ebony*, but this was the big leagues. And I was only twenty-five. Most beauty directors were in their late thirties or forties, except for Eva, the golden girl. How could I ever fill her shoes?

The next day I called Eva and I told her it wasn't the right time. I thanked her profusely and explained that it just felt too soon. I shared my concerns about word getting back to my current bosses. I just couldn't risk it.

"I totally understand and respect that," she said. "Well, if you change your mind, let me know. And let's definitely stay in touch. If it's not this job, something else great is going to come along—I know you are going to go on and do big, big things."

I hung up the phone totally at peace with my decision. In my mind and spirit, it felt like choosing between "chasing the sexy" and preserving my integrity—and the latter mattered more to me than anything else. But underneath the moral dilemma was a healthy amount of fear.

That night, I had drinks with Nadia and Kamil; both were young, Black corporate executives and the best leftovers from my life with Ex–Future Husband (well, them and my Interview Shoes).

When I shared my job update, Nadia held up her glass:

"Tonight we're toasting to Elaine for being *so* fabulous that she just turned down a job at *Vogue!*"

"It's *Teen Vogue*," I corrected her.

"Girl, whatever! It has *Vogue* in the title, okay?!"

We all laughed, and I went home at ease.

A week or two later, I ran into a well-known beauty publicist at a baby shower. She smiled coyly and said with a wink, "Sooooo. How are . . . *things?*"

"Things are great!"

"Oh, come on. Just tell me."

"Tell you what?"

"I had lunch with Eva."

"Oh, that's cool," I said as she waited for a bigger reaction.

"*And* I hear you're the front-runner for her job!"

"What? No, I'm definitely not." I tried to laugh it off nervously, but I started to blush. Always a dead giveaway if you manage to get a Black girl to blush. I hated the idea of my name being involved in any industry rumors. This was exactly why I didn't go out for the job. I tried to squash the idea: "You must have talked to her before I told her I decided I wasn't going out for it."

"Oh, don't be silly, Elaine. Whatever Eva wants, Eva gets."

On Monday afternoon I got a call at my desk from Condé Nast's HR department. After my conversation with Eva, apparently the higher-ups decided to forge ahead by seeking permission to consider me for the role from Cindi Leive, my esteemed editor-in-chief at *Glamour.* She did not have to give her blessing, but she did. This wasn't customary—especially at Condé Nast, which had earned a reputation for being competitive in those days, even among the leaders of magazine brands internally. But that was never Cindi's style. She was strong and diplomatic, and the kind of feminist who wanted to see other women rise. Thanks to her blessing, I was now being formally invited to interview for the *Teen Vogue* job. I froze while the voice on the other end of the line explained that Amy Astley, the editor-in-chief of *Teen Vogue,* would like to meet me on Wednesday.

The fact that I had originally turned this opportunity down and, without any effort of my own, it managed to come right back to me like a boomerang, reminded me yet again of Ex–Future Husband's Patois phrase: "What's for ya, cyan be un-for-ya." He wasn't for me. But maybe this job was.

AMY ASTLEY, THE FOUNDING editor-in-chief of *Teen Vogue*, had the most beautifully decorated corner office I'd ever seen. When I was ushered in by her assistant, she was perched behind her desk. I immediately recognized her signature blond bangs, pin-straight hair, and neat middle part from pictures I'd seen of her online. She stood up to greet me, flashing a sweet smile and stretching out a hand heavily decorated with architectural rings, which were easy to notice—as a former ballet dancer, she spoke with her hands. To my surprise, she possessed a buttery midwestern charm. She was a brand of nice I had never encountered before. Especially not in the fashion world.

I found my interview outfit on sale at Zara: blush-toned cigarette pants and a lightweight, lacy dinner jacket with three-quarter sleeves that looked very Céline. At least that was the goal. My one designer staple was my red-bottom Interview Shoes. I wore my hair in a low bun—just in case she was the kind of White person who gets distracted by big, curly hair. (You never know.)

During the interview, Amy and I landed on the topic of the young gymnast Gabby Douglas, who was currently being bullied on social media because of her hair, which had been labeled "unkempt" by certain detractors. Here was a star athlete who had earned her way into the Olympics at age sixteen, yet her accomplishments were sinking into the shadows of an unnecessary debate about her hair. Meanwhile, none of her White teammates were under that level of scrutiny. I couldn't help diving into a deeper discussion about how politicized and racially charged it was to speak about a Black girl's hair in this way—how unfair and sexist it was to distract from the talent of a young woman in sports by criticizing her appearance. White women in sports are rarely harassed about their hair in this same way. (Though any woman in politics has definitely had her share.) And powerful men almost never have to deal with the kind of ridicule that picks apart their physical appearance. But this? This was a child we were speaking about—I found it all outrageous.

Just as I had gotten myself worked up, I started feeling self-conscious that my passion might come across as unprofessional. But Amy leaned in. She seemed engaged.

Forty-five minutes later, as our meeting was wrapping up, she asked, "Elaine, do you mind just jotting down a couple of ideas? Anything you might like to write about for the magazine. And no stress. Just get it to me whenever you can. How does two weeks sound to you?"

Did I mind? Hah! Two weeks!? I had gotten so used to hiring managers handing me these lengthy multipart edit tests—assignments that assess your qualifications for an editorial job—that I never had more than a few days to complete. More than that, Amy's humble approach and our easy, in-depth conversation drew me in even more than the generous deadline. Her manner had a way of making me feel respected as not just another worker bee, but as a valued young leader.

Rather than doggedly pursuing this job for the sake of the big title and the prestige that would come with it, I saw the edit test as an opportunity to feel out whether it was a role I could truly fall in love with. I knew I had to find the love in the work in order to be any good at it. Plus, I secretly felt like a total fraud for not having my finger on the pulse of teenybop culture. Before that interview, I admit that I couldn't name one Selena Gomez song if my life depended on it!

That weekend, I gave myself a crash course on youth culture. I listened to every Selena Gomez, Ariana Grande, and Justin Bieber song I could find online; I went deep into the comment section on Tumblr and I finally made it a point to watch *Twilight*. I spent time with teenagers in my life, asking questions. The deeper I dived, the more excited I got. Story ideas started flowing, and my vision began to crystallize. Scrolling through blogs and flipping through teen magazines, I could begin to see the white space and the opportunity I had in front of me to bring a different perspective.

BEAUTY AND FASHION CAN be dismissed as superficial, but I was interested in exploring the deeper emotional connection that we have with how we present ourselves in the world. No matter what age you are, what socioeconomic background you come from, your culture, race, religion, sexual orientation, or gender, beauty is the great equalizer. It extends a unique invitation for connection. You can compliment a haircut and in minutes end up learning about someone's heartbreak, or remark on a shade of lipstick and somehow land in a discussion about politics. I would get stopped in the street daily by other curly girls looking to swap hair product recommendations, only to find myself in conversations about family and identity. Since I was a child watching my mom transform in front of the mirror before church, I knew beauty was about more than just products. So often, it's a reflection of how you feel, and how you want to be seen.

We can all transform through the power of makeup and hair, but young people in particular often use beauty as a tool for learning and loving themselves. Editorially, I saw beauty as a lens through which to explore identity, culture, self-expression, self-acceptance, and diversity. That, for me, made working in beauty endlessly inspiring. It felt like fun but important work, particularly speaking to young people who are still developing their sense of self and identity.

I got excited by the idea of making the kind of magazine I needed when I was growing up. One that reflected all different kinds of beauty. That broke down the hierarchies we see every day, and challenged the damaging beauty standards that convince so many of us from a young age that we aren't enough.

———

TEEN VOGUE FELT LIKE the perfect next step, one that was the culmination of everything I had learned in my career thus far—from *Ebony*, where I learned how to center the outside voice and celebrate diversity, even when the rest of the world was turning a blind eye, to *Glamour*, where I got my introduction to Condé culture and a crash course on writing for a major, mainstream publication. This was a chance to apply all of this experience for the readers I was most passionate about. The great news? I got the job. More important, I felt ready. I knew this role was for me, and I really wanted it—not just because it came with a sexy title but because I saw how I could make a difference.

MY HIRE REPRESENTED SOMETHING bigger than me. When the announcement hit the press, I learned from the headlines that I had become the first Black beauty director in Condé Nast's 107-year history. The fact that we were still celebrating these kinds of firsts in 2012 gave me mixed feelings.

I thought I was just a girl who worked hard to get a great job. To the rest of the world, I was a Black girl making history.

Seeing my race generate headlines in 2012 clarified the responsibility that came with this title. It called into focus what it meant for someone like me to assume a decision-making role that informs the kinds of images we see and the stories we tell. If I continued assimilating, hoping to blend in, I would be missing a massive opportunity to represent for communities that never had someone who looks like them championing their stories and their beauty from this seat before. It was time to start owning my superpower.

It also made it clear how far we were as a country from true equality. It reminded me that no matter how much you try to blend in, your race walks into every room before you do. This was not the postracial America news outlets claimed we were living in because of our Black president. And we were perhaps even further from a postracial reality in the editorial world.

At the time, I was the only Black editor on the masthead. But I saw the rare opportunity that came with that. I was finally in a position to help shift the culture internally simply by being who I was, and eventually, by hiring different kinds of people who might not get their foot in the door otherwise. I knew that I wanted to be a part of creating an even more inclusive magazine. Inside and out. All that would take time to unfold in baby steps, but we'd get there.

I had worked hard to land this dream job—a job I hadn't even been bold enough to dream for myself. But because it was handed to me with a profound and very public reminder of my otherness, it also came with a platform to use my voice in a new way. For the first time, I embraced what made me different—the very things that had made me feel like an outsider—as my superpower.

Rather than trying to be what I wasn't—in my work and in my life—I made a conscious commitment to fully own everything that made me who I am. Because those were the very things that made my point of view as an editor that much more valuable. It wasn't easy and it didn't happen overnight, but I set the intention.

M EANWHILE, IT WAS AS if I had inherited two jobs: the job of the beauty and health director, leading the editorial vision for that department, but also of the sole representative for people of color in a blindingly White slice of media. Because of that, I was often asked to speak as an authority on diversity.

A funny thing happens when you become what Shonda Rhimes has so brilliantly dubbed an FOD: First. Only. Different. There is an assumption that simply by being first, by succeeding in rarefied White spaces, your existence comes with built-in credentials that make you an expert on diversity and inclusion. And maybe to some degree it does, but sensitive topics surrounding race and gender are not easily unpacked in America, and the truth is we have to teach ourselves how to speak intelligently about them, just like anyone else. Yet we are expected to learn quickly how to walk the often precarious line between representing an underrepresented perspective without speaking in sweeping generalizations that trod on the White power structure that gave you the platform to begin with. At times it can feel as if you are being asked to carry the torch for an entire race of people who never had our voices, our experiences, our cultures represented with dignity in mass media. It's a dance you learn quickly because, ready or not, it comes with the FOD territory.

But the best part of being an FOD is the tribe that comes along with it.

Months after my promotion, the longtime CEO of BET Networks, Debra Lee, invited me to speak at her home in DC during their annual Leading Women Defined conference, alongside Keija Minor, who had recently made history as the first Black editor-in-chief at Condé Nast when she took over *Brides* magazine. Our back-to-back hires seemed to signal a changing tide in the industry's diversity conversation, a tipping point of sorts. Had Obama's election precipitated a sudden signal of progress? Were we entering a new day in publishing as we were in politics? What kinds of challenges had we experienced as Black women in fashion? How had we overcome them? Most important, what were we going to do with this opportunity? Suddenly these were the kinds of questions being hurled at me on stages and in media interviews.

The time it took me to reflect on these complex questions helped reframe what this opportunity could mean, not just for me professionally, but for those who, like me, had rarely seen themselves reflected in these pages. This job was not just writing about beauty products for a teen magazine—it came with the responsibility of representing for entire communities who had never been centered editorially within this system. It was a chance to use my role to magnify the margins of Black beauty.

"No matter how much you try to blend in, your race walks into every room before you do."

CHAPTER 15

New World Order

An artist's duty, as far as I'm concerned, is to reflect the times.

NINA SIMONE

O n my first day at *Teen Vogue*, I wore a butterscotch body-con dress from Zara that hit just below the knee. I layered it with a leather jacket and a black faux-fur vest. I splurged on a pair of Max Mara black patent booties I found at the Woodbury Commons outlet that laced up and anchored the look with the right amount of edge. My hair was, naturally, big and curly. Your girl was ready.

WHEN I ARRIVED, you could hear a pin drop. The hallways and cubicles were as silent as a library. Unlike *Glamour*, there were no Monday morning staff meetings where senior editors competitively pitched for page space, no enforced late nights during closes when stories went through endless rounds of edits as staffers peacocked around the office for their honor. No more cubicle chat about Engagement Chicken or raucous midnight singalongs to Aaliyah's *One in a Million* and other nineties jams in the art department after all the senior editors went home to their kids. Here staffers spoke in hushed tones around the office. Even though I was only a few floors away from my last job, I quickly discovered it was a whole new landscape of well-oiled systems, smaller teams, a more subdued office culture, and even more fantastic outfits.

Interactions with my new colleagues were perfectly polite but less frequent: There was an element of every man and woman for themselves, but not in any adversarial or chilly *Devil Wears Prada* sort of way; we just mostly kept to ourselves in our own offices. A couple of times a month, you'd meet one-on-one with the editor-in-chief to present story lineups inside the intimate silo of her pristine office. A director was expected to come in and to leave early; the office was empty no later than 6:00 P.M., to allow editors to make their evening Pilates or barre class or one of the many after-work events on the social circuit.

I was pretty stoked to find out that I had my own corner office waiting for me, one that came with its own water fountain. I was hydrated and happy, and filled with unexplainable pride whenever the Alhambra guy would come along to swap out those big blue plastic jugs.

Unfortunately, about a month into the job, an email from the managing editor went around, informing us of budget cuts, and to my deep dismay, in-office water fountains were among the first line items to get slashed.

Next were the reimbursable working lunches.

Then the town cars home.

One by one, all the little luxuries that peons like me looked forward to indulging in once we worked our way up a prestigious Condé Nast masthead were being taken away.

I begged and pleaded to keep my water fountain—as unsightly as it was, it had become a very personal point of pride. I was willing to cut down on jugs and I even offered to cover the cost on my own T&E (office lingo for travel and entertainment budgets). "Speaking of T and E," our managing editor deadpanned, "your budget is getting cut significantly, too. Sorry."

It was the year 2012: the glory days of print publishing seemed to be dwindling and I had only just begun my career climb.

I was the sole Black voice on the editorial team then and the website was still an afterthought with a digital staff of one. There was no way of knowing it then, but all of that was about to radically change.

It took time to get my sea legs at *Teen Vogue*—I didn't feel like a natural fit in such a sterile office environment. But the work itself was second nature to me. In fact, I'd never assumed a position that felt like more of a perfect fit. I walked into it with a self-assuredness that came from knowing this role was mine to redefine.

Part of my mission at *Teen Vogue* was to use my work to help young people see their differences as their strengths. It was important that I lived that mission, too. Like the reader, I was still very much experimenting with my identity and learning how to wield my newfound power as a young leader in a world I didn't fully understand. Coming into my own at *Teen Vogue* required me to take calculated risks—in my career, yes, but that fearlessness also manifested in experimental life and beauty choices, too.

I started dating a man twice my age, and when we went back to the fancy department store where Future Husband bought me my first pair of Louboutins, I decided to purchase my first "boss lady bag" with my own money—a large, classic black tote with gold hardware by Tom Ford. It was the first four-digit purchase in. My. Life.

I learned how to make my first fire. And hire.

I moved into a studio apartment on my dream block in the West Village—it was my first time living alone.

And I cut things off with the man I was dating who wasn't ready to fully commit—as a practice of walking at the first whisper. It was excruciatingly hard for me to pull that plug, but it was the right decision—and it made room for what was meant to be.

As with any other major transitions and growth spurts in my life, you could watch it all play out in my hair.

Over the course of the next two years, I dyed my hair green, bleached it blond, and then finally I chopped it all off for the first time ever. I wanted to shed anything that felt like a security blanket. Because my long, curly hair had become such a big part of my identity for so long, I was ready to challenge what society tells us about beauty: that you need long hair to be feminine, that Black girls with long hair should *never*, ever cut it because it grows so slowly that it might never grow back. (FYI: These are lies. Cut it off. Live your life. It *will* grow back.)

Still, I cried like a baby in the backroom the first time I saw myself, sans hair, in the mirror, and even called my old man ex for moral support. To which he replied simply: "The Elaine Welteroth I know is a boss lady. And bosses know it isn't the length of their hair that makes them beautiful or powerful." I let out a sigh and stood up to wipe my tears. "C'mon, I know you're not walking around with that boss lady bag and crying about a damn haircut."

The very first story I wrote for *Teen Vogue* was about my natural hair journey. I detailed my experience using hot tools and maximum-hold gels as a metaphor for shrinking and erasing parts of myself all throughout high school. It wasn't until my freshman year of college that I desperately missed the hair texture I was born with, so much that I finally decided to quit heat styling cold turkey. I went on a mission to coax my curls back to their naturally fluffy state. The piece explored how, for many of us, reclaiming our curls is a metaphor for reclaiming the parts of ourselves that we spend years killing off with actual irons and chemical relaxers.

That journey landed me in the expert hands of Rosie at Devachan Salon, a curly-hair mecca in downtown New York City. Rosie was a brown-skinned Brazilian woman of few words, but she had a magical set of hands and a skilled way with scissors. Her process was so ritualistic, so artful, and—in ways that seem almost silly to ascribe to a haircut—so healing. She'd start by sitting beside me at eye level listening to what I wanted, where I was in my life and with work, then she'd shush me, signaling that it was time for her to get to work—in silence. She'd move around my head as if she were doing capoeira with my curls. Her face always shifted into a pensive, quasi-meditative state before she strategically dove in. Rather than straightening and cutting for precision, she insisted on dry cutting curl by curl intuitively. This technique maximizes the bounce and shape of curly hair. To this day, her mastery of the curly haircut remains unmatched. I felt seen and celebrated in ways that feel almost too profound to attribute to a haircut. It was, for me, a spiritual experience.

Until then, my interactions with hair salons as an adult had been nothing short of demoralizing. I'd walk into White salons to the panicked reactions of stylists whose stunned expressions made it quite clear they had not been trained to service my texture—they didn't have a clue what to do with me or my thick, tangled curls. Or I'd walk out of Black hair salons—several hours into my weekend—with an aggressively heat-styled look weighed down by heavy products that often left behind oily spots on the headrest of my cab seat. There was no happy medium, no place for curls like mine to go and be understood. Which was why it felt so comforting to have finally found my tribe at Devachan, this multitextured oasis where curly girls came to get their hair loved on and nourished. Blowouts and heat styling weren't even on the menu.

"Let's make it big—*huge*," I told Rosie when I went to see her before starting my job at *Teen Vogue*.

That first day marked a significant turning point—personally and professionally, I was coming into my own. Gone were the days of heeding the call to shrink in order to fit a mold. It was time to break that mold altogether.

I was following in the footsteps of Eva Chen, one of the most beloved and revered young editors in the industry. Those were big (Prada) shoes to fill. I couldn't just swim in the middle of the stream now. I had to make waves. I remembered Harriette's advice: standout editors have a signature, and my signature should be my hair. This was the beginning of a new era—an era marked by big-ass hair.

I ended my first story ever for *Teen Vogue* with this: "I might have straightened my hair for every event in high school from picture day to prom, but for this dream-job debut, it's all about the curls. The bigger, the better."

The story ran in the February 2013 issue of the magazine with my picture next to it as my introduction to the readership of *Teen Vogue*. Based on the response from curly-haired girls—and their moms—all over the country, it clearly hit a nerve for tribes of Black and brown girls, mixed girls, curly girls who had all struggled to embrace their natural hair, too. Some even stopped me on the street to thank me for writing the story and were eager to share their own natural hair journeys and struggles with self-acceptance, too.

It wasn't that the story itself was particularly radical—after all, the natural hair movement was well under way by then. But the media's coverage of beauty still seemed so segregated that curly hair, and specifically Black hair, was rarely, if ever, covered in general market (read: White) magazines. There was a clear need for more cross-cultural content. Any time the deep yearning for representation was fulfilled, it felt refreshing and necessary—and whether on Twitter or in the streets, our young, vocal readership let us know it.

NEW WORLD ORDER

I<small>T WAS HARD FOR ME</small> to ignore how few decision-making seats in the media were occupied by people of color. Obama had just won his second term in office, but people of color in fashion were still grossly underrepresented behind the scenes, as were storytellers and image makers in the media overall.

I think back on my early days at *Ebony*, when I got the opportunity to witness the legendary model agent and image activist Bethann Hardison use her position as one of few influential Blacks in fashion to advocate for Black models. It was one of the most memorable moments of my early career, one that inspired me to use my position to be a changemaker, too.

Bethann was an agitator and a self-appointed hell-raiser. She's never one to shy away from confrontation—in fact, she used it as her tool for change. In the summer of 2008, she sent out letters inviting big-name designers, casting agents, photographers, and editors to come together for a candid conversation about fashion's diversity problem. Bethann was a well-respected mother figure to many in the industry; certainly no one wanted to be remembered by her for *not* showing up. So they came, likely thinking, "How bad could it be, right?" That little amphitheater in the Bowery Hotel filled up with a mostly White audience, some (according to Bethann) verging on racist. Then, one by one, she called out people by name for transgressions such as not casting a single Black girl in their shows or campaigns. It was a takedown, and a true sight to behold, especially as a young Black editor. As one of very few Black fashion insiders with real influence, Bethann made it her business to publicly agitate until decision makers felt forced to do the right thing.

And then the 2008 all-Black issue of Italian *Vogue* came out—featuring all Black models—and it set the industry ablaze. For a season, at least.

From that moment on, I knew I was put in this industry to serve as a change agent, too. I didn't want to just take up space at the table, I wanted to use my seat to shake things up. I also realized that in order to truly change an industry from the inside out, to rebuild broken systems, and to change hearts and minds, it takes more than just one voice and more than just one way. While I admire and revere Bethann—we need people who are willing to call out injustice, face-to-face, on the front lines—I recognized that my activism would look different. As an editor, especially now in an influential post, I had the power to help change the narrative through storytelling. In an era that applauds even the most superficial embrace of diversity, equating tokenism with progress, I was determined to use the opportunity I was given to make a difference by bringing more of my authentic self to the role. I'd had enough of feeling intimidated by self-important airs, sterile environments, and some of the stiff personalities in the industry.

As an FOD, sometimes just being yourself is the radical act. When you occupy space in systems that weren't built for you, *your authenticity is your activism*. But doing any radical work that has the power to shift systems—especially from within a corporate structure—requires allyship. Before I could go from assimilator to disrupter, I had to find my voice—and build my tribe.

I MET PHILLIP PICARDI BACKSTAGE at a show during New York Fashion Week, and within seconds we were belting out a nineties Mariah Carey ballad while the rest of the beauty editors looked on, confused but entertained. I didn't know him then, and he didn't know me. But any biracial girl and gay boy of a certain age have one thing in common: an obsession with Mariah Carey. And I do mean *almost* every incarnation of Mariah: White-passing Mariah, Black choir Mariah. Natural curls, no-makeup Mariah. Butterflies and rainbows Mariah. Urban makeover Mariah. Bone Thugs-N-Harmony *Breakdown* Mariah (aka when she earned her Black Card and the rest of Black America started claiming Mariah). *MTV Cribs* diva bathtub scene Mariah. And, okay, I admit she lost me right around *Glitter* Mariah, but many of my queer friends still live for this Mariah. Anyway, that is a (heated) debate for a different day.

Point is Phill and I had an instant connection, and when the beauty assistant role opened in my department, I woke up one morning out of a deep sleep remembering our exchange and asked HR to help me find him. He was an assistant at a beauty website and I thought he could be perfect for the job.

After interviewing him, I was certain he was the one—he loved makeup even more than I did, and as a boy in beauty, and a gay kid from a conservative town, we shared a passion for using beauty as a platform to celebrate diversity and to promote more inclusivity. We saw eye to eye and *clicked* immediately. I went to my editor-in-chief raving about him, hoping she would meet him and give her blessing for me to extend the hire. Her reaction surprised me: "A boy? In the beauty department?" Her point was that it was certainly not the most conventional first hire for my department, given that beauty editor jobs are mostly inhabited by women. I just remember thinking, "Wait, but *Glee* is the number one show on television for our demographic. RuPaul's *Drag Race* has legions of fans. I think America is *ready* for a male beauty editor." I was certain our readers were.

That this was even considered an unconventional hire reflects the cultural landscape at the time in "pre-woke" America, even in a creative industry. We desperately needed more diversity—of thought, of lived experience, of points of view—on our team.

"Trust me, you will love him," I told her. "If you aren't a fan after meeting with him, I'll go back to the drawing board."

Of course I didn't need to. She fell in love with him. Everyone did.

I WAS VERY INTENTIONAL ABOUT the qualities I was looking for in my first hire. In addition to searching for someone with an equally relentless work ethic who was strong in my weaker areas (i.e., someone who cared about beauty products more than I did), I was also determined to hire someone who felt like a piece of home at work. In retrospect, maybe that's because I still felt a little bit out of place in the office. I wanted to find someone who would help contribute to shifting the culture and shaking up the status quo. Someone who might even have the audacity to blast a little Mariah from their computer speakers in that quiet office of ours from time to time. Someone who had my back and who I could nurture and protect, too.

Phill started as my assistant, but from day one our relationship was so much more than that—we quickly became a dynamic duo. He was whip-smart, hilarious, fearless, and his charisma swept up the entire office. He also understood intimately what it meant to feel othered.

Phill was all of the things I was looking for, and more: I found someone who would eventually help me find my voice in the editorial world, and who made me feel less alone in it. I also finally had someone to confide in who recognized the microaggressions I was experiencing as the only Black editor representing *Teen Vogue* in a predominantly White industry.

Like the time I went on a business trip with my publisher to speak with the global heads of a number of major beauty brands. After a day of shuttling around the campus, I walked into a large conference room where I was prepared to share my insights with marketing execs over a "lunch and learn." A smiling White woman with short, highlighted newscaster hair stood up to greet me with a firm midwestern handshake and said, "Thank you so much for joining us and letting us shuttle you all over the place today. Gosh, you must be so tired. I know they've been working you like a *sla*—."

She caught herself before finishing the sentence and laughed nervously. Her offensive remark had landed like a thud, making everyone fidgety in their seats. Once again, my race made its way into the room before I had even spoken a word.

I wondered, "Would she have been conscious of her word choice had I not been Black? Would she have just finished her sentence if I were White? Had my Blackness made her nervous?"

I also wondered: "Am I being too sensitive?"

Eventually I excused it: "Maybe she didn't mean anything by it."

My pasted-on smile grew wary and my cheeks hot as I debated my next move. I felt the urge to rescue her from the humiliation unleashed by her own racist remark, to deflect the discomfort with a lighthearted joke. I knew it was an honest mistake, an extremely poor choice of words. But still, why was the onus on me to save her from herself when I was the one who was almost referred to as a slave in front of her all-White home office? I felt like I had just gotten jabbed. But I didn't know how to articulate or address it in a professional setting. Instead, I maintained that pasted-on smile, took a deep breath, and proceeded with the meeting as if it never happened.

"You have to be fucking kidding me," Phill practically shouted as I recalled the unfortunate "slave slip-up" back in the office. "I am so sorry that happened to you, Elaine."

His angry reaction surprised me. It honestly hadn't occurred to me that I could share this with a White person and be met with this kind of empathy. I had encountered and swallowed so many uncomfortable moments like those, but seeing his rage, I realized I hadn't ever processed my own.

When less overt but similarly uncomfortable microaggressions transpired in the office—like the code language used for a Black model's look being "too harsh" or her hair "'too Black," or a homophobic phrase used to describe a trans model's appearance as "too manly," or someone's body being considered "too big"—we'd commiserate behind closed doors and find a way to address it.

THOSE EARLY DAYS OF allyship were pivotal for me as a young professional and a person of color still learning how to navigate the corporate world. We had many long conversations over the course of working together that helped us both to really see each other and learn more about the world through each other's eyes. Through our friendship, I developed a deeper sensitivity and compassion for the experiences of LGBTQIA+ people in America; our relationship in the office gave me practice in learning how to be a supportive ally out in the world. Similarly, having grown up in a very White, conservative community in Boston, Phill said he became more cognizant of the insidious ways racism works in America through our friendship as well.

As I EXPECTED, PHILL quickly outgrew the position and eventually left *Teen Vogue* for a booming millennial women's website. But then six months later, he was back at *Teen Vogue*, this time as digital director—the youngest ever to hold that title. I was asked to help lure him back. For me, it felt like a second chance at continuing to shift the culture together—at least the one inside *Teen Vogue*.

By THEN I HAD built up enough trust and credibility in the office to start taking some bigger risks; I was beginning to carve out space for conversations about race and identity at the magazine. The office dynamics had also shifted. Loud music played on desktop speakers. Laughter filled the hallways. New hires were starting to fill the empty seats in the web department, and people were staying later and later. I'd linger longer in the art department, where we'd have friendly fights over the design of my pages. There was a buzz throughout the office: *Teen Vogue* had become, for me, an idyllic work environment for twentysomethings who were obsessed with the intersection between fashion, culture, and later, politics.

"Sometimes just being yourself is the radical act. When you occupy space in systems that weren't built for you, *your authenticity is your activism.*"

CHAPTER 16

Disturbing the Peace

When I dare to be powerful, to use my strength
in the service of my vision, then it becomes less and
less important whether I am afraid.

AUDRE LORDE

Earlier that year, I spent Christmas in Rwanda with Chloe—my first trip to Africa—and returned to the office with Senegalese twists down to my waist. I had never worn extensions in my life and this would be my first time wearing braids to work. I hushed the quiet voice inside me that was apprehensive. After all, I was a beauty director—experimenting with my own look was part of the job. At best: people would compliment my braids and we'd all move on. At worst: people would indulge in touching them or make some sort of ignorant comment, intended as a compliment.

In the year 2015, I'd hoped it wouldn't come to that.

But unfortunately, it did.

"Wow. *How* did your hair grow so fast?"

It was only my first day back on the industry-event circuit, and a particularly high-ranking fellow beauty director was gently petting one of my braids. She was still touching and marveling when she added, "Is this all yours?"

I was speechless.

There was nothing natural looking about these braids. They were woven with coarse Yaki hair so thick they couldn't be hemmed up into a ponytail if I tried, and so long that I would have beaten Beyoncé in a whip-your-weave contest. Not to mention, the last time she'd seen me, just two weeks prior, I was only three inches into my grow-out phase after chopping off my long, curly hair. (I know I said Black people's hair *does* grow back and all that. But come *on*, people—*no one's* hair grows *this* fast!)

I realize she didn't mean any harm, but I still couldn't help seeing the irony in that moment. The notion that a White woman who sat at the very pinnacle of publishing's beauty hierarchy could get there without ever being required to know the first thing about Black hair was still shocking to me. As a Black beauty director, I was expected to educate myself about every kind of beauty—paying particular attention to the Eurocentric beauty that was pleasing to advertisers and revered in pop culture. I'd edited multiple features about topics that don't necessarily apply to me, like stories recommending haircuts and shampoos for fine, straight hair like hers. But that a White beauty director couldn't tell the difference between a three-inch wash-and-go and twenty-inch twists? As my mother would say, "That's a crying shame!"

I swallowed the less-polite responses that flashed before my eyes and simply responded with a smile: "Oh, you of all people must know these are extensions."

NOT LONG BEFORE THIS ENCOUNTER, on live TV Zendaya was infamously struck with a very stereotypical assumption that the dreadlocks she proudly wore to the Oscars must have smelled of "patchouli" and "weed." At just eighteen, the star stood up for herself with a profound statement on social media: "Wearing my hair in locs on an Oscar red carpet was to showcase them in a positive light to remind people of color that our hair is good enough . . . to me locs are a symbol of strength and beauty."

It was a teachable moment for many.

Reflecting on the lack of education and respect for Black hair in mainstream culture, and after experiencing it firsthand, I wrote a story for the June/July 2015 issue exploring how Afrocentric hairstyles in White spaces can in itself be a form of activism. In it, I shared some of my own experience in Rwanda, spending six hours sitting on the floor of a hut getting my first set of traditional Senegalese twists—not just as a beauty experiment but as an exercise in connecting with a part of my heritage I had been disconnected from for most of my life as a Black American. And how returning to corporate America in them was my own way of pushing back against the internalized pressure to assimilate, because for generations Black people have been taught to conform, to wear our hair in ways that are deemed appropriate in White professional settings, to essentially strip away our culture.

I also referenced Zendaya's incident at the Oscars: "Zendaya's image and thoughtful comeback set into motion an important paradigm shift. Her bravery, pride, and eloquence helped bridge the gap between people on both sides of the cultural divide. All through the lens of beauty."

Because this particular Black hair story was pushing *Teen Vogue* into culturally sensitive territory, it was important that I was extremely thoughtful about every aspect of its execution. Black Twitter was alive and thriving by then, and no one wanted to get caught on the wrong side of it. As a teen magazine primarily known for publishing light fashion pieces at the time, taking on the politicization of Black hair was risky. Especially when our publication had been routinely called out for cultural appropriation in the past. As a result, some of the staff were afraid of the repercussions if we got it wrong. I understood the fear but I didn't want to give it the power to make me shy away from championing a story like this. Ultimately, going forward with it forced conversations internally that we wouldn't have had otherwise.

I found myself in meetings saying things like, "It's okay to say 'Black,' you guys. We don't have to whisper it. It's not a bad word."

And "We don't have to pull Bohemian looks just because she is a brown girl with braids. Can we try putting her in sporty, graphic swimwear? It's the summer issue."

I was also intentional about casting a model who resembled the story's hero, Zendaya, and I was insistent that she wear the same style of twists I got in Rwanda.

That shoot was the first time I felt like I was able to fully be myself on set. I was so proud to be telling a story that shed light on a topic I hoped would not only resonate with young Black girls but also educate our readers about the power of Black beauty. I was screaming "yasss" and high-fiving the photographer and the model the whole time. I was typically much more reticent at photo shoots, playing backseat to Marie, our creative director, but even she made it clear that this was my story, my shoot.

When the piece came out, the media went nuts.

But not in a good way.

It all started when someone on Twitter with a couple of hundred followers tweeted a picture of the story in the magazine with something to the effect of: "Cultural appropriation at its finest. *Teen Vogue* strikes again!"

The person who crafted the tweet assumed the model we photographed was White—and, countless retweets later, most of Black Twitter did, too.

"Why's your magazine so anti black?'"

"Shame on you @TeenVogue for appropriating protective hairstyles for black hair by putting them on white models."

The comments grew more enraged with every retweet—shortly there were hundreds of them. And then—*boom*. The UK *Daily Mail* ran a story about it.

Clearly, none of these detractors had even read the piece.

It was my first time putting my neck out and doing something unapologetically "for the culture" on a predominantly White platform. But the punishing outcome was the opposite of what I had intended—this was my career nightmare come true. I was crushed.

As I reviewed the pickup and watched my Instagram comments filling with angry messages, my heart sank. No one on the internet seemed to recognize that the story was tackling harmful stereotypes about Black hair, nor did they notice that a Black woman had written it, or that the biracial model we photographed in braids was as Black as I am. This was meant to be a celebration of Black beauty. Yet somehow my story had inadvertently offended the very community I was using my platform to represent.

I came home that night sick to my stomach and in tears. As I continued reading the comments, I spiraled lower and lower, feeling misunderstood, devastated, and humiliated.

Soon the model herself, Phillipa Steele, chimed in through my comments section, adding simply, "For the record, if anyone even cares, I'm half Black and half French." Not only did this revelation correct the error of how her race was reported online, it also seemed to beg the question: "Am I not Black enough to wear braids?"

After the model had confirmed her Blackness for those who were calling it into question, the argument against the story became less about her—and more about why *Teen Vogue* would publish a story about Senegalese twists and not show any dark-skinned Black women on the page.

On that front, I realized they were absolutely right.

I thought back over the process of how we had arrived at the rest of the photos: online we were able to publish the story as a photo diary with snapshots my friend Chloe took of me getting my hair braided by local women in Rwanda. We initially designed the magazine layout using those same images in a small sidebar, but when we learned in the eleventh hour that the images weren't high-enough resolution for print and therefore got vetoed by Anna, we resorted to a celebrity sidebar instead, which featured Zendaya (the story's muse), Zoë Kravitz (my braid inspo), and myself. All light-skinned women. And—this is the part that still gives me hives—a couple of White models wearing braids were sprinkled in, too.

Looking back, I realize that I was still operating in the mind-set of taking baby steps toward progress. I was so proud of the story itself and still in disbelief that the shoot even happened. But because of the tight deadline, I did not push hard enough for the kind of representation in the sidebar that I should have. In the age of the internet and splintered identity politics, imagery often speaks louder than the words—especially when it comes to beauty stories. Given that these braids originated in a culture where the women are dark-skinned, not being intentional about including them in this story was a critical mistake, one that I own completely.

As humbling as it was to see my well-intentioned piece get twisted up into a larger "anti-Black" narrative, it became a turning point for me as both a journalist and a young Black woman still finding my voice. It was one of the most painful lessons of my career. But I wasn't going to allow the blowback to stop me from telling our stories.

I WAS INSTRUCTED BY HIGHER-UPS at Condé Nast not to respond to the controversy, to just let it die down. Yet I felt like my professional reputation and credibility within my community was on the line. I couldn't watch us go down in flames over a story I wrote that was misconstrued in the press without addressing it head-on. I spent hours responding to some of the early detractors on social media. After the model confirmed that she was, in fact, Black, it prompted more reflective conversation in my Instagram comments about the issue of colorism in the Black community, as well as the gross lack of diverse representation of beauty in the media. Someone who was initially dragging the story ended up apologizing to the model once she realized that this was more layered than even she realized at first. Engaging in that kind of deeper dialogue with the reader for the first time felt necessary and important. Phill had rejoined the team right around this time, and with his encouragement, I decided to address the controversy in an open letter on TeenVogue.com.

The op-ed helped turn the tide by shining a light on how this piece ignited an important, nuanced conversation about race. In it, I wrote: "I will be the first to say that the industry still has a long way to go in addressing the deep need for more affirming messages. . . . As one of few Black beauty editors, it is a responsibility that I do not take lightly." I explained how the story came to be, and then added: "I relate to and understand first-hand what it feels like to be overlooked, to be disregarded, to be made to feel as if my voice isn't important and my beauty isn't desirable . . . because I am Black. I also know what it feels like to be ridiculed and rejected because, as a mixed-race person, I am somehow not Black enough."

If I could go back to coach my younger self, I would salute her courage.

But knowing what I know now, I would have also taken the statement further.

I would have specifically apologized to the readers for excluding dark-skinned women from the imagery and for featuring White women at all. I would have written: "I hear you, I see you, and I will do better next time."

LOOKING BACK, THE BRAID story controversy gets at every angle of the complexity of what it meant for me to be at *Teen Vogue* at that time. There was an untangling going on within myself, and in regard to my own relationship to assimilation. Braids became a complex metaphor for the knots in my own process of owning my identity, and understanding how to push through my own discomfort to properly represent for my community. As a journalist I was still learning how to use my platform and my voice to elevate cultural conversations around beauty.

As painful as this learning was, it was powerful and essential. It pushed me to become an even more diligent storyteller and a more conscious human being.

JUST TWO WEEKS LATER, the August *Teen Vogue* cover featuring three Black models hit newsstands, and the response was extraordinary. Suddenly, we were receiving widespread praise in the press and on social media for championing diversity with a cover that was lauded as "groundbreaking." Because I was the Black editor who penned the cover story, I was held up right along with it as a symbol of progress, a sign that fashion media was finally moving in the right direction. It was a redemptive moment that also felt a bit like whiplash.

It was our editor-in-chief Amy's idea to put Imaan Hammam, Aya Jones, and Lineisy Montero on the cover, and I felt lucky to have been given the opportunity to pen what would become such a landmark cover story for *Teen Vogue*. The takeaways from the experience offered invaluable insights for the whole team. Marie, our French creative director who led the shoot to success, said that she was taught there were three things that won't sell on a cover: models, anyone without household name recognition, and Black people. We had just done all three, and for what was typically considered a sleepy, end-of-summer issue when magazines often sell the fewest copies, but it became our highest-selling cover that year. It even beat out the issue featuring Kylie Jenner on the cover, which was previously our top seller.

Representation matters, this we know. It always has. But as the industry was waking up to the power of representation, I watched it quickly become a business imperative.

Yet with more and more diverse covers popping up over time, the focus on authentic representation behind the scenes was becoming even more vital. In order to change the stories, you must change the storytellers.

As the editor for the cover story, the February 2016 issue was another important opportunity for me to learn what it means to advocate for representation, both in front of the camera and behind it. With diversity becoming a larger focus for *Teen Vogue*, and across the industry, it became critically important that we were doing more than just commercializing the culture. And particularly in the business of image makers and storytellers, authentic representation begins with creating more opportunities for people of color behind the scenes. Because, as we well know, it takes more than a few token covers to incite meaningful change.

Back then, Amandla Stenberg was a young star who hadn't been in a major film since her small yet unforgettable role as Rue in *The Hunger Games* several years prior. But she had quickly become an important voice for her generation after her hyperintelligent Tumblr post "Don't Cash Crop My Cornrows" went viral, schooling the world on the issue of cultural appropriation. When we put her on the cover of *Teen Vogue*—and I asked Solange to interview her about what it meant to be proud and Black in 2016—it signaled a larger sea change editorially. Creating this issue was an opportunity: to rethink not just the stories we were telling, but who was telling them.

I got my editor-in-chief's blessing to call an editorial team meeting to brainstorm out-of-the-box ideas for the issue. I saw a chance to use this issue as a case study: What did we stand for now? What kinds of stories could be told here that weren't being told anywhere else? What would happen if we threw out all the old formulas and focused our efforts on carving out a new lane for ourselves as a platform that spoke directly to a wider

swath of issues facing young people today? In a crowded new media landscape, one in which magazines were quickly becoming passé for our younger
audience and where young stars were popping up on the covers of all the
other women's magazines, it was mission critical to rethink our approach. I
felt an urgency to pivot. And the stakes felt high.

Social media had become a window into what our readers were talking
about online: representation, intersectional feminism, environmentalism,
racial justice, gender equality, LGBTQIA+ rights, sexual and gender fluid-
ity, and beyond. Many of us on staff saw how we could expand the work we
were doing to mean more to a new generation of young people—the most
informed and the most diverse in history. We had to seize this opportunity
to speak to them more holistically about all aspects of their lives and their
identities, topics that were, for the most part, being overlooked by mainstream media.

That issue marked a turning point for *Teen Vogue* editorially.

For the cover shoot, I pulled inspirational images of Angela Davis in the
1960s—her full, round "freedom 'fro," turtlenecks, and wide-legged pants
were emblematic of Black pride and historically associated with the Black
Panther movement. The team liked the reference, but when it came to who
to book for hair, there was some debate.

Typically at *Teen Vogue*, the photographer—often a White man—had
the final say in determining the hair and makeup teams. The problem with
this process, as I saw it, was that it reinforced the same hires again and
again, making it harder for anyone who wasn't already considered a fashion
insider to break into the most exclusive editorial ranks. The unintended
consequence was that it became a form of systemic exclusion, one that pre-
vented diverse talent in particular from ever having an opportunity to break
in behind the scenes.

I realized that the only way to ever disrupt this system was for someone
at the magazine to advocate for new voices and, in this particular case, a
Black hair stylist. So I spoke up, insisting that it was necessary to the

integrity and authenticity of the story to hire a Black hair stylist, particularly given that our aesthetic references harkened back to the civil rights era. I held up the lessons we had all learned from the braid story as a case study for why this was so important.

"But we already have a Black wardrobe stylist on set. Isn't that enough?" No. It wasn't.

"We have a great stylist on hold who can do Black hair." That wasn't the point.

As we had all seen with the braid-story debacle, Black hair is political. The issue here was that we hadn't considered hiring any qualified Black hair stylists for a shoot that referenced one of the most iconic figures in the Black Power movement. To me, that was problematic. I was pushing for conscious inclusion because it was vital, but at the time it seemed to be perceived as an unnecessary complication and perhaps even taking a cover opportunity away from a credible, qualified White hair stylist who was more familiar— one who already had countless covers under their belt.

While it was uncomfortable to agitate the system, what I learned from the braid story was that it was my responsibility as an editor to advocate for every aspect of how my stories were told—and as a Black editor, ultimately I would be held accountable to my community if we failed them.

After heavy debate, we finally booked a talented Black hair stylist named Lacy Redway for the cover—and she killed it. Before then, she had been mostly relegated to booking celebrity hair jobs, which, because of the archaic, hierarchical system, often precluded her from being booked by the *Vogue*s of the world. Going in, you could sense that she felt the stakes were higher for her, like she had to prove herself on set.

On the morning of the shoot we headed uptown to the historic streets of Harlem. It gave me inexplicable pride watching all of the models with their big, unapologetic, signature curly Afros on our set—Amandla owning her cover-girl moment, Lacy instantly winning everyone over with her skill and charm, the fashion stylist Julia Sarr-Jamois pensively working her craft. And then, of course, there was my own little curly 'fro still bouncing back from the big chop, helping to guide the shots and conjuring good vibes.

So much of the work we do is valued most in hindsight, after it has been lauded and validated by the world. This demonstration of Black minds coming together to make art that celebrated our beauty and our excellence—it felt special, even in the moment. Nothing I had done professionally until that point compared to what it felt like to be a part of creating that Black girl magic.

WHEN SOLANGE'S INTRODUCTION AND the transcript of her conversation with Amandla landed in my in-box, I cried at my desk. It wasn't a quiet, cute little cry either. My body curled over in half, I held my head in my hands, and I wept. It was what Oprah would call the ugly cry. Solange's words were powerful and truly poetic: "There's a secret language shared among black girls who are destined to climb mountains and cross rivers in a world that tells us to belong to the valleys that surround us," she wrote. "So here we are, connecting as two nonconforming black girls."

And Amandla's words hit home, personally: "As a black girl you grow up internalizing all these messages that say you shouldn't accept your hair or your skin tone or your natural features, or that you shouldn't have a voice, or that you aren't smart," she said in the interview. "I feel like the only way to fight that is to just be yourself on the most genuine level and to connect with other black girls who are awakening and realizing that they've been trying to conform."

These were the kinds of affirming messages and images I needed to see when I was a little girl looking for examples of how to move through the world. As I reviewed the issue before it went to press, there were waves of joy, a sense of triumph. The knowing that some young girl would see herself in this work in a powerfully authentic way was the only indication I needed to believe that this issue had the power to touch hearts and change minds—because it pierced mine first.

When the cover story came out, not only did it unleash emotionally charged praise from masses of Black and brown girls on social media, it even got the support of one VIP Black woman named Beyoncé, who shared it on Facebook. The digital team cheered and I ran up and down the hallways like a maniac. We were all on a high.

Amy Astley was still the editor-in-chief then, and her commitment to diversity was notable—both in terms of empowering someone like me to have a voice at the table, and in her embrace of this even more inclusive direction for the magazine. Amandla was just one in a series of people of color cover stars, followed quickly by Zoë Kravitz and Willow Smith. With this succession of covers, and the broadening scope of feminist issues being covered thoughtfully in the magazine and on the website, which Phill was running by then, it was clear that something was shifting at *Teen Vogue*. You could see it on the covers. You could feel it in the stories.

The May 2016 issue was fronted by Willow Smith; inside we ran a feature that addressed cultural appropriation. Season after season, we had watched designers, celebrities, and magazines, including ours, get called out for appropriating looks from cornrows to bindis to Native American feathers to baby hairs, particularly around Coachella and during Fashion Week. I felt a mounting responsibility to address it—so we did, both by having hard conversations internally and then infusing that understanding back into the work we were doing as a team.

After initiating an open dialogue with the team about the sensitivities

around the issue of cultural appropriation and aligning on the need for revised practices in order to avoid being culprits, we decided to do a beauty
story that initiated a similar conversation with our readers. But rather than
purporting ourselves to be the authorities on the topic, we passed the mic.
For the first time, we cast real girls from routinely appropriated cultures to
be shot by a *Vogue* photographer for a story that explored the difference between cultural appropriation and cultural appreciation, *from their perspective.*
In a video, we asked these girls to explain the difference, in their own words.

With our brand's complicated past, it was a risky move that could potentially backfire—but we were all in it together. There was a sense of solidarity in taking this editorial step forward into a more culturally conscious
direction. And it was beautiful to see the meaningful collaboration across
departments. We were finding our voice, collectively. We had something to
say. And we were taking on one of our greatest creative risks to say it.

Each of the girls we cast for the shoot eloquently detailed what beauty
meant to them and their families, and how it was defined by their cultures:
a Native American girl named Daunette, who talked about the significance
of feathers in her culture; an Indian girl named Natasha described on camera the meanings of a bindi; a West Indian girl named Sashamoni spoke
about the cultural and religious significance of dreadlocks; a Japanese girl
named Eiko described the unique creativity of Japanese makeup styles; an
Afro Latina girl from New York named Leaf spoke poetically about her
baby hairs; an African American girl from New Jersey named Kyemah
spoke with pride about the power behind her Afro; and a Black, Chinese,
Irish, and Creek Indian girl from North Carolina named Brandi talked
about her experience as a multiethnic young woman who wears her natural
hair in braids on a conservative college campus.

The response from readers was incredibly encouraging and rewarding,
and it proved to us that we were moving in the right direction. We were
cultivating trust within the marginalized communities that we aimed to
celebrate.

———————

IN THE MIDST OF all this positive momentum, I received an email from Anna Wintour that made my heart stop. It was a meeting request:

"Dear Elaine, I've heard wonderful things about you and the work you are doing at Teen Vogue. I'd love to meet with you tomorrow. Anna."

I had to reread it to make sure I wasn't being punk'd.

THE FIRST TIME I saw Anna Wintour in person, I was running late to the office and had just finished bobbing and weaving my way through my morning commute while inhaling a banana for breakfast. As I entered the Condé Nast building, I searched the lobby for a trash bin. No luck. So I discreetly dropped the banana peel into my Chanel shopping bag that was doubling as my walking-shoe bag and proceeded into the elevator bank hoping no one would notice.

Of course, just as the doors were closing, Anna Wintour glided right into my elevator with her signature dark sunglasses on, standing mere inches away from me. Around us, spines straightened and noses lifted a little higher. Some cowered into their phones, pretending to disappear, myself included. I was anxious that Anna, the queen of fashion, might detect my smelly leftovers.

Sure enough, just before we reached the *Vogue* floor, in my peripheral vision I noticed Anna sniffing, looking around as if trying to detect the source of some foul stench—perhaps the one emanating from my bag. As the elevator doors opened, before exiting, she shot a disapproving look in my direction. I wanted to crawl into that same bag and die right there next to the discarded banana peel.

With the exception of that smelly elevator ride, I had never shared the same rarefied air as Anna, let alone ever been formally introduced to her. So when her email popped up, you could imagine the cold rush of panic that ran through my veins. Thankfully, I had Keija Minor, the editor-in-chief of *Brides* and the first Black person in that position at Condé Nast, to coach me through it. I called her immediately and took copious notes on the yellow sticky pad at my desk:

Meeting Anna Tips:

Don't wear black; she likes color.

Have an opinion; she likes people who have a point of view.

She will ask you about hobbies, what you like to do in your free time. Be honest but sound smart.

She's big on culture. Be prepared to talk about what Broadway shows you've seen recently, what book you're currently reading, what museums or art exhibitions you've visited—stuff like that.

Be yourself. She doesn't like people who cower in her presence.

Be confident. She can smell fear.

I thought to myself: "No pressure."

THE MEETING LASTED A total of seven minutes. It went well in the sense that I wasn't visibly nervous, I threw together a suitable lewk, and I was able to answer all of her questions confidently. (For inquiring minds: I wore a floral, A-line Balenciaga skirt that I purchased on deep discount at a sample sale, styled with tan Céline sandals and my signature leather jacket slung over my shoulders.) The meeting ended with her inviting me to come back with something to present to her, an idea, anything I thought we should be doing. It wasn't totally clear why, and there were no further instructions.

I admittedly spun out for a few days, before coming back a week later to pitch a platform specifically for young girls of color. I referenced *Suede*, a short-lived but beloved magazine for multicultural girls who loved fashion. (I still have my copy with Alicia Keys on the cover from 2004.)

The good news: I seemed to be building a nice rapport with Anna. The not totally amazing news: she wasn't going for my brown-girl-platform idea. But she did invite me to participate in a special project with a select group of other editors from various Condé magazines, where I was the youngest person in the room. It felt like I was being groomed. For what? I wasn't quite sure. Whatever it was, by the time I finished pitching my app idea weeks later to rave reviews from Anna and the company's decision makers, I was pretty sure I had just made it past the first or second round.

A FEW MONTHS LATER, Amy, my editor-in-chief, called me at my desk:

"Hi, Elaine. Anna is here and would like to see you for a minute. Can you come to my office, please?"

She rarely called me directly. I put on my heels and speed-walked to her office.

On my way over I spotted her in a cluster with Anna in the hallway.

Anna greeted me with a rare, gracious smile, then turned to introduce me to a tall, blond, well-accessorized *Vogue* executive: "This is Elaine. We are all so proud of the work she is doing here at *Teen Vogue*. She is—*prolific.*"

Anna locked eyes with me and grinned as she said this. I smiled back, but on the inside it felt like time froze:

Wait. Did Anna Wintour just call me PROLIFIC?

"In order
to change
the stories,
you must
change the
storytellers."

CHAPTER 17

New Highs, New Lows

It looks great on the internet.

THE INTERNET

T here is power in speaking your dreams into existence. Remember back in college when I spoke mine to M. Foss for the first time, thirty thousand feet in the air? Nine years later, it seemed that career dream was about to be realized.

But turns out, it wouldn't quite play out the way I had imagined it—or as it appeared to the rest of the world.

SINCE I SHOWED UP on the scene wide-eyed in 2008, the magazine world had entered into a state of steep and steady decline—but the fall was even more precipitous by 2016. Rumors of magazine closures were whistling around the hallways of most major publications. Dwindling ad revenue and annual layoffs had become the norm; the days of big budgets and bloated salaries were over. A new editorial mandate was felt across the industry: "Do more with less." Those privileged enough to hold coveted staff positions were frazzled, overworked, and fearful of losing their jobs. And so, there was a growing tension among the old guard, who were used to following rules that were changing in a new media landscape. These were all symptoms of a larger reckoning.

The internet had completely blown up the traditional flow of information, sending every major institution into a tailspin. Social media democratized content creation, giving a free platform to fresh voices and new players who no longer relied on traditional corporate structures for legitimacy or an audience. Because publishing powerhouses were notoriously late to pivot in the years leading up to the digital revolution, a great race for relevance had begun. No one knew exactly what was next, but everyone was desperate to be a part of it. As many media brands were left to grapple with their own mortality, the industry at large found itself at a critical crossroads: reinvent or die.

Because the shrinking attention span of young readers had been captured early by newer digital properties and personalities, teen magazines were the first to drown in the sea change—*Teen People, CosmoGirl, YM, Jane,* and *Sassy,* among others, had all folded under the quake of the internet boom, leaving just *Seventeen, J-14, Nylon,* and *Teen Vogue* standing.

It was 9:03 a.m. when I received an urgent meeting request from Anna Wintour's office. I was on set for an editorial beauty shoot, wearing baggy boyfriend jeans, chunky Balenciaga combat boots, a hoodie, and the leather bomber that had become my staple early on in my *Teen Vogue* days (long before my white boots!). I knew I would have to make a quick sartorial pivot.

Anna had two offices: one at *Vogue,* and one on the forty-second floor, the corporate suite that was widely known as the sequestered space she used to discuss serious matters that required privacy. Hires and fires happened there. While rumors had been swirling for months about possible leadership changes within the organization, I had no idea what was about to go down—but since I was being summoned to the fabled forty-second floor, I suspected that it was going to be a BFD.

I hopped into a cab and raced back to the office in record time to change into a more AW-friendly outfit. Luckily, I had a white oversized Helmut Lang blazer with laser-cut lapels hanging up in my office, but I had to quickly dip into the fashion closet to complete the look. (This was perhaps the very last job perk the dwindling economy hadn't yet claimed.)

ANNA'S OFFICE WAS A stunning open space with pristine, English country–style decor and wraparound views of the southern tip of Manhattan. As I walked in, the sparkle beaming off the Hudson River that spring morning was blinding. After a brief exchange of niceties, Anna informed me that my boss would be moving on to edit another magazine in the company, and that because of the phenomenal work I had been doing at *Teen Vogue,* I would now be its new editor.

Just like that, *Boom.* I was being tapped to lead *Teen Vogue.*

My eyes didn't flinch. There wasn't a single second claimed by shock or hysteria or dread—just a rush of readiness, grounded in a deep well of gratitude. This was a job I felt called to do.

Anna peppered in a few more compliments and shared how excited everyone was about what I would bring to this role. Then her congenial tone quickly became direct as she went on to explain that in addition to building on our recent editorial success and being the new face and voice of *Teen Vogue*, I would also be charged with turning the business around. I was to work closely with the sales team to bring my "best revenue-generating ideas" to the table. This was my mandate.

After congratulating me, she mentioned that for this, I would be receiving a ten-thousand-dollar increase in pay.

I think it's fair to pause here and say that the salary offer did not seem at all commensurate with the job I was being asked to do—not even in those days of deep budget cuts and nickel-and-diming. It was even less than what some beauty directors in the building were making at the time. And a fraction of what editor-in-chiefs in that same building made. I had come into Condé Nast well below market rate—because even a discounted offer back then still offered me a massive growth opportunity, plus a ticket out of *Ebony* and into the Condé castle where my contributions could reach a wider audience. But after five years of working hard to build up a name for myself, a portfolio that spoke for itself, and a more diverse readership that expanded into new communities, I believed I was worth more. I also knew better than to launch into a salary negotiation right then and there with Anna Wintour, who, as HR had informed me during my initial beauty director hiring, "does not discuss money."

While I felt enormous gratitude for the opportunity, I also had questions. I was still processing it all when Anna slid a press release announcing my appointment in front of me and asked that I read and sign it. She informed me that it would be hitting the press at 11:00 A.M. sharp.

I looked at the clock—it was 10:11.

Not wanting to come off as ungrateful before the most respected person in the industry, but feeling leery of signing anything under these circumstances without having time to consider what was being presented, I asked if I would be able to discuss the details of the offer with HR; Anna assured me that was exactly where I was being shuttled off to next. I managed a few babbly thank-yous before I escaped to collect myself in the hallway.

In the HR office, I learned quickly that there was more to the offer than immediately met the eye. I was told only then that I'd be splitting leadership responsibilities with my colleagues—Phill, the digital director, and Marie, the creative director, who had been longtime colleagues and friends by this point—and that we were all meant to work "as a triumvirate."

Not only was this arrangement a departure from industry norms, it wasn't the job I thought I had just been offered. Questions immediately flooded my mind: What did this new leadership structure mean? How exactly was it going to work? How would it be perceived by our team, the industry, and the world outside of Condé Nast? And then, of course, the question I still can't help but ponder: *Would* any of it have gone down this way if I were a White man?

Yet there was no time to consider the offer, to address my concerns, or to negotiate my salary. The announcement was going out at 11:00 A.M.—and if I didn't accept the offer as it was delivered, I was told they would simply take my name off the press release. It became clear that my promotion was happening on their terms—or not at all.

Growing up, my mom would say that sometimes life sticks you "between a rock and a hard place." It often went right over my head back then, but on that day it rang especially true, along with another one of her momisms:

"Sometimes you just have to take the bitter with the sweet."

I had dreamed of this day since those Saturdays in Claudia's backyard, and yet there I was, all grown up but feeling less like a powerful girl boss and more like a pawn on a chessboard. And I didn't know my next move.

From the lobby I called one of my trusted advisers to ask for advice, to which I was given a hard truth: "You really don't have any leverage here." He was right.

Before getting any clear-cut answers, before I even had a chance to review a formal offer letter, the press release went out with my name on it. And by 10:59 A.M. I was standing in front of the *Teen Vogue* staff as Anna announced the new leadership team. We were each prompted to say a few words. My voice shook as I cobbled together something seemingly on script based on what I could make of the corporate narrative I was being written into. But inside, I was struggling to make sense of what had just happened.

After the announcement, I was whisked off to lunch with my two team-mates, who were giddy about the news and what it might mean for their careers, but my mind was pulled elsewhere. Yes, I was thrilled to be taking on more responsibility, and to get this opportunity at twenty-nine years old was beyond even my wildest dreams. But I felt like I had just been rail-roaded into something I didn't quite understand, without any opportunity to advocate for myself. And because I was the only one getting a title pro-motion, I knew it would cause confusion.

I sat there in a haze, unsure what to do or to say that wouldn't take away from the high my colleagues were on. Something deep down in my gut felt wrong about this setup and how it might all play out. When I started to feel suffocated by the tightening grip of anxiety, I looked up to the sky to remind myself that God has a greater plan even for the things we cannot understand.

And when I reached for my phone to text my mom the news, I was sur-prised to find hundreds of incoming messages awaiting me. My in-box and social media timelines were flooding with praise:

Celebrities like Zendaya congratulated me over Twitter. Cultural lumi-naries like Ava DuVernay chimed in with support. Streams of readers piled on with notes of appreciation and admiration. I felt like I had just entered into an alternate reality. It took me several scrolls through resounding vir-tual cheer squads to uncover how all of Black Twitter suddenly knew my name. Then I saw the source: Essence.com broke the story as a "#BlackGirl-Magic alert" with the headline: "Elaine Welteroth Named Editor-in-Chief of *Teen Vogue*, and We All Rejoice." The story called out that I was only the second African American ever to hold this title. My face then appeared in a Twitter Moment next to this headline: "*Teen Vogue* Appoints Elaine

Welteroth Youngest Editor-in-Chief in Condé Nast History." Within hours, that headline became national news.

While I was still struggling to understand what my promotion even meant, the world was applauding me for making history.

I have thought back to that moment many times and grappled with a sense of shame and even blame over how powerless I felt in what from the outside looked like the most empowered moment in my career. Even years later, it's hard to untangle one feeling from the other.

As a culture, we love a celebration. We love a first. We hold them high. We all marvel at headlines and highlight reels. But we rarely discuss the marks and scars and bruises that come with breaking through glass ceilings.

Rarely do we talk openly about the tumult of the come up, the underside of a dream realized—rarely do we share that even good things can some-times play out in complicated, painful, and confusing ways. We feel pressure to post about the joy and the gratitude and the triumph of the biggest mo-ments in our lives—promotions, graduations, engagements, marriages, even childbirth—like it's all supposed to make us feel up, up, up. And we're supposed to keep quiet about the things that don't feel so good inside. But things aren't always as they appear. And even your biggest promotions can come along with some of your most bewildering blows.

In the press, I was being held up as a symbol of progress and exalted pub-licly as a token win for diversity (again). But behind the scenes I had been asked, on the spot, to assume an ill-defined position that broke from industry standards in a manner that I felt devalued my role and put three talented people in a difficult position. I was deflated, conflicted, and woefully unsure how to navigate this.

Our new setup was being presented internally as a novel, forward-thinking remix of the traditional leadership model in media. However, given my new title, my role at the brand, and my visibility in the industry, it appeared to me—and to the public at large—that I was being asked to do the job of an editor-in-chief.

Here I was being appointed as the face and voice of a media brand that promotes diversity and feminism as key tenets. Yet this level of responsibility was being handed to me without the "chief" title, or the salary, or the office, or the autonomy that had historically came with it. I couldn't help but feel tokenized.

Of course, I was grateful for the opportunity and the outpouring of support and excitement. Externally, this was seen as a win for the culture—and in some sense, I suppose it was. There was a tribe that had been following the work and who relished finally seeing themselves in it. And now, because of my promotion, young girls of color were seeing themselves in *me.*

As validating as it can be to receive recognition for your work and to be held up as a hero by your community, under these fraught circumstances, all the attention made me feel like a fraud. Overnight, without my control or permission, I was launched into the spotlight, where I would have to navigate an awkward dual reality. I worried how that would inevitably play out for the "trio."

Hours after the announcement and the subsequent Twitter storm, I was called in by a respected female executive within the organization who urged me to "just drop it" if I was planning to revisit the topic of a salary negotiation that HR swiftly shut down moments after my meeting with Anna.

I was stunned. This was a company that published stories every day touting feminism, women's empowerment, and pay equity. This was a time when movements were quietly assembling to empower women to advocate for themselves, in the workplace specifically. Yet even inside an industry where more women are at the helm than most, I was being encouraged to do the opposite, by another woman. I couldn't help but point out the hypocrisy:

"Doesn't this seem contradictory given that this company publishes stories every day encouraging women to advocate for themselves and to negotiate their salaries?" It was a bold comeback and I worried about coming across as combative to a superior, but I felt like I needed to stand up for myself—in my most gentle tone.

"Well, how much more money did you want to ask for?" she asked.

To be honest, I had no idea how to answer her question. Of course, I had read all those stories in the work and wealth sections of women's magazines that tell us "How to land your dream job!" and "How to get the raise you deserve!" but when I was put on the spot in real life, I panicked and made the most common rookie mistake: I blurted out a number off the top of my head. My number was only marginally higher than what I was already making.

I had totally lowballed myself. With a sinking feeling in my gut, I realized she'd pass that number on to HR.

ONE LESSON I LEARNED the hard way: *Never* give your number before you're ready to. Do not allow anyone to force you into a negotiation that you haven't had time to prepare for. You can simply say, "I'd love to take the night and come back to you on that first thing." If I had someone coaching me, I would have been so much more prepared in that moment. But I wasn't. I had no coach and no idea that this happens all the time—especially to women. Even more often to young women of color.

Women are taught to work hard and to play by the rules. We are taught to never overstep, to stay in our lane, to keep our head down, to go with the flow, to never be too loud or disagreeable. Not to be bossy. Not to be pushy. We are not encouraged to know our worth, let alone to demand it. We are not given the tools to fight for ourselves or taught to challenge authority. Instead, we are taught—in subtle and overt ways—to give up our power, to take what we can get, and to be grateful. Whatever it is, whatever it takes, you just do it. And you do it well. With a smile. Whether it feels good or not. Women aren't taught to get comfortable with making people uncomfortable.

These outdated survivalist lessons have been projected onto women—and reinforced by women—for generations. But this wasn't 1950. And I was not raised to be a shrinking violet. Still, I had never confronted anything like this. I felt like I was being badgered into a corner that I didn't have the tools to fight my way out of. I felt bullied by superiors who had legitimate authority over my livelihood. The hardest part was that I *really* wanted this job. It felt like it was part of my purpose. I couldn't bear the idea of walking away prematurely. But I also couldn't imagine doing a job that encourages women and girls to advocate for themselves if I didn't have the space to advocate for myself—I believed in practicing the principles we printed.

I WENT HOME THAT NIGHT and phoned a friend—a White, wealthy, male friend who was born into the kind of privilege that comes with tools I hadn't yet inherited. In the sworn cone of silence, I shared with him what happened, and he told me to go back in to ask for exactly what I thought I was worth—even if I had given the female executive a different number, even if I thought it would sound ridiculous.

"Say it anyway," he insisted. "Stop thinking about what they'll say."

Every time I hit him with my stream of what-ifs, he remained steady:

"Do it anyway." This became my mantra as I tried to push through the mounting fear. I stayed up all night researching salary comparisons and preparing a script that attempted to maneuver around as many plausible rebuttals as I could anticipate. I just kept whispering to myself: "Do it anyway."

There are times in our lives when we can all use a good hype man. But this was different. I realized his self-assuredness was the result of years—generations even—of privilege that afforded him the leverage of walking away from any deal that wasn't to his advantage. He lived in a penthouse apartment in the West Village that his family owned, had gotten grandfathered into fancy internships at the White House, had been exposed to only the best schools, and had rubbed shoulders with the brightest since preschool. None of this is to say he had never faced hardship. But for the first time ever, I was getting to see inside the mind of someone who had only known a world where the cards were usually stacked in his favor. I was being coached into a kind of mind-set that felt foreign to me as a young Black woman, as the first in my family to graduate college, and as the youngest person ever to hold the position I was being handed—but it was critical going into my first major negotiation in corporate America. His was a confidence I couldn't learn overnight, although dammit if I wasn't going to try.

I was not a victim or a quitter. I was raised to work hard. While the circumstances of this perceived win made me feel small, I felt connected to and held up by something bigger: Remembering that I was in a position to represent for a much larger community of people that had never been recognized in this way gave me my power back when I felt powerless over my circumstances. The overwhelming support of Black Twitter and my friend's advice helped me believe I could go back in there and negotiate more favorable terms in order to keep doing the work I was put there to do. Their support gave me leverage I didn't initially think I had. Leverage I do not believe I would have had otherwise.

I slipped back into my skin that night, found my voice again, and woke up *ready* to use it.

However, I recognized the wisdom in choosing my battles. I had to decide what I was willing to "fall on my sword" for.

For me, it was a salary that gave me a sense of dignity in doing the work I was being asked to deliver—knowing that I would continue to overdeliver, as I had since I was hired. And so I went back the next day, with the strength of my entire community at my back, feeling taller walking in than I had the day before.

I managed to secure an ever-so-tiny bump in my salary. Though it was never just about the money, and a tiny bump could not resolve what would inevitably become a more complicated situation.

Being a young, Black, female leader comes with nuanced challenges under any circumstances; add to that the inevitable layer of confusion following the announcement and the duality that became mine alone to manage. However, there is no leverage like proven success. A year later, I'd eventually get everything I wanted: the official title, the corner office, a more commensurate salary.

But first I had to do the work: I had to make lemonade.

"Women aren't taught to get comfortable with making people uncomfortable."

CHAPTER 18

Lemonade

I go forth / along, and stand as ten thousand.
MAYA ANGELOU, "OUR GRANDMOTHERS"

From all of my closed-door talks over the years with successful people of color, female leaders, young innovators, and especially Black female bosses, it seems there is a universality to some of the challenges we face in the workplace.

We all come up in a world that is set up to make us feel that we are not enough— so we strive even harder to earn respect, we put in the overtime, we bend history, and we stretch ourselves thin to reach and exceed the expectations of the powers that be. We rise to every occasion. We strive for excellence. Because that is what Black women do. We take what we can get, and we make magic happen. We make lemonade.

When we achieve it, we are often told we are "too much." "Threatening." "Intimidating." "Entitled." "Bossy." We are told we "take up too much space in the room." We are asked to "tone it down." To "be grateful." I heard all of these things directed at me, either to my face or behind my back, in the stormy months leading up to and following that promotion.

The higher up we get, the more apologies we are expected to make for our power. It can feel demoralizing, exhausting, and unfair. At times, your very existence and survival in these spaces can feel like an impossibility. But the tactics used to keep us small are nothing new. For generations, women— Black women especially—have been overworked and underpaid, overlooked and underestimated.

And, to paraphrase the great Maya Angelou, still, like air, we rise.

Over the course of the next year, our teamwork spoke for itself, and when I was asked to stand on stages and accept awards—as the face, the voice, and the mind behind a movement—I did. But despite what it may have looked like on the outside, it proved to be the most difficult chapter of my career. Our internal reality quickly became mired in corporate politics; I often came home depressed and in tears. The mechanics of the early days remain blurry, as if I were moving through a thick, uninspiring fog, searching for a way to establish a new normal. Every decision was made by committee. Each step, a compromise. It was difficult for all of us, for different reasons. The goal of the setup I'm sure was for each of us to have the space to operate from our respective zones of genius. But at times it felt like we were three friends being pitted against one another. We learned quickly— the hard way—exactly why having a singular leader is the norm.

The saving grace was that our leadership team had a common vision and passion for what the future of *Teen Vogue* could be. We dug into the work. We were already off to a running start, plugging in fresh perspectives, pushing the brand into new territories, integrating the intersectional identities and interests of a new generation of young readers. We set forth on a mission to do more than just entertain; we created a platform that empowered, educated, and amplified underrepresented voices. The work that came out of *Teen Vogue* over the course of that year dramatically shifted the narrative in media.

Still, it was challenging internally, and some days it demanded a strong sense of humor to pull through: I recall arriving early to a boardroom one day as executives filed in. We were chitchatting, waiting for the meeting to begin. Finally I said, "Are we waiting for anyone else?" To which the woman next to me turned and replied, "Yes, we are waiting for the editor-in-chief." Clearly, with my big, curly hair and youthful take on executive-realness office style, I wasn't the image of a boss she had in mind.

"Oh. Great. Well, then let's get started. I am the editor of *Teen Vogue.*" I smiled back at her, letting out an easy laugh that defused the discomfort in the room.

ONE OF THE BRIGHTEST silver linings of my promotion was being welcomed in by high-profile, high-ranking female executives of color who'd all faced similar trials and slayed similar dragons. It helped put my experiences into context—I was part of a greater tapestry of women who were rewriting the rules, refusing to blend in, rising up to advocate for what they believed in, commanding respect, and not just leaning *in* but leaning *on* one another for support along the way. This was a tribe that supported each other fiercely both publicly and privately during the dark times.

FOR THE FIRST MILLION-DOLLAR deal I helped broker for *Teen Vogue,* I tapped Bozoma Saint John (aka Boz), a powerful, well-known Black female marketing executive. We had cultivated a relationship long before either of our promotions to prominent positions at zeitgeisty companies. Before our first formal meeting, where our teams would discuss a potential partnership, I met with her one-on-one for what she called a "pre-meeting."

Boz schooled me with a boisterous belly laugh. "Girl, this is what White men have been doing on the golf course for decades. Anything you need—and I mean *anything*—you can call on me."

These words were like salve at the time.

She continued. "Okay. So talk to me. What do you want to do? How can I support you? What can we do together?"

Rather than putting tiny white golf balls across sprawling green hills, we were doing a business kiki in her plush office, with fur throws, myrrh incense burning, and Jill Scott playing (turned up a little louder than elevator friendly). Not only had I never been privy to a pre-meeting, I had never borne witness to a corporate powerhouse quite like her.

Television shows, movies, and advertisements would have us believe a boss is a tall, suit-wearing White man—like the White paper Dad I selected for my preschool project. Even today, if you were to ask kids what a "boss" looks like, they might describe someone who resembles Donald Trump. Boz was refreshingly the opposite. Which makes watching her take up all the space she wants in her office, and in the world, pretty damn revolutionary.

Boz IS A CHARISMATIC, six-foot-tall, dark-skinned Black woman with extravagantly long hair; she wears red lipstick, long lashes, and her highest metallic open-toe heels to work on any given Tuesday. In a society that routinely squeezes women and people of color into constricting boxes for approval, Boz is unapologetic about doing things her own way—and she doesn't waste time being bothered by anyone else's desires for her to tone any of it down. Every flashy long nail, every figure-hugging office look, every inch on her towering heels represented a head-to-toe embodiment of a woman enjoying the freedom of bringing her authentic self to work every single day. Even through her Instagram handle @BadassBoz and her signature hashtag #WatchMeWork, she was creating space for a brand-new executive archetype—one that in turn gives the rest of us permission to bring our whole selves to work, too.

In our business negotiations, Boz's ideas were as bold as her outfits and her social media presence. She wielded her power differently than I'd seen before: She was about collaboration, not competition; innovation, not copycat ideas; genuine support, not backbiting.

She put me at ease and embraced me like a younger sister. Her leadership style was refreshing. And invigorating.

This was my colorful induction into the POC C-suite sisterhood. I felt like the Black Alice in an all-new corporate Wonderland, just taking it all in.

By the time our teams finally met, Boz and I had already aligned on the major points of the deal I had in mind. We greeted each other and let the meeting play out as if our offline kiki had never happened. She and her number two, also a Black woman, reacted positively and bolstered my ideas in the meeting. Ideas that I had a difficult time rallying support for internally. They spoke without code switching, centering our voices in a way I had never seen play out in a business setting. These were subtle gestures that redirected the power dynamics in the room. And, if only for a day, it was empowering to see those rules being rewritten by powerful Black women.

Meanwhile, in that meeting, for the first time in my career I observed the White advertising executives from my team shifting in their seats the way I used to at Ogilvy. Out came the Black vernacular, the awkwardly inserted "girl," the high fives. It was an instinct I understood, having spent much of my life and career navigating rooms in which I was the only one. Anyone who's ever worked in a male-dominated space or has experienced being the minority in the room at least once understands this pressure to fit in.

While I cringed through parts of that meeting, I walked away with more tools and some fresh insights on how race, gender, and power intersect in business.

We also left Boz's office with a major multiplatform deal in the works— my first since becoming the new editor of *Teen Vogue*.

THE NEXT DAY, THAT same colleague and I had a dinner meeting with Kenya Barris, the creator of the hit television sitcom *Black-ish*. Back when I had shared my crazy idea to build an integrated television partnership around our upcoming cover featuring Yara Shahidi, the teenage star of the show—while the rest of the room fell silent—my colleague had immediately supported me and called on one of her personal contacts to help get us the meeting. The big idea was to, hopefully, get *Teen Vogue* woven into an episode where Yara's character Zoey lands an internship at the magazine.

When my business lead and I arrived at the restaurant, I was ready to pitch the new mission and ethos of *Teen Vogue* to him: why we mattered in this cultural landscape, how—very much like the show—we were leading intergenerational conversations across racial divides. Just as I was about to whip out all the covers that demonstrated our commitment to celebrating diversity, Kenya interrupted me.

"As a Black father to three Black daughters, I just want to thank you for the work you're doing at *Teen Vogue*." I was stunned into silence. I was shocked he even knew what we were up to at *Teen Vogue*. Moments like this one reminded me that what we were doing mattered. That we were making a difference.

"I have a favor to ask you actually. I promised my daughters I'd get a selfie with you since they are mad I didn't bring them with me to meet you," he continued.

We all laughed.

When I pitched my idea, his response was "This is the easiest 'yes' I have given. Yes. Let's do this."

That meeting was a slam dunk.

We finished with a guaranteed TV integration deal with the most watched sitcom on primetime television and the promise of a million-dollar deal with one of the most powerful brand partners in the world. Kenya even invited me on the spot to appear onscreen in that *Black-ish* episode, to play myself as Zoey's boss at *Teen Vogue*—which terrified me, but it was another way to bring visibility to the brand.

We should have been popping champagne bottles. Yet on the way home, my business lead was staring straight ahead, slouching in her seat, seemingly weighed down by something.

"What's wrong?" I asked. "That meeting could not have gone better."

"This is your ticket. I saw it in their eyes," she said. "They would do anything to support you. It's just, that would never happen for a White girl like me."

I was so taken aback and confused that I asked her to come again. That this was her takeaway from our successful business trip together was baffling to me.

This was presumably her first time experiencing what it is to be the minority in a meeting, and her White fragility was already showing. It hurt most because of how close we had become and frankly how supportive she had been—especially in helping me bring this idea to life. It reminded me of that childhood slumber party, when I learned how quickly a sense of safety in a relationship could be interrupted.

In that moment I felt as though her comment had just reduced all the years of hard work I invested into building my career from scratch—and this early success in my new role that directly benefited both of us—to the color of my skin. As if she had not benefited from her fair share of race-based privilege in America throughout her entire life. As if Black people in leadership positions aren't almost always the only ones of color in decision-making rooms, working twice as hard to overcome the cultural bias that cannot be stripped from any interaction in the business world or otherwise in this country. As if I had not had to work twice as hard for the equal respect throughout my life—even now in this very seat of power that I was being asked to split three ways.

———

I MIGHT NEVER BE ABLE to adequately decode that comment, though the sentiment stung deeply. But I also couldn't allow it to slow me down. In the moment, I chose instead to bite my tongue in order to stay focused on all the positive momentum underneath us.

Ironically, when I received the *Black-ish* script for our episode, the working title was "Black Nepotism." (You can't make this stuff up.)

In the episode, we see Zoey's father, an ad exec, observing the egregious ways in which his White colleagues enjoy the benefits of nepotism. But when he finally has enough power to give his own daughter a leg up in the working world with an internship at *Teen Vogue*, he grapples with mixed feelings. When we operate the way White power has operated for generations by opening doors for our own, is it considered nepotism? Or is it just leveling the playing field?

I shot the episode and after it aired, I organized a screening and moderated a panel discussion with the show's creator, Kenya; the lead actress, Tracee Ellis Ross; and, of course, our cover girl, Yara Shahidi, to unpack the nuanced themes this episode introduced. We discussed the shifting power dynamics at play when more people of color are working their way into leadership roles than ever. With these decision-making seats, diverse leaders—like us—have an opportunity to level the playing field in a world that has for generations been rigged by the dominant power structure, which, at least until the norms change, is indisputably wealthy, White, and male.

They say art imitates life. *Would* an idea like this have been greenlit and executed with such ease if Black people had not occupied our respective decision-making seats in media? Serendipitously, our *Teen Vogue* episode of *Black-ish* had a comedic way of underlining a new seismic shift in the media zeitgeist—and some of the myopic perspectives I was grappling with in my own office.

"That is what Black women do. We take what we can get, and we make magic. We make lemonade."

CHAPTER 19

Weight of the World

To be a Negro in this country and to be relatively
conscious, is to be in a rage almost all of the time.
JAMES BALDWIN

I was asked once about my "moment of truth," the singular event in
my career that shaped my perspective or prompted me to look at
my work through a new lens. Without hesitation, my mind went
back to July 16, 2016, the morning I watched seven bullets penetrate thirty-two-year-old Philando Castile's body during a traffic
stop as his fiancée and their young daughter sat beside him in his own car.

There is something indescribable about the feeling of watching another
innocent human being get shot to death by a cop, the very people we pay to
protect us. The bloody scene was captured on Facebook Live from Philando's fiancée's mobile device and was streaming right into the safety and
comfort of my own home. After the series of police shootings targeting
Black men that had made headlines that summer, this particular murder
rocked me to my core. Since George Zimmerman's 2013 acquittal after killing
Trayvon Martin, an innocent seventeen-year-old boy in Florida, I knew if

history was any indicator, the officer who had just killed Philando would not be held accountable.

The wall I had unconsciously built up over time to shield my heart in the aftermath of stories like these—the wall that had enabled me to do my work, to read the news, to continue moving through the world without being paralyzed by sadness and rage and mourning—finally cracked. That morning I broke down: I cried for Trayvon Martin, Eric Garner, Michael Brown, Tamir Rice, Freddie Gray, Sandra Bland, Alton Sterling, and Philando. I cried for every Black mother who was living this kind of real-life horror story. I cried for my brother, my family members, my boyfriend, for every Black man and woman I loved who could end up like they had.

I also thought of my own mom, and the expression she raised me on for as long as I can remember: "Life ain't fair, baby girl. The sooner you get used to it, the better."

Philando's death unearthed the darker truths underlying these words, ones that my mother had repeated throughout my life to prepare me for a world that would not necessarily do right by me or by those I love.

I could barely get out of bed that morning. I felt wounded by this news in a way I couldn't fully explain. It was as if the weight of the world was sitting on my chest—an unavoidable pain and anger I had managed to put away for too long.

On my walk to work, still in a haze, I expected I might find a face with eyes red like mine, another body visibly shaken, or maybe even some protests breaking out. For anyone paying attention, for any feeling human, I imagined this news would have a similarly intense effect.

Instead, I arrived at the office to find it operating like it was business as usual.

Perhaps I should have been less surprised when just days after that shooting, the #AllLivesMatter debate came up at a small meeting and I found myself explaining #BlackLivesMatter to a table full of White staffers. In the midst of feeling the heartbreaking loss of these lives on a personal level, I searched for the appropriate language to capture why All Lives Matter was such an offensive, dangerous point of view, one that further endangered Black lives.

As alone as I felt in those moments, I knew I wasn't alone in those conversations. They were happening all over America—at dinner tables, on college campuses, and in other workplaces.

But that day I could no longer just push through as if it never happened or electively look away for the sake of self-preservation. I had to do something. I felt compelled to find a way to put this pain to work.

As writers, as magazine editors, as people with public platforms, we are the cultural agenda setters. We signal with our editorial decisions what the priorities are. And so I sent out an email inviting the staff to participate in a silent protest hosted on *Teen Vogue*'s social media platforms. On a stack of poster board, I wrote the letters #ITCOULDBE with a black marker and commissioned a videographer. "It could be" was a prompt to illuminate how the issue of police brutality touches each of our lives.

I WAS MOVED BY THE variety of people who showed up at the conference room that day, and seeing the different ways that they connected to this issue. Kyle, a fashion assistant, wrote #itcouldbemylittlenieces. Sue, a beauty editor, wrote #itcouldbemyidols. Ella, our digital editor, wrote #itcouldbemybestfriend. Phill wrote #itcouldbemyboyfriend. Emily, a digital beauty editor, wrote #itcouldbemycoworkers.

And every Black editor on staff—of which there were now many, including myself—wrote #itcouldbeme.

It was hard not to notice who felt compelled to participate and who did not. The silent voices were the loudest.

When I saw some of the senior White staff missing from the sign-up sheet, I visited their offices with a one-on-one invitation. "It would mean a lot if you participated in this," I said, gently encouraging them to consider what it would mean if they used their influence in a moment like this to raise awareness, to show solidarity.

Times like those, I felt most acutely that I had a responsibility to use the platform I was given to advocate for issues affecting my community.

In the days, weeks, and months that followed, I had a hard time thinking about anything but that image of Philando's lifeless, bloody body. Perhaps even more painful, I could not unhear or unsee his four-year-old daughter begging her mother to calm down so she would not get "shooted" as well. I wept for Philando as if he were my own boyfriend—because it so easily could have been.

WHEN JONATHAN, THE NERDY-GLASSES-WEARING, science-studying private-school boy I met in church choir as a teenager all those years ago, reemerged in my adult life while hunting for a job in New York City, we met up for a drink. By then, he was post–grad school at Stanford, and had grown into a broad-shouldered, beautiful man. He still had that infectious, sweet smile and skin as smooth and rich as dark chocolate—and I quickly found him to be the kindest man I had ever met.

We fell into a different kind of love. One that was sturdier, safer, and more like home than anything I'd ever experienced. At the time, I had just cut off all my hair and I was swearing off men for a while after my breakup with the older man. I was trying to focus on bettering myself, by myself. But Jonathan was unrelenting in his pursuit. Even with two blown ACLs he'd join me for long runs when I was training for my first half marathon. Even when I refused his help, he was there during my big move into my first "grown up" apartment that I was determined to live in alone. We hung out for months before we ever even kissed. And once we did, it was pure (rom-com) magic. We became official when he showed up with fruit and flowers at the finish line of my Brooklyn Half Marathon, and two years later on Christmas, he asked me to marry him.

In the days following Philando's death, I kept flashing back to the time Jonathan took out the trash in my West Village apartment. It was a hot summer night around 9:00 P.M. and he was wearing a tank top. He was not even ten feet from my doorstep, on his way back from tossing out the trash in the back of the building where the garbage receptacles were stationed, when one of the neighbors, a young White Wall Street type, came around the corner and nearly crashed into Jonathan. From inside my apartment, I heard a grown man yelp; there was an unmistakable brand of terror in his voice. My heart stopped.

I opened the door just in time to see Jonathan's arms fly up in the air, a position Black men are trained from a young age to assume to make White people less frightened of them.

"I live here. I live here. I'm not going to hurt you, man," Jonathan explained.

The man grabbed his chest, catching his breath. "Jesus. You just don't expect to see some big Black guy in here at night. You really scared the shit out of me coming around that corner like that, man."

I stood in shock at the ease with which the man rationalized his own knee-jerk racism. That he would casually excuse his racial profiling of Jonathan, insinuating that a Black man like him had no reason to be in a building like ours. That he felt no shame in blaming Jonathan for his own misplaced fear and fragility. Surely, he seemed to assume, we'd all understand his cause for concern: How dare he be Black? And in the West Village? And at night?

But the part that enraged me most—and that keeps me up at night still—is that in the moment Jonathan *excused it* and feigned empathy.

"It's all right. I get it," he said to the guy.

The thought that in 2015 in New York City a young, professional,

Ivy-educated Black man (who, at the time, still wore the biggest, geekiest glasses) was absolving some White bro for being terrified by his very existence made my stomach turn and my blood boil. It still does today.

I wanted to go after that man. I wanted to demand that he apologize to Jonathan for insinuating that he had no place there. Why was Jonathan expected to apologize for that man's terror, which under different circumstances could have resulted in the senseless loss of his own life, like so many other Black men in America? That toxic brew of White privilege and unexamined White fragility *still* makes me stew. I wish Jonathan could retract his apology.

But that isn't the world we live in. The truth is, Jonathan's response to this kind of interaction was both a learned behavior and a survival mechanism. And it was nothing new. For generations Black men have been trained to surrender, to apologize, to appear as "nonthreatening" as possible, to smile, to assimilate, to overachieve, to do whatever you can to remind White people of their humanity—but even then there are no guarantees of safety.

JONATHAN WAS ONE OF twelve Black kids in his graduating class at a private, all-boys college preparatory high school, where he was a top student and a prized point guard on the basketball team. He had already been accepted to Morehouse College on scholarship when, at an away game at a predominantly White school in a much more conservative region of California, he was wrongfully accused of throwing a rock that hit a White female student. Her family pressed charges against him.

Instead of encouraging their son to accept a plea bargain—an option that inevitably leaves so many Black boys behind bars for crimes they did not commit—Jonathan's father, one of very few Black engineers in Silicon Valley, and his mother, a registered operating room nurse, hired a top attorney. His whole community rallied around him: Each court appearance was filled with busloads of his church family, friends, and teammates, who went to support him as he defended himself. As an innocent Black boy, going up against a wealthy White family in a rigged justice system represented a faith-based roll of the dice. But it was the decision his parents made from a place of power, not just to preserve their son's future, but to represent for every innocent Black kid who didn't have the resources to fight for themselves. After a grueling nine-month battle, he won the case.

But as I witnessed that night in the West Village, much like that time in graduate school when he was stopped and frisked by cops while he was on lunch break during intensive cancer research at Stanford, this wouldn't be the last time Jonathan would have to defend his honor. For too many Black men in America, this is part of an everyday lived experience.

If this could happen to Jonathan, what about those without the education, the resources, or the power to defend themselves?

Even as the celebrated editor of a magazine, I knew there was very little separating me and my family from Philando's story.

Just weeks after being installed as the new editor of *Teen Vogue*, I was flying to visit my grandmother in Rochester for her seventieth birthday. It was a late-night flight that had been repeatedly delayed, so by the time I arrived at LaGuardia Airport, TSA was closing down and no one else was there except one male TSA officer and a nice couple who tried to convince him to let us through. The officer claimed we all arrived too late—even though we had more than an hour until our flight's revised departure time. The couple, who happened to be White, continued urging him to reconsider closing the gates on us: "How can you close before the last flight?" Finally he caved, but when I moved in to get in line with them, he stopped me and said, "Where do you think you're going?"

"What do you mean? We're on the same flight."

"No. I said *they* could go through. Not you."

Eventually, he let me through, but not without a series of snide comments.

By the time I was in the security line with all of my belongings in bins on the conveyor belt, I had enough.

When he made another rude comment, I said, "Wait. I'm sorry, what did you just say?" I was challenging him but I also carefully managed my tone to prevent the situation from escalating.

Within seconds of speaking up to him, he ordered me to get out. When I refused, he picked up the bins with all of my belongings and threw them forcefully across the room, clearing the gates. Then, from behind the conveyor belt, this tall, overweight man charged me, his eyes bulging as he pushed his broad chest against me and physically forced me out while yelling in my face, "Get out!"

As he slammed the clear door shut in front of me, the couple watched, shaken, unsure of what to do. He demanded they continue walking through security or he would make sure they wouldn't get on their flight either.

I stood there frozen, looking through tear-filled eyes at all of my personal belongings strewn across the floor. Afraid of what the man might do next in this empty airport with no one else around to check him, I called my mom. She encouraged me to hang up and call the police immediately, but before I even got the chance, two airport police officers showed up. That power-tripping TSA officer had already called them on *me*. Clearly, he had told them a very different version of the story.

As I gave them my report, I was physically shaking and barely getting the words out when one of them interrupted me and said, "Wait. I think I've seen you on TV."

The mood shifted.

"Are you famous?" the cop asked, trying to make an extraordinarily ill-timed joke.

The moment before, I was being questioned like someone who had committed a crime. And to the TSA officer, it seemed I was just another Black girl he thought he could mistreat without consequence. Now all of a sudden I was being treated with dignity and respect, when two minutes earlier I had just been stripped of both. I watched the cops' faces light up as they asked what I did for a living, and I wondered how this incident might have played out differently had they not viewed me as some sort of VIP.

SOME DAYS MY EXISTENCE felt like a bizarre paradox. I was still learning how to navigate my own new normal, one in which I could go from a meeting with Anna Wintour to being harassed and hemmed up at an airport with armed cops questioning me until one of them realized I might be famous. From getting stopped on the street by a young woman who called me her inspiration and nervously asked for a selfie, tearing up after we hugged, to my fiancé being threatened for simply existing in the West Village after dark.

Experiences like that airport incident and Jonathan's racist encounter while taking out the trash left me reeling, wondering *when does it stop?* In my experience, no amount of money, title, or education makes any difference if you are a person of color in America.

I went through all the proper procedures to file a formal complaint against the TSA officer. I even went to the airport to ask his manager to review the tapes, only to find that they had been deleted. They were apologetic, but I was told there was nothing they could do. It was my word against his.

Unsurprisingly, he was reprimanded but ultimately kept his job, with no accountability in place for his actions.

I hardly told anyone about this incident. I knew no one would understand. I was embarrassed and angry and I wasn't interested in sympathy. I wanted—and needed—to channel my frustration into effecting change through my work.

"I felt compelled to find a way to put this pain to work. As writers, as magazine editors, as people with public platforms, we are the cultural agenda setters. We signal with our editorial decisions what the priorities are."

CHAPTER 20

The Ones We've Been Waiting For

Change will not come if we wait for some other person or
if we wait for some other time. We are the ones we've been
waiting for. We are the change that we seek.

PRESIDENT BARACK OBAMA

For the first time in my adult life, young people all over the country were being ignited by political unrest that was reaching a fever pitch. The presidential run between Donald Trump and Hillary Clinton was heating up, and so many of the human rights issues our readers cared about seemed to be at stake. Up until then, there hadn't been a mainstream media platform to amplify the youth voice on these issues. *Teen Vogue* was becoming that. Story by story, issue by issue, we were working together to change what it meant to be a teen publication at a critical turning point in history.

Phill's digital strategy was laser sharp, introducing more political stories that struck a balance between hard-news reporting and analytical think pieces, stories that infused public discourse with an intelligent, empathetic youth perspective. It was the kind of journalism pundits never expected of a magazine brand that spoke directly to young people.

As the site grew, expanding into news and politics, the complexion of the newsroom became more and more diverse, as did the content. The website developed into a launching pad for award-winning content like Not Your Fault, a series led by our badass wellness editor Vera Papisova, which created a safe space online for the stories of sexual assault survivors and their allies. Her wellness vertical centered nonbinary identities and championed important conversations like consent from a progressive, sex-positive, intersectional feminist lens.

The new *Teen Vogue* was giving voice to people and perspectives that had been routinely marginalized in mass media. All without abandoning our core fashion and celebrity DNA.

That summer we photographed two young women for the cover of the December 2016 issue who I felt embodied the spirit of *Teen Vogue*'s new direction: Yara Shahidi and Rowan Blanchard. Each had become a role model and thought leader for their generation. I spent time getting to know these two remarkably astute, questioning, brilliant young women over virgin mojitos at the Four Seasons Hotel in Los Angeles. We spoke for hours around a wooden table under the LA sun, discussing this new, more inclusive era of activism, the importance of checking your own privilege, the power of representation, and what it would mean to see the first female president elected. It was poignant and edifying.

Rowan made a point that day I've thought about often and referenced many times since: "The thing about privilege is, oftentimes you don't even have to think about inequality when you don't have to face it." They might have been nearly half my age at the time, but they were wise beyond their years. I came into that conversation a fierce champion of them both, but I walked away a more enlightened human being.

In that same courtyard, I shared french fries with Chloë Grace Moretz, who studiously broke down her reasons for campaigning for presidential hopeful Hillary Clinton. We debated Clinton's policies and then seamlessly shifted into how she was balancing school and work with first love. These were the kinds of fluid conversations we wanted to have with our readers, who, we knew, were so much more than the selfie-obsessed generation many adults had written them off as.

For my first issue as editor of *Teen Vogue*, an issue that—thanks to our creative director Marie's hard work—was shot exclusively by women photographers and featured the trailblazing *Rookie* founder Tavi Gevinson on the cover, I introduced an editorial franchise called In Conversation, to host meaningful cross-generational conversations between female thought leaders of different eras. Listening in as Amandla Stenberg and Gloria Steinem discussed the intersectional fight for Black liberation and feminism was the kind of career highlight you work your whole life for.

"There is no such thing as white feminism. If it's white feminism, it doesn't exist," Gloria shared. "The world is divided between two kinds of people. The people who divide people and those who don't. And those who don't are growing in number."

At a time when our world felt more divided than ever, these were the voices and the stories that gave me hope.

THERE WAS NO PROVEN model for the seemingly radical changes we were implementing at *Teen Vogue*, and yet no one was telling us to pull back from the direction we were going in or to temper our coverage of the issues we knew mattered to our audience. But not everyone got it. Especially not right away. The staffers were all drawn in by different issues, but not everyone working at *Teen Vogue* considered themselves activists. There was a silent minority in the building, a quiet bastion of resistance to some of the more overtly liberal stands we were making. Not everyone was as eager to see us tackle topics like racism, homophobia, Islamophobia, immigration reform, police brutality, and reproductive rights. Most of us were still trying to understand the complexity of these issues for ourselves. (Remember, this was the same year that we sat around a table breaking down why #AllLivesMatter was offensive and problematic.)

I understood that sentiment, and how fear can service silence. But as I saw it, we were all in it together, in an ongoing process of waking up to how we could be better journalists, better allies, and better citizens in a world in turmoil.

WHEN DERAY MCKESSON, a modern-day civil rights activist, came to speak to the leaders of Condé Nast that same year, he said, "We are not born woke. But rather, there are moments of awakening for each of us." While the term "woke" became a defining term of 2016, I appreciated his refreshing explanation, which clarified that "wokeness" doesn't work like a light switch. You don't just turn it on and *boom*, "You're woke!" Instead, it is a process of learning, listening, stripping away the blinders that privilege puts on, and exposing yourself to suffering that doesn't always affect you in order to act from a place of understanding and empathy.

I remember thinking that was what *Teen Vogue* could be in the world; we could exist to create moments of awakening. At a critical turning point in our culture when so many of us were seeking truth and authenticity, we had an opportunity to mean more to our readers and to the world. We wanted to give a voice and an inclusive home to the most diverse and informed generation of young people in history who are smarter than they've been credited for, who care deeply about the issues of our time. By breaking down false binaries and inviting new voices to speak out on issues that matter to young people, *Teen Vogue* was becoming a media brand that validated and celebrated all aspects of their identities. This is a generation that wants to know how they can support the Black Lives Matter movement *and* learn about the best bronzers for their skin tone. Who want to be educated and not just entertained, who crave authentic representation, not just superficial tokenism. Collectively, we saw how we could expand the intersection where all of these values and interests could coexist.

OUR COVER FEATURING ROWAN and Yara holding hands with fists up fatefully hit newsstands on Election Day 2016. That image and their hopeful words took on new meaning in a moment that was, for many, clouded by defeat. Millions of people around the world—including many of our readers—were devastated by Hillary Clinton's loss and what it meant for the plight of women, girls, and people of color. It felt like an out-of-body experience, waking up to the news of Trump's win. I walked to work that morning under a thick, ominous grey sky, feeling the weight of the world even heavier on my heart. When I got in, Anna called a meeting for *Vogue* and *Teen Vogue* staffers to gather in a conference room. Many faces were red and slick with tears as she offered moving remarks that challenged us to turn this painful page together.

As much as I shared in the agony over this loss and what it signaled about the even darker days ahead of us, something else crystallized for me in that moment that I couldn't help but feel dejected by.

The sudden outcry among mostly White women in our office reminded me of the pain I'd been feeling most acutely since the tragedy of Trayvon Martin's death and George Zimmerman's acquittal in 2013, long before the streak of slain Black bodies became trending hashtags. It seemed to confirm my sense we'd been living in two different Americas all along.

BECAUSE MANY *TEEN VOGUE* readers were waking up to their own political power—whether or not they were of voting age—Trump's win ushered in an urgency to continue to use *Teen Vogue*'s platform as a vehicle to educate, enlighten, and empower.

Not long after the 2016 election, when Lauren Duca wrote a piece for TeenVogue.com titled "Trump Is Gaslighting America," which subsequently *blew up the internet*, it became proof of what we at *Teen Vogue* always knew: young people aren't afraid to call BS on an administration that abuses its power, and their voices are crucial.

Rowan and Yara's guest-edited issue that centered around youth activism was still on newsstands when Duca's on-the-pulse story went viral and became the singular tipping point that put *Teen Vogue* on the map as a serious player tackling political news. It was a watershed moment for the brand. Thanks in large part to the success of Duca's zeitgeisty piece, we sold more copies of that issue than any other that year. Within weeks, *Teen Vogue* gained supporters like Dan Rather, and Phill and I ended up on *The Daily Show with Trevor Noah*, talking about the brand's transformation. In a climate where magazine sales were plummeting, our digital traffic shot up from 2 million to 12 million and our print subscriptions suddenly jumped by triple digits, a trend that continued on through the next year as we rolled out the magazine's redesign—a collectible new size (inspired by the dimensions of an iPhone)—and a new quarterly frequency that focused on creating bigger moments around what our readers cared about the most.

This was a media phenomenon no one saw coming—not even us.

Vogue's rebellious little sister had started a fire that couldn't be stopped.

In UNDER A YEAR, *Teen Vogue* went from being seen as a cautionary tale—just another teen title doomed for defeat in a struggling economy—to a new, exemplary case study of a youth-focused, mission-driven media company that doubled down on a new direction in a politicized climate and attracted a more engaged audience. Outwardly, our team of young underdogs was undisputedly—and rather unexpectedly—killing it.

But behind the scenes there was growing division internally and a corporate culture that emboldened certain double standards that made the work environment more and more crippling over time. Despite the challenges, my MO was to just focus on the work, which we did to great success. But when I was still expected to operate in an underresourced three-headed leadership split, even after I became the only one left whose sole focus was overseeing *Teen Vogue* (the other two members of the trio had been pulled to oversee digital and creative efforts across other titles), I had enough. I loved the work and the young people I was doing it for, but I could no longer stomach making it look good to the world when it wasn't good for me inside. As a brand, we had risen to prominence for activating and empowering young women and people of color—but it became clear that we were editorializing values that were not reflected in the company culture.

ANYONE WILL TELL YOU the greatest leverage in any negotiation is a successful track record and a genuine willingness to walk away. And I was. As my discomfort within the company steadily grew, a new set of dreams beyond the Condé castle were forming inside me. It was bittersweet, but I was readying myself to walk in the direction of those dreams.

A year following my first promotion, with a brand turnaround under my belt, I went directly to Anna to thank her for the incredible opportunity. I had no intention of asking for what I, frankly, felt I had earned honestly, so instead I expressed gratitude for the chance I was given to help lead the team to success. I underlined my pride in exceeding expectations under less than ideal circumstances. But this time, without a script and without fear, I was honest with her about my daily experience navigating dual realities:

being held up as a token symbol of progress for doing a job that I was not formally empowered to do.

Then, less than twenty-four hours later, Anna had given me everything I had hoped for originally: a commensurate salary, the official editor-in-chief title, and even the big corner office that typically comes with the job of leading a magazine brand.

IT WAS A BITTERSWEET win, but a big win nonetheless. I knew it wasn't going to solve the more systemic issues at play. But what was most validating about that exchange was having the opportunity to feel seen and heard in a way I had not necessarily anticipated.

I accepted the new offer, this time under more favorable terms, because I recognized that there were still more dreams worth chasing from this post. That night, I wrote a bucket list of goals and I gave myself to the end of the year to accomplish them.

"Young people aren't afraid to call BS on an administration that abuses its power, and their voices are crucial."

CHAPTER 21

Burning Out

There is no glory in a grind that literally
grinds you down to dust.

EVE EWING

The job of an editor-in-chief is a lot like plate spinning: I was juggling a number of high-stakes editorial and experiential projects, and was busy building brand extensions that would create more revenue opportunities and hopefully help keep the lights on at the magazine, while also keeping us striving to be an industry leader.

I was successfully delivering against my mandate, and moving big, meaningful projects forward when it happened. I had already hired the very talented Rajni Jacques, my colleague from my *Glamour* days, as fashion director, and then quickly recruited Lynette Nylander, who hailed from London's cool-kid crew at *i-D*, as my deputy editor—both Black women with impressive credentials. Not because they were Black or female, but because they were the best candidates for their senior-level roles. And because we all have a responsibility to lift as we rise. They came in with fresh perspectives and an eagerness to push the new mission forward.

All the while, I was still up against ever-tightening budget constraints, a shrinking staff, and some of the same systemic issues that made work feel like an uphill battle.

As a result, I was too busy to sleep, too frazzled to eat, and TMI: I had developed a bizarre condition where I felt the urge to pee—all the time. It was so disruptive that I went to see a doctor, thinking it may have been a bladder infection.

Instead, I found myself standing on a scale in my doctor's office being chastised for accidentally dropping nine more pounds. These were precious pounds that my naturally thin frame could not afford to lose without leaving me with the kind of bony body only fashion people complimented. My mother frequently pointed out that I had become "scary skinny," which I can assure you is never intended as a compliment in the Black community. Ask many Black people what their ideal body type is and you'll likely hear the words "booty," "hips," "curves." I've dreamed of having curves my whole life, and would give anything for more "meat on my bones" to fill out my clothes.

My doctor, a young Black woman whom I had become quite fond of and developed a friendly rapport with over the years, was now asking me to explain the same thing my mother had for years: *Why couldn't I manage to keep meat on my bones?*

As she sat me down and fixed her hazel eyes on me, a concerned expression spread across her face:

"What is your average daily calorie intake?" she asked.

I was tempted to defuse the tense moment with a joke, but her deadpan expression advised otherwise.

Instead, I responded politely: "Is this an actual question? C'mon, really? Does anyone know the answer to that question?"

"We have talked about this before, Elaine. Did you ever see that nutritionist I recommended?"

Clearly I had not, otherwise I might have had my calorie-tracking note-book in tow. I spared her any slick remarks this time and simply shook my head no.

"Do you have a history of any kind of eating disorder?"

This question jarred me. I wanted to respond, "Why would I *want* to be this skinny?"

"Are you taking any illicit drugs?" she proceeded, ignoring my exasperation.

Okay, now she was really trying my nerves. My pride had already been shot, but asking me if I was a drug addict felt like an affront. Did I really look *that* unhealthy?

"I am here because I have to pee all the time," I reminded her.

"What about chronic stress? Would you say you're under any undue stress?" she queried.

"What woman in New York City is not under stress?" I shot back, buffering my indignation with a coy smile. "Of course I am stressed."

"Well, frequent, potent urges to urinate can be associated with certain types of anxiety."

"Wait. What?" My heart sank a little.

"How are things going at work?" She cocked her head, genuinely concerned.

Before she could even finish her question, my mouth started involuntarily curling, twisting into that inconvenient, uncontrollable ugly cry. My harried facade was crumbling. I was breaking down.

I COULD NOT SAY EXACTLY when it began, but I was so tightly wound that my body would visibly bounce in my office chair throughout the day. My crossed legs trembled so much under the table during meetings that they would often cause the table itself to gently quake. Colleagues had begun to take notice, too, tapping me to remind me, no longer in whispers, "Elaine, go to the bathroom."

It became a running joke around the office: "Wait, before we start this meeting, Elaine, are you sure you don't need to use the restroom? It's okay. Really. We'll wait. Nothing interesting will happen until you're back, we promise."

Everyone would laugh.

"*God!* Peeing is such a waste of time!" I'd say, only half joking, before making a mad dash out of the room. I'd hiss, "Ain't nobody got time for thissss!" as I ran around the corners of the hallway, barely making it to the stall in time.

During this time, I developed another bad habit: I'd frequently lug my lunch around all day long but never actually eat it. I went from meeting to meeting carrying a soggy biodegradable container that my assistant fetched from the cafeteria, but I never finished any of the meals inside it. My assistant and deputy editor would take turns reminding me to eat. Jonathan would stuff bananas and a breakfast sandwich in my purse before work, and would periodically call the office to ask my assistant if I had touched them. I felt like a child, helpless and incapable of satisfying my own most basic human needs: feeding and relieving myself. And now the doctor was telling me that they were not funny quirks: these were red flags.

Still, I had all kinds of excuses: I was simply too busy to eat or pee. Too busy to pay attention to my body. Too busy to breathe. There was too much coming at me. Too many people, decisions, and tasks demanding my attention. But that day, I learned that unconsciously depriving myself of food or feeling too overstimulated or too restless to eat were indicators that I was not managing my stress properly.

My mom would occasionally call to badger me. "How many times do I have to remind you that you are no good to anyone if you are not good to yourself?" she'd say to me. "You have to take care of number one, Lainey. If you don't take care of your body, it won't take care of you." The combination of losing weight so rapidly and constantly having to pee were, I learned, my body's way of telling me that my life was out of alignment; I needed to slow down.

Which explains why whenever I did make it to the restroom, you would be hard-pressed to get me out. Those bathroom breaks were the only uninterrupted moments of my day, when I could answer emails in peace, think clearly, or decompress without someone barging into my office. It is clear to me now that as a young woman who had quickly risen up the ranks, becoming responsible for the work of people who were once my peers, I was struggling with creating boundaries. I had become so engulfed in the work—and in proving myself—that taking care of myself never even made it onto the to-do list. #Selfcare sounded good in theory on the internet and in our magazine's pages, but I wasn't making it a priority in real life. By the time the daily whirlwind slowed, it would inevitably be 9:00 or 10:00 P.M., the office mostly cleared out, but I always had more to do.

The truth is I had formed these bad habits long before my time at *Teen Vogue*. I had been running myself ragged my whole life. Since those days managing the salon in Claudia's backyard, I've always been on the go, with business to handle, shit to do, big dreams to chase.

In the process, I've missed out on some precious life moments. Like the evening Barack Obama was elected to office.

THAT NOVEMBER NIGHT IN 2008, as the streets of Harlem erupted into an all-out parade that poured onto 125th Street and swelled into an impromptu block party, I was in the *Ebony* offices until after midnight, watching the news alone from my desk rather than joining my friends at the many parties popping off throughout the city. I was beaming with pride, very much feeling the weight of the moment but not the urgency to put my pages down. That kind of historic evening happens only once. Yet somehow I chose to stay in my seat, toiling away at stories on pages no one would ever remember—not even me.

Around that same time, I came home late one evening, as usual, and collapsed in tears at the dinner table, all the work I had taken home strewn around me. My peers back then praised me for "killing it," and I had accumulated enough pictures with celebrities at the ripe age of twenty-five to make my Facebook friends envious, but inside I felt empty. I had lost sight of who I was outside of work. I rarely spoke with my closest friends and family—except my mom, who never allowed me to get too far out of her reach. Thankfully, I had Offy, my roommate, who was like a younger sister to me.

That night, during my meltdown, she was my soft place to fall:

"Elaine, oh, my God. Are you okay? What is wrong? What happened?" she asked, genuinely concerned.

"All I do is work," I said. "I'm so frustrated that I don't ever have any free time, but I wouldn't even know what to do with it if I had it."

My dramatic diatribe went on and on: "I feel like I'm not even interesting when I go to these fancy work dinners—like I have nothing to say anymore. I don't know my favorite restaurant, let alone my favorite new book. Offy, you read all the time. How? I can't remember the last time I finished reading a full book!"

I erupted into the kind of sobs someone cries when they've lost someone they love.

And I had.

Myself.

I'd lost her in the day-to-day grind. In the process of becoming the woman I always wanted to be, I forgot that it involved becoming a whole person, not just the success story I had been trying to write my whole life.

Fast-forward seven years, and there I was: same situation, higher stakes. I was thirty years old, engaged, and living with Jonathan in Brooklyn. As the editor-in-chief of *Teen Vogue*, which in a tumultuous political climate had quickly amassed a cult following, young women were now stopping me in the street daily to say how much it meant to see someone like me in that role and to thank me for doing stories they could see themselves in. This was the culmination of what I was working toward my whole career, so why did it feel so fraught?

I LEARNED THE HARD WAY that there is a thin line between being a hard worker and a workaholic—someone who buries herself in work and inadvertently avoids participating in her own life. In hindsight, it is clear that I have always possessed tendencies toward the latter. What began early on as a kid's overcorrection to her parents' struggles manifested into a fear of failure that drove me into a relentless, myopic race with myself, one that had no end in sight. I found myself in a pattern of perfectionism. Always striving, even for what would ultimately prove to be futile missions—relationships that became toxic and jobs I had outgrown. When you are invested in building something you believe in, and you know there is no safety net if you fail, it is all too easy to lose perspective. It is by no means a bad thing to be ambitious, but I needed to develop healthier habits in order to be truly successful.

THROUGHOUT THIS TIME, I committed even more fully to a practice that had been giving me solace since my early twenties: meditation.

It started with an invite on group text: My friend Namik found a Groupon for an hour-long guided meditation at a decidedly unglamorous holistic center in Union Square. I'd tried to meditate many times before, and had even met and interviewed the great Deepak Chopra, but it had never really "worked" for me.

That evening, though, I went through exercises in which I let go of busy thoughts and began to connect more fully in the present. The constant hum in my mind, which so often felt like a beehive housing thousands of busy bees, was quieting. I saw the "golden light bloom into a cocoon" around me just before the meditation practitioner began describing it. When we finished, I opened my eyes feeling more clear, and with my mind quieted, centered, and more peaceful. Here at this hole-in-the-wall meditation center, I learned how to harness the power of mindfulness.

Since then, I'd been a regular.

Every Tuesday, following the thirty-minute guided meditation, I'd participate in a "healing clinic," which basically consisted of sitting still in a chair while one of the ladies who worked at the center performed "energy work" that looked like Reiki. At the end of it they would deliver a personal message that was always eerily on point.

One night, when I was twenty-six going on twenty-seven, and going through a breakup, I received a message that struck me to my core and has stayed with me through every season of my life since: *When the music changes, so must your dance.* It was the most beautifully worded truth, a profound lesson reminding me to trust my instincts, to let life guide me, and to never stay anywhere doing the same things longer than I was supposed to. It did more than just help get me through one of the hardest heartbreaks of my twenties, it would eventually help me get through my biggest professional breakup, too.

THE SUMMER LEADING UP to that humbling moment in my doctor's office, I was asked to host a discussion at Soho House in Chicago for our then cover girl Solange's website, Saint Heron. The panel was on "the plight of women artists of color and our brilliant influence on the art world despite efforts to deter our shine." The most eclectic, fly, young crowd came out to hear from genius female artists Jamila Woods, Fatimah Asghar, Safia Elhillo, and Eve Ewing.

When the topic of self-care came up, Eve, an academic, writer, and visual artist, said: "There is no glory in a grind that literally grinds you down to dust."

This hit home for me.

I was perched on a director's chair under a spotlight, looking polished and put together in an ankle-length, satin, earth-tone dress, rocking a perfect twist out and highlighted cheekbones—but I was dead behind the eyes. How could I, *how dare I*, talk to these kids about self-care and creativity? I was so tired I felt like I was in a dream state, disconnected from my words and my body. I was barely present, distracted by the burdens I had carried with me from the office more than seven hundred miles away.

There is no glory in a grind that literally grinds you down to dust.

After I left the doctor's office that day, that line was on replay in my mind. It was as if I were reconnecting with a truth I had buried.

I was burning out.

Early on in my New York life, I was asked in an interview what my career mantra was and I answered with a tongue-in-cheek paraphrase of a quote from *Crocodile Dundee* star Paul Hogan that I had found on Google: "Bite off more than you can chew and chew it as fast as you can." I stuck by that motto for years, repeating it on stages, whispering it to myself during all-nighters, doling it out as advice to mentees. I practiced what I preached, except, ironically, when it came to actual food.

I wish I could go back now and revise that *Crocodile Dundee* career motto that is still floating around on the internet with my byline. Now, at thirty-two, better advice would be: "Bite off only what you can chew. Take one bite at a time. Chew thoroughly. Swallow fully. Breathe. Make room for the next bite. Find time to laugh. It's better for digestion."

Not as pithy, I know. But this is the mind-set of a marathoner, the pace of someone who understands the difference between a sprint toward short-term wins and the stamina required for long-term success. Growing a sustainable career that withstands the test of time requires consistent energy that builds momentum over time. But when you have been running nonstop on a hamster wheel toward a goal with blinders on, you might not know how to slow down, let alone get off. Even when you need to.

But your body and soul have a way of telling you when the music is changing.

I have always had a hard time letting go of things, whether it's my stubborn habit of attempting to reseal a chipped nail with a top coat or allowing boyfriends who've gone bad to linger like leftover food in my fridge. It is perhaps the downside of being born with will like steel. But one of the things turning thirty taught me was that there is hustle and there is flow; and you cannot successfully achieve one without the other.

"There is hustle and there is flow, and you cannot successfully achieve one without the other."

CHAPTER 22

End of an Era

Crises are nature's way of forcing change—breaking down old
structures, shaking loose negative habits so that something
new and better can take their place.

SUSAN L. TAYLOR

W e were a month out from our very first *Teen Vogue*
Summit—a dream project of mine that was nearly
sold out. The idea was to create an interactive safe
space for the incredible, like-minded young activists,
creators, and innovators who had formed a commu-
nity online around our new mission. It wasn't about just sitting in the audience and listening to high-profile people talk at them for an hour or two.
The vision was to bring them together in real life for an immersive experience to meet one another, build important connections, and be inspired by
women they looked up to. I wanted to host meet-ups all over the country in
smaller markets as drumbeats that culminated in a large-scale, weekend-
long event in Los Angeles, one that would include off-site career excursions,

scholarship opportunities, mentor sessions, interactive group breakouts, and intergenerational keynote conversations with their sheroes. The whole team was excited about it.

We were also days away from announcing a special issue guest-edited by Hillary Clinton, which we had been working tirelessly on for months. It was a project for which we had commissioned pieces from esteemed feminist writers like Gloria Steinem and Roxane Gay, as well as organized a historic roundtable with the would-be first female president in conversation with five of the brightest young women from our 21 Under 21 list (Phill had dreamed up this list as a way to recognize young changemakers across industries).

Meanwhile, the understaffed digital team was juggling even more demanding daily deadlines and continuing to crank out smart political stories for the website that kept *Teen Vogue* in headlines. (One particularly controversial sex-ed piece written by wellness editor Vera Papisova earned us a literal roast from an outspoken anti-LGBTQ, conservative Christian fundamentalist YouTuber called Activist Mommy, who burned *Teen Vogue* magazines at the stake—literally—in an actual firepit on a video that was watched by millions. A perceived win for us all.)

We were on a roll: Our sales team had also just come to terms on a multimillion-dollar deal that enabled us to publish a bonus issue in partnership with a single major advertiser—the kind of sweet deal that hadn't happened since print's glory days. I had just secured a lucrative book deal for the brand. We were in the final stages of design just before rolling out a merch line in a partnership that I had forged with Urban Outfitters. We were in development on a first-of-its-kind social-only content platform with Nike—the list goes on and on.

ONE OMINOUS FALL DAY, not long after I went to see my doctor, I was in the office prepping for a big meeting where I would be presenting my vision for the future of *Teen Vogue* to the Condé Nast executive team. Originally, this meeting was intended to serve as a topline overview of big ideas—not tied to numbers, no revenue projections, no specific strategies, "just keep it focused on the big ideas," I was told. And so I did.

Just two days before the presentation, I was called into a very brief confidential meeting with higher-ups where I was informed that the CEO was intent on closing the magazine, and it would be wise to prepare a profitable road map for a digital-only business.

The news was delivered to me as a matter of fact, stripped of emotion or any explanation. This was not a conversation—this was simply a last-minute heads-up to pivot the direction of my vision for *Teen Vogue*. As the leader of the brand, deep in the weeds of running the day-to-day and intimately connected to the audience we had galvanized, I knew on a gut level that pulling the plug on the magazine this abruptly after a year of record growth and with promising new ventures on the horizon was ill advised. From my perspective, there was too much at stake, and it would send a counterintuitive message to the marketplace after all the momentum we had amassed, particularly during a time of great decline across the rest of the publications. I didn't believe it was the right decision.

Instead of pivoting on a couple of days' notice to craft a pitch I didn't believe in, I decided I would go in there with a clear-eyed approach to put up a fight for what I did believe in—even if it was a losing battle.

As a wise New York City black-car driver and former military vet once told me, sometimes there is more honor in losing a battle with dignity than in winning a war without it. I armed myself with levelheaded conviction, logical strategy, and the best revenue projections I could muster last minute.

Despite the mixed messages I had been given leading up to the big meeting, I headed in optimistic, but with a stiff upper lip, intent on making my objectives clear. As I stood in front of an all-White, mostly male executive team in a sterile boardroom, I presented a roll-off strategy for print that was less abrupt and allowed time for the brand extensions to grow into stronger bases for the business. As I laid out my case, Anna spoke up in my defense: "I think what Elaine is proposing makes a lot of sense."

Still, the already chilly atmosphere turned ominous. There was firm resistance to any notion of keeping the magazine going for any amount of time. As the meeting neared the end, I leaned forward, steadying myself on the chair at the head of the table, and locked eyes with the CEO. I took a deep breath, and went in for one final push:

"If the company is not prepared to invest in the future of *Teen Vogue*, would you consider allowing me to help find an investor who is?"

It was a bold move, especially in that setting. "Condé Nast would retain majority stake, but this way we can secure capital to ensure the brand's future and sustain its growth," I continued.

"Thank you. But no," he huffed. "I will not be selling any part of a brand with *Vogue* in its name."

And so it went. My hopes for *Teen Vogue* were dashed. But my larger goals were called into focus. I had left it all on the field, as they say. No one could say I didn't. I could walk out of that room with my head up high.

I BELIEVED IN WHAT WE had built. I believed in our mission. Our team had done what no other editorial team had before and in record time. During a critical turning point in our world, one where young people were rising up and using their voices to advocate for human rights issues that affected them and their communities, *Teen Vogue* was changing the narrative and providing a platform to elevate perspectives that had previously been pushed to the margins by mainstream media. We delivered on a progressive vision for what this brand could come to mean in a splintered world.

I loved and nurtured *Teen Vogue* and was proud to have helped usher it into a new era. I was proud of the whole team. But I also saw the limitations within Condé Nast. And I felt called to do more—outside of those walls, beyond just this one media brand.

Teen Vogue had put me squarely on the path to pursue new dreams. After the *Black-ish* episode, I seized the opportunity to moonlight as a TV writer and I cowrote an episode of *Grown-ish*. I had top agents from two major talent agencies circling. Before there was any talk of print closing, I already had a whiteboard in my office filled with new goals and big ideas that I was talking to my inner circle about—ideas that included testing the waters beyond Condé Nast. Deep down, it was almost like the decision to close the magazine was divine confirmation that it was time for me to step out on faith and to turn the page on this chapter of my career.

But Condé Nast and Anna presented me with offers to stay, and even a chance to create my own role within the company; they were enticing opportunities that were worth considering.

The good news: while it was sad to let go of the magazine, I had options. It was up to me to decide which direction to go in. At least I had time to figure it all out. I was assured no announcements would be made about the closure before the *Teen Vogue* Summit, which was now in less than thirty days.

THE BAD NEWS WAS I still had to pee. All. The. Time. And I was sure that the extra-added pressure of the imminent magazine closure and not being able to share this news with my staff was making my anxiety more acute. My doctor recommended going back in for tests.

It was 8:00 A.M., and I was lying on my back in an unflattering baby-blue paper smock, peering down at my signature white boots in stirrups while a cold, metal object was taking snapshots of my cervix.

Just then, my *Teen Vogue* Google Alert went off on my phone: *TEEN VOGUE SHUTTERS*.

I was spread-eagled and shivering, holding my iPhone close to my face. I had been assured this news would not become public until after the Summit and that I would be able to deliver it to my team on my own terms. But somehow it leaked early.

I closed my eyes and thought about the people on my team who were also reading this—and how confused and panicked they'd be about what it might mean for their own budding careers. I thought about the readers who were rooting for and empowered by the brand's radical reinvention. The rumor mill that was already speculating that I might be taking over *Glamour*, a magazine I loved but that I had no interest in returning to.

Tweets were already popping off in my timeline, questioning how the only turnaround teen title making big waves and gaining momentum with progressive messages in a politicized climate could, at its height, be closing. Magazine lovers saw it as just another casualty in a losing battle for print. Media insiders viewed it as a natural progression for a youth-focused media company in the digital age.

For me, it represented the death of a dream.

Oprah says the hardest thing about breaking up is never just the end itself. It is the death of the dream. Whether it's a promising romantic relationship, a cherished friendship, or a dream job, in the end, you can't help but daydream about the *if onlys* and *what-ifs*. You mourn what *could have* been, until you are forced to confront what it is: over.

At that moment I had to let go—of the false notion that I could control how life unfolds, of the belief that I could somehow prevent my team and the dedicated readers from feeling let down. I surrendered to the God that had gotten me this far. To whatever lesson I could only learn this way—on my back, shivering in a paper smock.

On the other side of fear is freedom—but you have to be willing to look it in the face.

During the taxi ride back to the office, feeling fragile but somehow steadier, clearer, and more present than I had in months, I called home. I was expecting to hear my mom's voice, but instead my dad picked up.

"Heya, Lainey," he said. "Mom filled me in on what's going on on the work front. I wanted to tell you: don't let them beat you down with all that bullshit. It is the kind of thing that could break a person. It happened to me at Lockheed, and it ain't worth it. So don't you let them take away that smile. Know that your ol' dad is here praying his ass off for you, okay?"

I hadn't quite realized until I heard his familiar deep baritone voice that this was one of those rare times in my adult life that I needed my dad.

I needed to hear him say it would all be okay. That they were all assholes who didn't know a good thing when they had it (even if it wasn't that simple). That I could always come home if I wanted to (not that I ever would). That I had a light in me I could not let them dim. That I had a family that was so proud of me they could hardly stand it. And that he couldn't wait to see me for Thanksgiving. The simplicity of those words was the grounding I needed in one of the most destabilizing moments in my career.

When I finally reached Condé Nast, instead of entering the building, I perched myself on the edge of a concrete bench near the perimeter of the 9/11 memorial fountain facing the front doors of my office. And I did what I always do whenever life lets me down: I looked up at the same blue sky that stretched past the shiny high-rise tower, and into the clouds that promised it would get better. I trusted that there was so much more than this for me.

I made an executive decision that I would not enter the building until I could address my team about the news directly. I called Condé Nast's corporate communications, and was told "It's a leak. It has not been confirmed. For now, it is business as usual."

But I could not just stride into my corner office and pretend that I didn't notice the confusion that would surely be teeming from every cubicle outside my door. I knew every move I made would be read into by the staff for clues of their fate. Anything I did would be reinterpreted and regurgitated by the rumor mill, which was already running amok. I'd had enough of the rumors. And I had finally had enough of outside circumstances dictating my moves. I needed to find a way to reclaim my agency in an uncontrollable circumstance. After that kind of news leak, it wasn't business as usual for any of us, and I wasn't going to pretend that it was.

From the concrete slab outside the office, I made my point of view clear on calls with the powers that be, until a second story went out—this time with the CEO unexpectedly confirming the news. We were finally all in agreement that there was nothing left to hide behind.

It was go time.

I asked my office to send out a staff meeting announcement, and before I knew it the conference room had quickly filled up with frightened faces. Instead of reading from the corporate script, I chose to craft my own. There was no reason to follow the rules, rules I had spent the better part of my career rewriting.

The words I expressed in front of my team exist now only in hazy recollections, on some piece of scrap paper I've since lost, and in the memories of those who were there pressed up against one another in that conference room. Whatever I said was delivered with sincerity and landed in a way that left a hushed silence hovering in the air.

That is, until, thankfully, our longtime creative director, Marie, who I considered my comrade, sliced right through it with a misguided champagne pop. The cork screeched through the air, making a staffer duck.

Marie had often waxed poetic about what she viewed as my uncanny ability to speak confidently in front of crowds, but the truth is I always admired her—not just for being insanely good at her job, but for being the kind of partner who could take the piss out of people and cut through tense moments like these with a well-placed joke. Or in this case, a champagne plug. I felt grateful to have her by my side through that moment—through it all.

Suddenly, shitty news aside, there we were again, sipping champagne from red cups, procrastinating on getting back to work. Condé's young, motley crew partying 'til the wheels fell off, just as we had done so many times throughout the bumpy, exhilarating ride.

It turns out it wasn't the end of anything, but just another twist and turn on the journey. We didn't necessarily know what was ahead, but for everyone in that cramped conference room, it was the start of a new beginning.

"There is
more honor in
losing a battle
with dignity than
in winning a war
without it."

CHAPTER 23

A Dream Realized

Nobody tells you what to do when your girlhood
dreams bump into your womanhood dreams.

CLEO WADE

In the days leading up to the *Teen Vogue* Summit, I was excited but also queasy from all the unanswered questions in my mind about the future. So many of my professional and personal dreams had been realized in record time, and yet I found myself still mourning the death of the dream that I had for the future of *Teen Vogue*. I'd just delivered the notice to my team about impending layoffs, and while it was made clear to me that Condé Nast wanted me to stay at the company, I had mixed feelings about that, too.

As flattering as it was to have Anna Wintour, of all people, essentially offer me the chance to write my own job description for a new venture that we were now knee-deep in conversations about, once the idea was greenlit by the company, something just didn't feel right. I felt paralyzed rather than motivated. With the demise of the magazine came a growing sense of completion, a restless readiness to expand and explore beyond the four walls of the Condé castle.

I had been operating for nearly a decade inside the confines of a corporate structure that was shrinking and constantly restructuring to manage its decline. It had become soul crushing. Ultimately, I decided that if I was to stay, in any capacity, I would prefer to move into a contract role that allowed me the freedom to take on outside projects as well.

Anna generously gave me her blessing. "I just want you to feel good about this, Elaine. Remember, I want you thinking big."

I had no shortage of opportunities in front of me, inside and outside Condé Nast, but absolutely no clarity on what step to take. It wasn't easy weighing my options while preparing to stand on the biggest millennial-pink stage of my career for an event franchise I willed into existence with my incredible team. It wasn't easy knowing I was considering walking away from that powerful platform for good.

So, unsurprisingly, the stress of those weeks leading up to the Summit took a toll: I wound up in my hotel bed with a 104-degree fever and a throat so sore it hurt to speak. I could hardly lift my head off the pillow.

One of the agents I had met at CAA, Christy Haubegger, sent two cartons of hot soup to my hotel room, along with a plethora of immunity-boosting juices. It was the kindest gesture, given my immune system was as jacked up as my state of mind.

Once my fever broke, I dragged myself to the Soho House to meet her for dinner, hoping it'd help generate some semblance of clarity on my next best career move. We had been introduced by a close mutual friend, another woman of color executive and a power player who knew the professional crossroads I was at. That dinner felt less like a traditional agent meeting and more like one successful woman extending herself as a resource to another. While there was an undertone of potentially doing business together, she was also coming to me as an adviser and friend.

"Oh, honey. Well, at least you look pretty good for feeling so terrible," she teased. "Don't worry about doing the whole entertaining-me thing—I'll do all the talking. Okay? We need to get you back in bed ASAP."

It was precisely what I needed. While I was wrapped up like a fever-stricken pig in a blanket, sipping hot tea with ginger, overlooking the twinkling nighttime majesty of Hollywood's rolling hills, Christy hooked me with the first line of her career story: "So, the way I see it: there is work, and then there is your life's work. My goal was to build my life around the latter."

She went on, sharing gems from her own transition from the magazine world to Hollywood, first as a film producer, then as a high-powered agent who had infiltrated the system specifically to bring the sorely underrepresented Latin perspective to the masses. It was the same mission that had led her to start *Latina* magazine years prior. As the founder of the first and only national magazine brand for Latinx women, Christy is a true trailblazer. A Mexican American woman who got her law degree but found the work soulless, Christy became increasingly frustrated with the lack of representation for her community in mass media, a frustration that pushed her to take a major bet on herself and her community. It led her to start *Latina*, which she grew and then sold before heading to Hollywood to help nurture the careers of some of today's most in-demand Latin artists, including Jennifer Lopez, Eva Longoria, and America Ferrera.

Christy's trajectory was yet another inspiring, real-life example of a successful woman of color who, like Harriette, used her gifts to carve an inspiring career path that was connected to a greater purpose. And, like Harriette, Christy arrived in my life at precisely the right moment.

It was the kind of pep talk I needed.

I still didn't know what I was going to do next, yet after talking with Christy, I knew I was on the right path.

But first I had to get my butt to the Summit.

DAY ONE OF THE Summit went off without a hitch. I felt energized by every single one of the more than five hundred *Teen Vogue* readers I met who had traveled from all over the world to be there. I kicked off the morning onstage rallying the inspiring tribe of young changemakers to announce themselves—as artists, as activists, as innovators. Then everyone was dispatched to assigned shuttle buses that were waiting to take them inside a range of companies in the LA area—from Facebook to Netflix—where they could meet female executives and see the inner workings of how business gets done behind the scenes. In the evening, we heard from all twenty-one of our 21 Under 21 rising stars, who were appointed to our annual list for making a positive impact on the world through STEM, the arts, and activism. After months of nurturing a strong relationship with Toms, the social impact shoe company, I joined CEO Blake Mycoskie onstage to announce that they were generously offering surprise scholarships to five girls in the audience, totaling a hundred thousand dollars.

It was the kind of day that reacquainted me with my Why.

Just when I thought nothing could get me down off that high, I was pulled into an urgent meeting with a small roomful of Condé Nast's execs and the public relations team. They informed me that two big interviews had been lined up for the next day: *The New York Times* and the *Los Angeles Times*. "The reporters might ask about what your plans are now that the magazine is closing," someone said.

My body immediately tensed up. They were putting the pressure on, urging me to commit to staying on with the company and to announce the venture that had not yet been adequately fleshed out.

"I'm sorry, but we are not in a position to announce that *tomorrow*," I said plainly. "How could we? We haven't worked through any of those details. I don't even have a contract yet."

By then I was savvy enough to advocate for myself. Thankfully, I had also collected a stellar lineup of advisers—including a powerful lawyer who I would learn to lean on more and more as this unfolded. She's the only Black female attorney with her own firm in Hollywood. And a total badass.

That night, I talked through my options with what would later become my all all-female team. They made it very clear that their unanimous vote was for me to walk away from Condé Nast, for good.

I was then left alone in my hotel room to wrestle with my thoughts.

It was the night before day two, the pinnacle of the Summit, and I was restless. I tossed and turned in my king-size bed before waking up at 3:00 A.M. drenched in sweat and swimming in uncertainty.

I called Jonathan, the only other person (besides my mother) I knew I could call in the middle of the night and who had been by my side throughout all of it. As soon as he picked up, I broke down crying, so hard that I couldn't speak.

"I was supposed to know by now," I eventually managed to say.

In true Jonathan form, he got all scriptural on me, affirming that I was in a storm but reminding me that it is always darkest before dawn.

"Sometimes it takes reaching the summit to see what's on the other side," he said. I swear this man of mine is like an old sage wizard, even at three in the morning. I still do not know how he conjured up coherent sentences at that ungodly hour, let alone this kind of deep, off-the-cuff poetic advice. All I know was that I immediately felt more at ease.

This was the effect he had on me from day one. This was the difference between the adrenaline of puppy love and the chaos of chasing what seems right on paper. *This* was real love. Real love that wakes up in the darkest part of the night to redirect you toward the light. Real love that calms every roaring wave inside you with a certain steadfast grace, powerful enough to remind you of your own strength.

Thankfully, I was able to fall back asleep. I woke up a few hours later to the most beautiful sunrise and a renewed sense of peace. I felt buoyant and grateful, and even though I still didn't know what I was going to do next, I knew somehow with certainty that everything was going to be okay.

MY MOM DECIDED ON a whim to fly down last-minute to be there for the Summit. I was already backstage blowing my nose and getting miked when

I heard her voice. She was holding court in the greenroom with all of the VIPs, many of whom were my personal friends. Her infectious laugh injected a shot of joy into everyone in her path—but no one needed it more than me. Just feeling her energy and hearing her voice made me feel like everything was right in the world.

She came charging around the corner where I was tucked away, prepping for my speech. "Look at my baby!" There was no stopping an enthusiastic mother intent on laying her eyes on her (grown-up) child before a big moment.

"Girl, this dress is the one, okay?!" She reached for my waist, which was belted tightly into a leather, millennial-pink Proenza Schouler dress, and threw her head back, letting out a joyful squeal: "You look marvelous, darling!" Then she winked and leaned in close, feigning a whisper: "I see all those balled-up tissues up in here. But hey, at least no one would know you were laid up in bed for the last four days looking like who done it and what for!"

Some things never change.

My mom was the only one in the whole world who knew how far I'd come—from the chatty three-year-old pageant princess to the stressed-out thirty-year-old wreck of a woman crying my eyes out in bed with a fever just three days earlier. Now, here we were, in a defining moment of my career. I was back on my feet, polished and put together, finally feeling like I was in charge of my life again.

She was the one holding my hand and cheering me on every single step of the way. As together as I felt, I know I never would have made it this far without her. (Corny jokes and all.)

She pulled me in for another tight hug. Then our mother-daughter moment was interrupted by a firm grip on my arm.

"Elaine, the secretary is here and would like to say hello."

My mom's eyes bulged as she covered her mouth in disbelief.

Hillary Clinton was on the premises.

Secretary Clinton and I had met recently in New York City on the set of her *Teen Vogue* shoot. Her saying yes to guest-editing that issue was one of my biggest career goals come true. During that session, we captured the secretary in conversation with five young women from our 21 Under 21 list of girls changing the world. Instead of delivering a conventional image for the cover, Marie suggested we create a collage of Clinton's face, spliced with a subversive depiction of the American flag. It was young, rebellious, and unapologetically political. We did not know when we designed it that it would be the last newsstand cover of *Teen Vogue* magazine in its print iteration. But it made a damn good curtain call.

That day at the Summit, Hillary Clinton greeted me with a warm embrace, and I thanked her for being there. It had taken months of back-and-forth and navigating through uncertainty before arriving at a firm yes from her team. But there she was, our keynote speaker, in a teal print suit by Argent, ready to kick off our Summit from the main stage.

A nearby photographer who, like every other body backstage, had to get Secret Service clearance, snapped photos. As we did our step and repeat poses, Secretary Clinton leaned in close and whispered, "I can't wait to hear what's next for you." I was genuinely caught off guard. I can't recall what I said in response, only that it was met with a wink and affirming nod from her, followed by:

"I'd love to sit down with you and talk with you some more after all of this. I'll talk to my team and make sure that happens. Let's be sure to stay in touch."

It wasn't even 9:00 A.M. and I was already having a surreal exchange with Hillary Clinton.

I ushered my mom over to say hello—Lord knows what that woman talked to the secretary about, but they were belly laughing and holding both hands in all of their pictures together.

Then the exquisite Yara Shahidi and her mother arrived. Yara was wearing a structural lime-green sweatshirt and studiously holding a clipboard filled with questions for Secretary Clinton that she had written herself. She beamed from ear to ear and spoke a mile a minute about how she had just finished

James Baldwin's *The Fire Next Time* and stayed up cramming to prepare for this interview. She claimed she was a nervous wreck, but it didn't show one bit.

Yara's meteoric career trajectory from playing the sassy teenage daughter on *Black-ish* to a real-life activist, thought leader, and voice of her generation had run parallel to *Teen Vogue*'s recent ascent. They seemed in some ways inextricably connected. Her voice, like *Teen Vogue*'s, had awakened the world to the power of young people at a critical time in history. The *Teen Vogue* cover that we had shot together over a year ago—which was her first major American cover and just the first of many to come in a career that was quickly blooming—reflected a sense of hope we all so desperately needed. And now, Yara was moments away from taking the *Teen Vogue* stage to represent on behalf of Gen Z in an exclusive conversation with the would-be first female president of the United States herself.

I had the honor of introducing them and couldn't wait to listen in.

When it was go time, I said a quick prayer and marched out to the stage to greet the hundreds of girls who had come to participate in what felt more like a movement than a live event. What had all started as a line item on my career bucket list was now a beautiful reality. I walked onstage to roars, applause, and high-pitched cheers, and stood in awe, feeling that I was living in total alignment with my purpose.

In that moment, I was all flow.

All of the seeds I had planted, everything I had been striving for, all I envisioned this brand to be—*this* was the perfect culmination of all of that, and then some. I could walk off that platform knowing for sure I had done what I came here to do.

LATER IN THE DAY, the film and TV director Ava DuVernay arrived in all of her glory. Her presence is a power all unto its own. A year back, someone had asked me, "Where do you see yourself in five years?" I told them, "My next dream is to work with Ava DuVernay one day—in any capacity." I was only semijoking when I said, "I would seriously pay to intern for her."

Ava's work was waking up America. I was spellbound by *13th*, her hard-hitting documentary that tracked the roots of mass incarceration and the prison-industrial complex back to a loophole in the Thirteenth Amendment, which rendered the abolishment of slavery as a conditional freedom rather than an absolute human right. The film's raw, journalistic approach to truth telling was what we needed, not only to unpack how we got here, but to feel and create our way forward.

So when we got the news that Ava had agreed to be on a Summit panel with Rowan Blanchard and Storm Reid, the stars of her forthcoming film *A Wrinkle in Time*, I told my team that we wouldn't need to find a moderator: "I got that one!" Having my own personal career icon show up and work her magic on this crowd of young people eager for inspiration brought me so much joy. Onstage we talked about redefining mentorship and using your art as activism; and then Rowan, Storm, and I collectively fangirled over Ava.

OUR FINAL KEYNOTE SPEAKER was the honorable Maxine Waters, California's progressive senator, known endearingly to liberal millennials and Gen Z as "Auntie Maxine." Backstage, she was doling out hugs and boomerangs before taking center stage with actress and activist Amandla Stenberg. By the end, the young, politically charged crowd was riveted, chanting along with her: "Impeach Forty-five!"

These intergenerational conversations had become a central feature of the magazine under my editorship. Bringing that to life onstage, and looking out of the sea of completely enraptured faces, connecting with their heroes, was a total dream come true.

AT ONE POINT IN THE AFTERNOON, I was around the back corner of the building when I heard someone calling my name. I turned around and saw Ava DuVernay waving her arms in the air and smiling. She was on her way to her car after her panel and just so happened to spot me.

"Girl, what are they doing with the magazine? And why?" she hollered at me from across the parking lot. "More importantly, what are *you* doing? And how can I be down?"

I laughed in disbelief. My shero was asking *me* how *she* could be down. I seized the moment. "Yooo. I'm the one trying to be down. Let's do coffee!"

"Coffee? Girl, come on over to my house. Imma cook you a meal."

"Are you serious?" I responded, no chill whatsoever.

"Yes, I'm serious! You're in LA often, right? Ask Rowan to connect us and come over next time you're in town."

I managed to play it relatively cool, but inside I was geeking out. When your career idol invites you over for dinner, you don't wait until you find yourself in the neighborhood; you plan your next trip back *just* to make it happen.

THE EVENT ENDED THAT evening with the illustrious Rupi Kaur reciting poetry from a glowing outdoor stage to a rapt audience beneath a pitch-black sky. Those of us left in the audience were wrapped up in blankets, lounging on bean bags with new friends, now joined together under the stars. A poetic ending to a perfect day.

It was the mic-drop moment of my entire career to date.

A DREAM REALIZED

AFTER I SAID ALL my thank-yous, gave all my hugs, and collected all my boomerangs, my mom snatched me up to go get dinner. We piled into a car and drove up a series of dark, windy Hollywood roads.

Normally I would have questioned where we were going, but I was too lost in thought reflecting on a day that meant more to me than anyone even knew. Then the car stopped outside a huge white gate, in front of a beautiful Hollywood home tucked away in shrubs. When I saw my girlfriend Aurora James, a designer who had spoken at the Summit earlier that day, emerge with a sneaky smile, I assumed she had planned a small dinner for me and I was so touched.

"Wow! You really got me," I said, thinking a couple of my closest friends might be inside.

As I made my way up the steep hill, staggering in unsteady heels, I saw a mansion lit up on a cliff with a massive pool in place of a front lawn.

"Wait, what is this?" I was so confused. "Whose house is this? Do I know them?"

Right then, the gate swung open and an unexpected roar rattled me: "SURPRISE!!!"

Familiar faces were lining the upper and lower levels of the terrace, smiling and cheering. There was Rowan and Yara standing beside Beyoncé's ingenues Chloe x Halle, the sister act who had performed at the Summit earlier in the day. There was Cleo Wade, one of my close friends and a poet who had collaborated with me for our very first experiential issue launched the year prior. There was the activist DeRay Mckesson, whom I'd commissioned to write a heartbreaking love letter to Jordan Edwards, a fifteen-year-old Black boy shot by the police in Balch Springs, Texas. I spotted the original Girlboss, Sophia Amoruso, who had opened up the doors of her HQ to young *Teen Vogue* fans during the career excursion on day one. There was Amani Al-Khatahtbeh from *Muslim Girl*, who we had tapped at *Teen Vogue* as an expert on issues that directly impact Muslim communities. There was Nadia, the best gift Ex–Future Husband gave me; after we split ways, she stood by me and helped me navigate every hurdle in my career since. Then among many more familiar faces I saw Rajni and Lynette, my sister-circle at *Teen Vogue*—and I was overcome with emotion.

Every single person there was an inspiration to me and had contributed in special ways to my time at *Teen Vogue*, as an ally, a coconspirer, or a dear friend. And they were all there to celebrate with me.

I imagine some of them might have thought they were there to toast the Summit's massive success, knowing that I had toiled over it for months. Others assumed they were there to celebrate my birthday, which was just days away. Only I—and a handful of my closest confidantes—knew that this moment was much bigger than both to me.

As the music blared and the beat dropped, my mom trailed behind me, squealing, and more and more of my people's faces came into focus. Then Aurora, who had secretly planned the entire thing, handed me a shot, and everyone cheered. I raised the glass to the crowd and thought, "This is how you end an era."

Not curled up in a ball crying.

Not giving away my power by laboring over my next move.

Inside, a candlelit seated dinner awaited. There were three or four rows of long, narrow wooden tables with jewel-toned, embellished pillows for seats—framed by 360-degree floor-to-ceiling windows overlooking LA. The night sky was all lit up. Everywhere I looked there was somebody I loved.

After dinner, Aurora made a heartfelt toast. Still holding up her glass, she asked: "Who else wants to say something?" Silence. No one moved. I reached for the mic to let everyone off the hook with a joke about how no one needed to say anything more because they already had me out here feeling like the Black LC (Lauren Conrad), only this time on the final episode of *The Hills.*

Then out of the corner of my eye I saw Amandla Stenberg stand up. She talked about what being on the *Teen Vogue* cover meant for her personally and professionally. It had opened up new doors by allowing the world to see her in a new light. "You allowing me to see myself so authentically gave me permission to be myself. What you've done for all of us is so powerful."

As she sat back down, rejoining a table full of the new young Hollywood, brown girls, queer girls, smart girls—one by one, people I adored, admired, and respected rose to speak.

Rowan was too shy to grab the mic, but shared with me in a private moment: "I'm looking around, and I'm recognizing that all of these friendships I've made in this crazy Hollywood world are through you and because of *Teen Vogue.* I met them on a *Teen Vogue* shoot or at a *Teen Vogue* event. And I was on the cover because of you. My identity has been celebrated because of you. And now I feel so lucky that you're like a big sister to me."

When Lynette and Ranji stood up, I really lost it.

They were the two Black women I had hired to help lead *Teen Vogue* alongside me. They were both very much in the trenches with me and epitomized grace under fire. And they were the only ones there who knew all of what was going on every day behind the scenes over the last few months.

Rajni told stories about how far we had come together since our *Glamour* days, and how honored she was, especially as a Black woman in this industry, to be appointed fashion director, and how many times she got stopped even just that day at the *Teen Vogue* Summit by young brown girls who were awed to see not one, not two, but multiple Black women at the top of the masthead at *Teen Vogue.*

Then Lynette grabbed the mic and said, "You were the best editor-in-chief I ever had. You're the real deal. You elevated all of us."

I was a mess of tears by this point. Everyone who spoke that night saw and appreciated why *Teen Vogue* mattered. But earning the respect and admiration of those two Black women especially was both humbling and redemptive. That for me was everything.

We spent the rest of the night swaying around the piano, belting out Roberta Flack and Aaliyah hits during moonlight karaoke. My mom even hopped on the mic to serenade us young folks with her Mahalia Jackson-esque rendition of "Amazing Grace."

That night I let go of worrying, and I gave in to the joy of dancing into my future, no longer afraid of what was on the other side. That night gave me closure on my childhood dream realized. If the awards and external validation that comes along with public praise ever meant anything, this moment meant more than all those honors combined.

I was elated. And at peace.

This is how you end an era.

"Sometimes it takes reaching the summit to see what's on the other side."

CHAPTER 24

Brave Enough

Wanna fly, you got to give up the shit that weighs you down.
TONI MORRISON, *SONG OF SOLOMON*

I woke up the next morning to my mother's smiling face lying beside me in the hotel bed. I was exhilarated and exhausted, and ready to recap the night. It all felt a little bit like a dream.

After tying up loose ends from the Summit, my mom and I dutifully headed over to the CAA offices, a shiny, supersized tower in Beverly Hills. Christy and co. had invited me to join what I understood to be a meeting of the minds among select women across the entertainment industry who were focused on women's empowerment initiatives and creating more equity in the business. I didn't have many more details than that, likely because I was too consumed with Summit stuff to absorb much more. I said I would be late and was assured it was totally fine—a "come as you are," "whenever you can make it" sort of thing.

But then I walked into the amphitheater-style screening room and spotted Shonda Rhimes, Tracee Ellis Ross, Rashida Jones, Lena Waithe, and tons of women producers and female studio execs. I instantly recognized that this was a bigger deal than I thought, so I tiptoed in, hoping to take my seat without causing a disturbance or attracting any undue attention.

Just when I had settled in as quietly as possible, still mortified that I was so late, one of my soon-to-be agents at CAA, Maha Dakhil, dashed across the room to greet me.

"It would be great if you said a few words," she urged.

"Oh. No, no. That's okay. I just got here. I'm still playing catch-up. But thank you," I whispered, hating the idea of delivering an impromptu speech in a foreign environment in front of some of the most intimidating people in the world, especially when I was the late girl in the room and still piecing together why everyone was gathered.

Then my lawyer, another organizer of the meeting, appeared, insisting that I address the group. I declined again, practically shooing her away. "You sure? Everyone here would really love to hear from you," she asked one more time, before finally giving up and walking back to her seat. I still wasn't quite sure what I was attending. And how dare I casually pop in at the end to speak when these women have been in here all day rolling up their sleeves? I just wanted to settle into my seat and listen.

But just after Shonda Rhimes finished her remarks (which flowed out of her like she was some combination of tenured professor and impassioned revolutionary), Maha was back—this time with a mic.

"Everyone, here with us today is the incredible editor-in-chief of *Teen Vogue*, Elaine Welteroth! She would like to say a few words."

Suddenly I was standing in front of the most important women in Hollywood with a mic in my hand. There was no time to panic, so instead I just trusted myself and let it *flow*.

By then, I'd figured out that this was the beginning of the #TimesUp movement and this powerful collective of women were brainstorming ways to organize a mutipronged movement to eradicate abuses of power against women in the workplace. I still have no idea what I said, but when I finished, the room erupted in applause and cheers. My mother held her hand up for a high five.

"You go, girl! That was excellent, you hear me?"

Something about it felt like a sign that the future was even bigger than any of the options I could see in front of me. This was a time for women to rise up together.

Not long after, I strategically found myself back in LA for a week of meetings—but let's be real, mainly I had my aims set on reconnecting with Ava.

I had not yet decided whether to stay with Condé Nast or walk into the unknown, completely untethered. I was waiting for the contract from Condé Nast—we had hammered out loose terms of a deal but I wanted to review the numbers before making any firm decisions—when I heard back from Ava's office. "There is a God," I whispered to myself, letting out an exhale of both relief and hope. I needed some wise counsel. We arranged to meet up at her house that night around seven.

Jonathan dropped me off that evening, and we said a quick prayer in the car in Ava's driveway. We prayed that God would take away the nerves and remove any intimidation, ego, fear—anything that would stand in the way of connection.

"Now go, baby, go," Jonathan rooted me on as I stepped out of the rental car. I felt like a grade-schooler going to hang with a "big-time" upperclassman.

Ava opened the door and greeted me with a warm, sisterly hug, welcoming me into her home. It was beautiful, like a contemporary African American museum, filled with stunning art. She gave me a quick tour and then said, "Let's go sit on the couch."

A bowl of popcorn and cozy blankets awaited us.

"So, what's your story?" Ava asked. "You're a total rock star over there killing it at *Teen Vogue*, that's clear. But I want to know more about you."

Ava might as well have been an oracle. Her eyes have a way of seeing inside of you; her presence invites you to unfold.

I told her my story: How I grew up not seeing myself in magazines, which led me to want to make my own. The aha moment that happened at twenty when I learned about—and stalked—Harriette Cole, and how she became my conduit into the business. I told her about the excitement and serendipity of that first day of my internship shooting Serena Williams, when I spoke up and found my voice on set. I told her about my journey to and vision for *Teen Vogue*; about the young audience I had fallen in love with and felt passionately committed to. I shared the difficult stuff, too: the tension that comes with being the only one in the room, the office politics, the duality of public perception versus the private reality of newfound success. In retelling my journey—and all the ridiculous, relentless, brave things I did to arrive at this moment—I found myself saying over and over again, "Who was that girl?"

Looking back, I'm a little mortified by just how much I told her. But Ava took it all in stride: "I feel connected to you—I feel your story, I feel your passion, your verve." Then she said, "Okay, so what do you want to do next? Because this is so clearly just the beginning for you."

There it was. My least favorite question rearing its head again. Exactly ten years after it first confronted me when I approached college graduation.

I told her about the venture I was in talks with Condé Nast about. I hadn't ever shared the details aloud to anyone—and I still was very unsure if I would actually go through with that plan—but I figured this was as good an opportunity as any to test how it felt rolling off my tongue. Especially in conversation with someone whose opinion I trusted immensely.

I thought it might sound impressive. That I had this great big plan with the support of a big company, and Anna Wintour, behind it. In a sense, I was going to make my longtime employer my first client—isn't that everyone's dream? Most people just looking for the shiny thing to grasp onto in conversation would have easily been like, "Great! That sounds awesome."

Not Ava—she was unimpressed.

"But *why* would you do that?"

Her question took me by surprise. I did not have an answer.

"What's the story?" she asked. "I always like to craft the story."

I could see her wheels turning.

"Okay, so you are this smart young Black woman who has been killing it at *Teen Vogue*, someone we have all loved celebrating. Then you did that incredible Summit, and you killed that, too. But since they chose to close the magazine, now you can go off and do your own thing. Whatever *you* want. You don't need Condé Nast for that."

I was, yet again, in a rare moment of speechlessness. She was right.

"You know what I think?" she asked.

Of course I wanted to know!

"I think a better end to this story is . . . 'Elaine leaves Condé Nast.'"

She used her hands to emphasize each syllable as if it were being read in lights, and then paused for emphasis.

"*That's* the story I want to read. You know why? It's powerful, and decisive."

In that moment Ava was shining a light on my truth. For me, the Summit had symbolized completion of an extraordinary era in my career. I was thirty, standing on the other side of some of my wildest dreams. Some of them I hadn't even thought to dream at twenty-one. I had checked off every single bucket list item—and then some. My magazine career mission had been fulfilled. Now I just needed the courage to believe there was more on the other side. That I was enough on my own—without the title, the media brand, the corporate structure. That I could fly on my own and reach even greater heights than I ever could from within the confinement of those walls.

But while my spirit had all but decided that I was moving on, I hadn't yet said the words. I was still too gripped by fear.

"You should be a little fearful," Ava told me. "That's good. It's a motivator. We all feel fear when we're about to do something great."

Before we said good-bye, Ava looked up at me from across her kitchen counter and said, "You sat in front of me today and I heard you say, 'Who was that girl who stalked Harriette and found her way into that magazine career? Who was that girl who spoke up during that shoot?' Well, I'm looking at her. That girl is *you*. She's the same girl who walked into my house, sat on my couch over there, and decided to tell me her story. *That* story, that way. You're still *that* girl. So do the things *that* girl did to get to where she wanted to be."

When Ava got up to say good-bye, she swept me into her arms and gave me the biggest hug. Then she told me something I will never unhear: "I think the universe is calling you to be a little bit braver right now." She said it with the kind of conviction you cannot manufacture.

I let out the exhale of all exhales; I didn't realize just how much I needed that hug. And that divine confirmation.

That conversation gave me clarity. It settled all the restlessness in my spirit. I now knew—for sure—exactly what I had to do. That same girl who obsessively chased a magazine career from California to New York City always knew this day would come. It was time for me to close the door on my first dream in order to start building the next.

I WENT TO SLEEP THAT night with the kind of peace I had been chasing for months.

The next morning, I woke up to find the contract from Condé right there in my in-box; the details I had been waiting weeks to review.

I looked at Jonathan and laughed. "Look at God."

It was too late.

All I could hear was Ava's voice: *The universe is calling you to be a little bit braver right now.*

I was ready.

On a sunny day in January 2018, I delivered my resignation to Anna Wintour in her private office on the forty-second floor, and for the final time, I walked out of the building where my first big dream came true.

She was extremely gracious and supportive of my decision. I thanked her for the life-changing opportunities she'd given me. Then, to my surprise, she stood up to give me a hug. "Call me anytime. I mean it."

Immediately, I felt lighter, freer.

My mission at *Teen Vogue* was to make young people whose voices had been marginalized feel seen, centered, and celebrated. Anna had given me the space and permission to fulfill that mission. I did what I came to do.

I had done enough.

I was enough.

And I was ready for more.

"The universe is calling you to be a little bit braver."

Just the Beginning

No matter how far a person can go the
horizon is still way beyond you.

ZORA NEALE HURSTON, *THEIR EYES WERE WATCHING GOD*

Our lives are a series of dreams realized.

We don't say that enough.

Instead, we repeatedly ask children, "What do you want to be when you grow up?" As if one answer, one dream, one career path can define you throughout your whole life.

The truth is, job titles are temporary. But purpose is infinite.

There are no destinations, no happily ever afters in real life, no glossy pots of gold at the end of the rainbow.

There are only new beginnings.

Just as you reach your first summit, you'll find a new horizon awaits, one with new mountains to climb, new peaks and valleys to wander across. Trust that life will continue molding you, challenging you, and readying you for your next adventure. But only you can choose to walk away from what no longer serves you, to leave what you've already conquered, and to step boldly into what's next.

When you find yourself existing in the space between dreams realized, parts of you will feel too big for where you are, while other parts of you will feel too small for where you're going.

Go anyway.

Do not wait.

Do not wonder if you can.

Do not ask for permission.

When you get lost, it's okay to stop, to look up, to look within for the answers—they're always there.

And when the world tells you to shrink, *expand*.

Remember:

You have done enough. You are enough. You were *born* enough.

The world is waiting on you.

Acknowledgments

My *More Than Enough* journey started long before I ever put pen to paper for this book. And it will continue long after these pages find their way into your hands. But in many ways, this book has already done its greatest work by bringing me back to my roots in profound ways and introducing me to actual Earth angels who helped me grow exponentially throughout this process. There is no better way to bookend this year-long effort than with gratitude, with which I am filled to the brim.

To my family: Thank you for letting me share pieces of you with the world and for allowing the words on these pages to open up an even deeper dialogue between us. Mom, my honorary editor-in-chief: In the thirty-two years we've been "in business" together, this acknowledgment might be the only piece of published copy I haven't called home to read to you first. Money cannot buy that kind of support—or benevolent tolerance of my neurotic work habits. Thank you for making me into the woman I was meant to be. I would be lost without you. After reading this, I hope you know that you are the true (s)hero of my life story. I have always thought the world would be such a better place if everyone had a mom like you. I can only hope that this book has multiplied your mothering so that it might minister to millions of other people's lives, the way it has mine since day one. Dad: This book never would have been had you not seen the writer in me. Thank you for giving me your blessing to tell my truth. Thank you for being the first in the family to read it cover to cover and for affirming—yet again—that my words matter to you. That "you have arrived" text was quite literally the best validation a daughter could ever dream of receiving from her dad. I'm grateful that this book has brought us closer and ignited healing. Thank you for teaching me the meaning of amazing grace. Eric: My big-hearted, heavy-handed older brother. The yin to my yang. Naturally, you were the only one bold enough to ask me to my face why the hell I'd write an "autobiography" at thirty-two. ("Isn't that something old people do?") Tbh, valid question! Some days I think I wrote it for the same reason you play punk rock. It wasn't so much a choice as it was simply something I felt like I was born to do—no matter what anyone might say. This process has reminded me that we are more alike than we think. Thank you for being a constant example of the bravery it takes to dance (mosh?) to the beat of your own drum (electric guitar?). I love you for life and I will always be (dancing!) in your corner.

My dearest friends: A very stylish and remarkably talented writer-editor named Chioma Nnandi, who was the first friend to read my manuscript, once said in her insanely charming British accent: "Writing a book seems a bit like scraping the very bottom of your soul. And then sharing morsels from the deepest parts of you with the world." You were not lying, sis. I couldn't have done it without the encouragement of extraordinary friends who joined me on this excavation, either by making yourselves available for hours-long phone calls and emergency text messages or by way of our little reading circle in my living room. You know who you are. You helped me see my story in new ways and your advice informed much of what made it onto these pages. Solid Six: I love each of you for a million different reasons. Misti Blue: You kept the wheels of my life and my business on track while I was off-roading to birth this baby. NO ONE rides harder than you. Tracy: Thank you for being my memory bank, my compass, my soul mate, and the mirror that always reflects back what matters most. Natalie: Your prayers and our sisterhood have gotten me through so many of life's tests, this book included. Don't worry, I'll save the dirt from our early adventures in NYC for my first "fictionalized" work. ;) Brooke, Offy, Chloe: Ours is the greatest love story never told. Perhaps that's the next book to write. Brooke, I can always trust the truth in those eyes. It was your vision of me dancing in the sky that we aimed to replicate for this cover. Offy: Without you I never would have survived my twenties and lived to tell these stories. Thank you for living through the most heart-wrenching chapters with me and being the sister I needed. Chloe: This process only reenforced for me that you are a true friend of my mind, my heart, and my soul. Thank you for all the times you knew exactly what to say. And for hyping me when necessary! "The Aunties": Lynette, Chioma, Rajni, our sister circle is sacred. So is our text group. Y'all have gotten me *through*. Team captain of The Aunties, Lynette Nylander, my former deputy editor, my once work wife, my forever friend: You came into my life for reasons far greater than either of us could have ever known at the time. I'd never give you the satisfaction of knowing this until now, but I may not have a book title, a through line, or a cover image if it weren't for you swooping in to save the day. I owe you endless champagne! Marie Suter: Cheers to the many lessons and laughs, and life after Condé. Thank you for elevating my taste and training my eye. You sharpen everyone around you. Forever grateful for your friendship. Madeline Poole, you are the MVP on so many levels. I would be lost in the sauce without your creative genius. Jacq Harriet, maker of book cover dreams, I am honored that you leaped at the opportunity to work together for my most personal cover shoot to date. Thank you for visually capturing the spirit of this book. Coree Moreno, Alana Wright, and Vernon François: You are more than my glam fam; you are true friends. There isn't anyone else I'd rather glow up with. Chad Sanders: I know Jonathan thinks you're his best friend, but you're my person, too. Thank you for lending your mind, your time, and your notes, which sharpened this book and challenged me to drill deeper. Aurora James, my beloved friend and trusted "coworker": Thank you for somehow making space in your very full life to join me in the all-consuming obsession that is book-making, and for being the go-to I could always count on for a sanity check. Your support and astute feedback pushed me to put even more of my soul on the page. Cleo Wade: I'm eternally grateful to have watched you flourish through the delivery of your own book baby first and to have learned from your inexhaustible grace. Thank you forever for weighing in on the biggest life and work decisions I've made over the last couple of years. I'm inspired by your mind and I'm fed by our friendship. Amandla Stenberg, Rowan Blanchard, Yara Shahidi: I might be older than you, but each of you has been a huge source of inspiration to me. This book is, in part, a testament to how powerfully you are already shifting the world for the better—including mine—just by being authentically you. Never stop pushing. Never stop questioning. Never stop showing up. Malala Yousafzai: I was just sitting down to start writing this book when you successfully lulled me away from my desk and swept me off to Brazil for the adventure of a lifetime. Spending that sacred time with you and all of the brilliant, resilient young girls of color we met along the way was like fuel for my creative process—you reminded me who I do it all for and why. Thank you for being a lighthouse for girls everywhere. *Project Runway* fam: Thank you for getting me through the last leg of this process with a new adventure that was so much fun, it never felt like work.

My mentors: We are only as sturdy as the shoulders we stand upon. I am fortunate to stand atop oak trees. To my teacher Dr. Michele Foss-Snowden, aka "my M. Foss": As if helping me get through college wasn't enough, it was your encouraging texts, uplifting baby pictures, and heart-to-heart convos that fueled my stride to the finish line on this book. Thank you for arming me with the tools to be a deeper thinker and a more analytical writer, and for forcing me to speak my dreams into existence. You are the kind of fairy big sister I always wanted. Harriette Cole, my first boss: This book represents a full circle moment for us. I will never stop thanking God for the twist of fate that led me to you and whatever it was that moved you to usher me into my first big dream. I wouldn't be where I am had you not taken a chance on me first. Thank you for still being just a phone call away, even after all these years. Your constructive editorial feedback in the critical final hour made all the difference. Anna Wintour, Amy Astley, Cindi Leive, and every woman boss I have had the privilege of working for: Thank you for every opportunity you gave me to learn from you. Each of you has opened doors for me, changed my life in meaningful ways, and shaped the kind of leader I strive to be. Ava DuVernay: Your words, your hug, and your encouragement, especially that fateful day, changed the trajectory of my life in ways you may only know now after reading this book. You are one of my North Stars. Thank you for supporting me, for seeing me, and for allowing me in to see you, too.

My team: Long before I wrote the first word of this book, I said a prayer and set an intention that—above all else—the process would be beautiful. That prayer was answered in full, only because of the extraordinary angel-people I was fortunate enough to have with me on this journey. Marya Spence: from the very beginning, there was you. You saw this book in me before I could even put words to this dream, and you wouldn't give up on me until it was a reality. You delivered on every promise. You fought for me. You even fought *with* me when necessary. And now, here we are at the finish line together like you always knew we'd be. Forever grateful for you, my fierce, loving literary agent and friend. Thank you for guiding me through a world that felt so foreign to me, and for leading me into the open arms of my dream team at Viking. Meg Leder: You are the embodiment of grace under fire. If I knew editors like you existed, I might have had the confidence to do this first book thing sooner. I deeply appreciate your indefatigable support, your vast experience and skill, and your deep well of patience (I know I tested it), but most of all, your generosity. You've had my back in ways that I will forever be grateful for. Looking back, this book was always meant to be ours to create together. In you I've found more than an editor; I am honored to call you a friend. And to Shannon Kelly, thank you for everything you've contributed to this book, from rolling up your sleeves and digging into the nittiest of grittiest details to chasing me on email to keep us on track. You rock. Everyone should have a Liz Welch in their life! I can genuinely say that I never could have completed this herculean effort without your hand to hold. You are the linchpin that kept this project together, holding me up and keeping me in the light, all while digging deep into the dirty work with me. It is your unwavering belief in this book that kept me moving toward the finish line. You are a wizard and a godsend. Truly, one of the greatest blessings of writing this book has been getting to know you. Through this process you have quickly gone from complete stranger to friend, aunt, sister, THERAPIST, and my closest confidante. Along the way, you made me feel seen in ways few ever have. And I see you, too. What a magnificent joy and blessing it has been to have your brilliant mind and stunning heart by my side throughout this ride. Please thank Gid and Bella for generously sharing you with me! To the dream team of publishing: It is a great honor to work with you and to join the ranks of Viking's esteemed authors. Your skill and savvy are only matched by how much you care. So much gratitude to Nina Shaw "attorney-at-law" and my CAA team, led by the badass Christy Haubeggar, for pushing me out of the nest and insisting that I fly. Gratitude to David Levin and Ellis Beber for keeping my financial life in order so that I can dive freely into these creative adventures. To Amanda Silverman and my Lede ladies: Thank you for protecting me and my story and ensuring that it's delivered into the world with precision and with love. Abi, Ashley, Jasmine, Faith: Thank you for taking care of me while I was in my writing hole. Above all, I thank you for those small, in-between moments of encouragement that meant so much. Team *Teen Vogue*, past, present, future (but especially circa 2012–2017): I am endlessly grateful, proud, and honored to have worked alongside each one of you. (You know who you are.) Fighting for what we all believed in was worth it.

My person: Jonathan, my love for you begins at the end of words. You are simply the best part of everything. Everything I am, anything I do, is 100 percent better because of you. They say you protect what is sacred. Well, in these pages I saved the best of us for *us*. Yet more than anyone, you sacrificed to help me make this dream come true. Throughout too many twenty-hour writing days spent hovering over my laptop, you fed me—physically, mentally, and spiritually. You honored my work as if it were your own. You share me freely with the world, and when it breaks me, there you are at the end of every day with that smile, helping me put the puzzle pieces of life back together again. You hold each and every one of my stories never written. I love you with my whole heart. Thank you for doing life with me.

Finally, to you, dear reader: We often hear about the fight for a seat at the table. Thank you for joining me at the first table that was mine to build. For you. For us. I can't wait to meet you all.